Performing Chinatown

ASIAN AMERICA

a series edited by Gordon H. Chang

Performing Chinatown

Hollywood, Tourism,
and the Making of a Chinese
American Community

William Gow

STANFORD UNIVERSITY PRESS
STANFORD, CALIFORNIA

Stanford University Press
Stanford, California

A version of Chapter 1 was previously published as "Chinatown Pastiche: The Chinese Village at the 1893 World's Columbian Exposition," *Journal of Urban History* 50, no. 2 (March 2024) © Sage Publications.

A version of Chapter 6 was previously published as "A Night in Old Chinatown: American Orientalism, China Relief Fundraising, and the 1938 Moon Festival in Los Angeles," *Pacific Historical Review* 87, no. 3 (Summer 2018): 439–472. © University of California Press.

Printed in the United States of America on acid-free, archival-quality paper

Library of Congress Cataloging-in-Publication Data

Names: Gow, William (William Edward), author.
Title: Performing Chinatown : Hollywood, tourism, and the making of a Chinese American community / William Gow.
Other titles: Hollywood, tourism, and the making of a Chinese American community | Asian America.
Description: Stanford, California : Stanford University Press, 2024. | Series: Asian America | Includes bibliographical references and index.
Identifiers: LCCN 2023036811 (print) | LCCN 2023036812 (ebook) | ISBN 9781503638099 (cloth) | ISBN 9781503639089 (paperback) | ISBN 9781503639096 (ebook)
Subjects: LCSH: Chinese American entertainers—California—Los Angeles—History—20th century. | Chinese Americans in motion pictures—History—20th century. | Chinatown (Los Angeles, Calif.)—History—20th century. | Hollywood (Los Angeles, Calif—History—20th century. | Los Angeles (Calif.)—Social conditions—20th century. | United States—History—1933–1945.
Classification: LCC F869.L89 C52 2024 (print) | LCC F869.L89 (ebook) | DDC 979.4/9405—dc23/eng/20230913
LC record available at https://lccn.loc.gov/2023036811
LC ebook record available at https://lccn.loc.gov/2023036812

Cover design: Michele Wetherbee
Cover photograph: Johnny Yee poses with a tourist in his rickshaw in China City while his brother Swan Yee takes a photograph. Los Angeles Daily News Collection, UCLA Special Collections, ca. 1938. Creative Commons, Attribution 4.0 International License.
Typeset by Newgen in Adobe Garamond Pro 11/14

To my friends at the CHSSC.
This book would not exist without you.

Contents

Illustrations

Acknowledgments

It is fitting that this book began with an invitation to make a movie. In 2003, I interviewed community member Gilbert Hom about his time as a student activist at UCLA in the late 1960s. At the conclusion of our interview, Gilbert invited me to work on a documentary with the Chinese Historical Society of Southern California (CHSSC), a nonprofit in Los Angeles Chinatown run entirely by volunteers. I joined the project and went on to co-produce the documentary with my friend Jenny Cho. Our video, *Revisiting East Adams*, focused on a Chinese American community that existed near East Adams and San Pedro Streets in the 1930s, 1940s, and 1950s in what is now South Los Angeles. That project was my introduction to the CHSSC and to many of the topics discussed in this book.

For the next eight years I worked as a public-school teacher in Southern California while volunteering with the CHSSC as a board member and community historian. During this time, Gilbert became my friend and scholarly interlocutor. In 2007, I founded and directed the CHSSC's Chinatown Remembered Project. With that project, I trained local high school and college youth in community history methodology and then paired them with Chinatown elders to document the history of Chinatown in the 1930s and 1940s. Gilbert helped identify many of the community elders that my team interviewed. Many Chinatown Remembered interviews feature prominently in this book. Sadly, Gilbert did not live to see *Performing Chinatown* in print. To this day, my research remains indebted to him. Without

Gilbert's invitation to join that documentary project in Chinatown twenty years ago, I probably would never have written the book. Thank you for all your mentorship and guidance over the years, Gilbert. Rest in peace.

At the CHSSC and in the Chinese American community of Los Angeles, my thanks go to Eugene Moy, Linda Bentz, Jenny Cho, Kelly Fong, Isa Quintana, Vincent Huynh, Fenton Eng, Katherine Kwok, Dr. Ruby Ling Louie, Dorothy Hom, Tyrus Wong, Ben Fong, Eleanor Yee, Peter SooHoo Jr., Jennie Lee Taylor, Charlie Quon, Marian Leng, Esther Lee Johnson, Stanley Mu, Camille Wing, Donna Young, Nancy Thai, Genie Moon, Scott Chan, and Annie Luong. I also acknowledge all those who worked on the Southern California Chinese American Oral History Project in the late 1970s and early 1980s, in particular Suellen Cheng, Beverly Chan, Bernice Sam, June Mei, Emma Louie, and Jean Wong. Their foundational community scholarship made *Performing Chinatown* possible.

This book would not have happened without all the teachers and friends who supported me well before I was accepted to graduate school. To the many San Francisco Unified teachers who inspired me in my youth, but especially Mr. Woo, Mr. Spellicy, and of course Coach Feibusch, thank you. Chris Abalos, Matt Lethin, Sherman Chan, Alfredo Mazariegos, and Bruce Howng have provided lifelong support and continued friendship. At NYU a special thank you goes to Professor Rebecca Karl for providing the mentorship that inspired me to go on to graduate school. Since our years as undergraduate activists, Sarah Polaski and Usman Haq have provided stimulating conversations and political debates.

From my time at UCLA, I would like to thank Meg Thorton, Irene Soriano, Marji Lee, Stacey Hirose, Valerie Matsumoto, Don Nakanishi, Thu-huong Nguyen-vo, David Yoo, and Robert Nakamura. I would not be the educator I am today without Glenn Omatsu: thank you, Glenn, for being an example of what an Asian American Studies practitioner can be. You transformed the way I think about education and its relationship to community. My fellow UCLA Asian American Studies students shaped my academic thinking during this pivotal moment in my educational journey. They include Dean Saranillio, Jenny Cho, Sharon Heijin Lee, Bene Ferrão, Anthony Yuen, Camillia Lui, Francine Redada, and Tad Nakamura.

To my many public school teacher colleagues, including Rene Semik, Jaime Jimenez, Daniel Escalera, Adrienne Karyadi, Ned Acker, Amy Bisson,

Amy Beeman-Solano, and the late Don Hedrick: thank you for great lunch-time conversations and for all you do in teaching the next generation. It is not easy. I would not have found success as a teacher at the college level without our work together at public schools in my twenties.

So many people at UC Berkeley helped make this project possible. I am deeply appreciative of the staff of the Ethnic Studies Department, including Latonya Minor, Maria Heredia, Dewey St. Germaine, and Jennie Imazumi. The many faculty who discussed this project with me include Ling-chi Wang, Christian Paiz, Richard Candida Smith, Chris Zepeda-Millan, Keith Feldman, Ula Taylor, and Lok Siu. For their intellectual support and lively conversation, my thanks go to Katie Keliiaa, Rachel Lim, Jeff Yamashita, Mihiri Tillakaratne, Daniel Woo, and Evyn Espirtu.

Heartfelt appreciation goes to Weihong Bao and Michael Omi. Your feedback helped make this a better project. A special thank you to Cathy Choy and Shari Huhndorf. I could not have picked more supportive men-tors at UC Berkeley. Cathy and Shari, you read multiple versions of every chapter, commented, and provided detailed feedback. You both exemplify mentorship.

My work is built on the support of the many librarians, archivists, and staff at institutions across the country who helped me locate primary source material: Sine Hwang Jensen, Lily Castillo-Speed, and the rest of the UC Berkeley Ethnic Studies Library; Kim Zarate and Joelle Warlick at the Chinese American Museum of Los Angeles; Linda Bentz, Amanda Galvez, and Andy Tan at the CHSSC; and Li Wei at the Huntington Library; as well as the staff, librarians, and archivists at the Los Angeles Public Library, the Margaret Herrick Library, UCLA Library Special Col-lections, the UCLA Asian American Studies Reading Room, the Special Collections Library at Princeton University, the Rare Book and Manu-script Library at Columbia University, the Hoover Institute at Stanford University, the Special Research Collections Department at UC Santa Barbara, and the California State University, Northridge, Oviatt Library Digital Collections.

Numerous scholars and colleagues have taken time to advise, support, or discuss my research. Thank you, Bill Deverell, Merry Ovnick, Greg Robin-son, Jack Tchen, Scott Wong, Teresa Barnett, Jan Lin, Isa Quintana, Kelly Fong, Laureen Hom, Lawrence Lan, Lon Kurashige, Daryl Maeda, Judy

Wu, Peter X. Feng, Denise Khor, Josh Sides, Melody Herr, Judy Yung, and Takeo Rivera.

Living in San Francisco and then Sacramento, yet spending so much time in Los Angeles, I am grateful for the many families and friends who supported my research trips and opened their homes to me. They include Lisa Chee and Mike Deaderick, Tim Brocket, Sharon and Dave Phosolly, and Jenny and Genaro Mejia.

I spent three incredible years as a lecturer at Stanford. Cindy Ng of the Asian American Activities Center welcomed me in my first quarter there. Stanford's Asian American community will never be the same now that you have retired, Cindy! Thank you also to Jerald Adamos and Latana Thaviseth for your support and for all you continue to do for students and the community. In American Studies, thank you to Shelley Fisher Fishkin and Amy Potemski. In Asian American Studies, I thank Jeannie Tsai, Vivian Yan Gonzalez, and Calvin Cheung-Miaw. My special appreciation goes to Gordon Chang for mentorship and guidance during my time at Stanford and since I left. I would not be the scholar I am today without you, Gordon. Finally, heartfelt thanks to all the Stanford students I worked with in various capacities and particularly those who advocated for my position and for Asian American Studies more broadly. Stanford has an endowment larger than the annual GDP of a small nation. It is past time for it to use part of that endowment to adequately fund and staff the Asian American Studies Program.

Thank you to all my friends and colleagues who advised me during my five years on the job market, including Jih-Fei Cheng, Bene Ferrão, Denise Khor, and Kathy Yep. If I had not secured a tenure-track job, *Performing Chinatown* might never have been completed.

The last two years as a tenure-track professor at Sacramento State have been a dream for me. I thank my colleagues in the Asian American Studies Program for their support: Bao Lo, Tim Fong, Wendi Yamashita, and Greg Mark. Thank you, Annette Reed, for your leadership of the Ethnic Studies Department. In the office, I want to acknowledge the staff who keep our department running: Palesa Mosupyoe, Annalise Harlow, and Rena Horse. My thanks to the incredible students at Sac State, who have pushed me to become a better teacher and scholar.

My appreciation goes to the blind reviewers at the University of California Press and Stanford University Press, as well as the reviewers at the

Journal of Urban History and *Pacific Historical Review* for their comments on articles and drafts of *Performing Chinatown*. At Stanford University Press, my acquisition editor, Margo Irvin, provided needed support throughout the project. Thanks also to Cindy Lim at the press for her assistance, and to Erin Ivy for copy editing.

I would like to recognize my family, both immediate and extended. My late Uncle Richard Chee was the first person to ever tell me that an Old Chinatown existed in Los Angeles now buried underneath Union Station. It is fitting that *Performing Chinatown* opens with an anecdote about his life. Thanks to all my relatives in the extended Gow, Chee, Gee, and Pettey families. To my younger brothers Eddie and Max—my first training as a storyteller came while playing *Dungeons & Dragons* with you in our basement. Part of me wanted this book to open in a tavern on the edge of an enchanted forest, but I did not think that would pass peer review. Thank you to my mother-in-law Shu-Chen and my late father-in-law Hong Chi, who provided support and childcare that allowed me to complete my Ph.D. Both my parents Bruce and Ola Jane, but especially my mom instilled in me a love of learning, reading, and writing early in my life and always supported my goals no matter how unattainable they sounded. I would never have moved to New York to major in cinema studies as an undergraduate had my mom not supported my dreams. Thank you, mom. You continue to inspire me.

Of course, my eternal thanks and love go to my life partner Mary for supporting my crazy goal of returning to school to get my Ph.D. in my thirties and then moving to Sacramento when I finally received a tenure-track job. Thanks for your patience with all the weekends I spent at the CHSSC, in random archives around the country, and locked in my room writing this book. You supported this project in ways big and small. I never would have completed it without you. It's been a wonderful twenty-year ride so far, and I cannot wait to see where our future together takes us!

Finally, a deep-felt acknowledgment goes to my two boys Malcolm and Miles, who have never known their father as anything but an academic. This book may be dedicated to the CHSSC, but my life's work as an Asian American Studies practitioner is dedicated to you. I do this work so that the two of you can grow up in a world where you see your identities, and Asian American history more broadly, represented in your public school education in ways I never did as youth. Representation alone will never save us, but it does matter. It remains one of the many building blocks we need to create a more just and equitable society for all.

To everyone listed above and to all those I forgot to mention, thank you. All of you in your own ways contributed to this community history.

Sacramento, June 2023.

A Note on the Romanization of Chinese Names and Places

Before the 1965 Immigration Act, most Chinese immigrants spoke Cantonese or one of the village dialects from the Sze Yup (*Siyi*) or the Sam Yup (*Sanyi*) region of the Pearl River Delta. Despite this, the field of Asian American history generally uses the *Pinyin* system of romanization when writing nineteenth and early twentieth century Chinese names and places in English. This academic convention is borrowed from the field of Asian Studies. There are multiple reasons for our field not to use *Pinyin* as the default, particularly when referring to the period before 1965. *Pinyin* is based on Mandarin, a dialect that few Chinese immigrants spoke before that year. As a result, this form of romanization produces English spellings far different from the ones commonly used in English-language sources produced between the late nineteenth century and the mid-twentieth. Furthermore, many second-, third-, and fourth-generation Chinese Americans, who speak no Mandarin and read little, if any, Chinese, often see the English spellings of their ancestral villages, ancestors' names, and in some cases even their own names changed by historians to fit contemporary scholarly conventions. In contrast, *Performing Chinatown* uses the original English romanization of all Chinese places and names with *Pinyin* in parentheses. This will allow community members, their families, and their descendants to recognize names and places without knowing Mandarin or being familiar with the arcane debates over Chinese romanization that occupy academics.

Performing Chinatown

Introduction

My great uncle Richard Chee was many things in his life: a US military veteran, an aerospace engineer, a UCLA Bruin, and an avid sports fan. For a moment in his life, Uncle Richard was also a Hollywood performer. As a Chinese American born in Los Angeles' Old Chinatown who came of age in the 1930s and 1940s, my uncle appeared as a background extra in Hollywood films. His first opportunity to perform on screen came when he was a student at Belmont High School. He and his friend Willie Quon landed roles as extras in the 1943 wartime comedy *Rookies in Burma*.[1] Sixty-five years after this background appearance, Uncle Richard still recalled his experience fondly, even as he remembered losing his entire first paycheck playing cards with other Chinese American extras on set.

Richard Chee was not alone in performing in Hollywood. Charlie Quon found his way into the Paramount film *China* (1943). The future Hollywood animator Tyrus Wong appeared in the background of *The Painted Veil* (1934). Esther Lee performed as a background player in *Keys of the Kingdom* (1944).[2] Of course, any Chinese American in Los Angeles could have performed in MGM's 1937 cinematic adaption of Pearl Buck's novel *The Good Earth*. In the mid-1930s, MGM Studios built a Chinese Village in the San Fernando Valley replete with rice fields and water buffalo, and then sent buses to Chinatown to pick up extras. The press reported that more than a thousand extras appeared in *The Good Earth*. If this number is true, it is equal to a third of the approximately three thousand Chinese Americans the US Census estimated lived in Los Angeles in 1930.

Hollywood films were not the only place Chinese Americans in Los Angeles performed. Some performed for their day jobs in China City, the short-lived tourist attraction developed by Christine Sterling near the Los Angeles Plaza. China City re-created the set from *The Good Earth* alongside magic shows, rickshaw rides, and Chinese lion dances. Other Chinese Americans, like the members of the Los Angeles Mei Wah Girls' Drum Corps, performed at China relief festivals held in Old Chinatown after the outbreak of the Second Sino-Japanese War in 1937. For this generation of Chinese Americans in Los Angeles, performance for primarily White audiences was a defining aspect of everyday life.

Performing Chinatown: Hollywood, Tourism, and the Making of a Chinese American Community traces the relationship of Chinese Americans in Los Angeles to performance for movie audiences and tourists during an era when the government excluded or restricted Chinese immigration.[3] Although it covers the period from the late nineteenth century through the mid-twentieth, its focus is on the pivotal years between 1931 and 1945. During this moment of tumultuous global change, Chinese Americans experienced the Great Depression, the outbreak of war in the Pacific, and the official repeal of the Chinese Exclusion Act. In Los Angeles, they witnessed the destruction of Old Chinatown to build Union Station and its replacement by two competing Chinese American tourist districts: Christine Sterling's China City and a separate development, New Chinatown, built by Chinese American merchants under the leadership of Peter SooHoo.

In this historical context, *Performing Chinatown* asks: How did popular representations and economic opportunities in Hollywood inform life in Los Angeles Chinatown? To what extent were the rights and privileges of citizenship and national belonging related to such representations? And in what ways did Chinese Americans in Los Angeles use performances of racial difference to shape their social and political standing in society? In answering these questions, I build on the growing research on Asian American public performance as a site for the contestation and creation of social power.[4] Thus, the book centers what I call "Chinatown performances."

I define Chinatown performances as the prepared or rehearsed actions of Chinese Americans primarily for White movie audiences and tourists that shaped popular ideas of race during the era of exclusion and restriction.[5] Chinatown performances were almost always undertaken for profit. I understand that even certain "mundane" activities enacted by Asian Americans could take on theatrical qualities and thus create racial meaning, but I do not focus on these behaviors.[6] Instead, I examine public performances that Chinese Americans intentionally imbued with racial meaning for tourists and movie audiences.[7] With the exception of Chapter 5, which looks at the wartime performances of the actor Richard Loo, I focus not on famous performers but rather on seemingly everyday members of the Chinese American community whose public performances attracted the attention of popular audiences. In examining this history, I am cognizant of the ways in which the construction of racial difference is always connected to other axes of identity—in particular the relationship of race to gender and nationality.[8]

Too often today, people understand race to be a fixed, ahistorical, biologically determined category that stands outside of popular culture. Because they believe that race is fixed, popular critics often take one of two approaches in discussing Asian American representations: they debate the accuracy of a given racial representation,[9] or they discuss whether a portrayal is positive or negative.[10] These approaches have dominated popular discussions of Asian American representation in film over the past few decades. For example, journalists have asked whether *The Joy Luck Club* (1993) depicts Chinese American men too negatively,[11] if Justin Lin's portrayals of Asian American youth in *Better Luck Tomorrow* (2002) are excessively violent,[12] and whether *Crazy Rich Asians* (2018) accurately represents the diversity of modern-day Singapore.[13] While there is nothing inherently wrong with any of these questions, I take a different approach.

As a work of Asian American social and cultural history, *Performing Chinatown* examines the role that Chinatown performances played in shaping, challenging, and creating dominant ideas about Chinese Americans in the popular conscience. In doing so, it demonstrates the ways these performances constructed ideas about race and, in turn, how these ideas shaped the lives of everyday Chinese Americans. I am informed by a large body of scholarship that studies the way popular culture assigns racial meanings to human bodies—skin color, phenotype, hair texture—and how these meanings inform the distribution of social, economic, and political resources.[14] The sociologists Michael Omi and Howard Winant call this process "racial formation."[15]

In tracing the history of racial formation, I examine Chinatown performances in the context of immigration laws meant to exclude or restrict Chinese immigrants.[16] Beth Lew-Williams has convincingly argued that the actual exclusion of Chinese immigrants from the US lasted only from 1888 to 1943.[17] However true this may have been in a strictly legal sense, between 1875 and 1965 a larger set of policies restricting Chinese immigration shaped representations in popular culture. These policies began with the passage of the Page Act in 1875, which sought to limit the immigration of Chinese women, and continued through the passage of the Chinese Exclusion Act of 1882, which prohibited the immigration of Chinese laborers.[18] The Magnuson Act of 1943 officially ended Chinese exclusion, but only allowed 105 Chinese to immigrate per year, making it largely symbolic. The true end of Chinese immigration restrictions came with the passage of the Hart-Celler Immigration Act in 1965. Chinatown performances constantly engaged this larger apparatus of immigration policy in the period between 1875 and 1965.

Given this background, *Performing Chinatown* conceives of racial representations in popular film and in Chinatown for tourists as intimately connected to restrictive immigration laws. Rather than thinking of the law and popular culture as separate spheres, I consider popular representations of Chinese Americans one of the foundations on which this racist legal policy was built. Stereotypes of Chinese immigrants as a threat to mainstream middle-class society became common tropes.[19] Yellow peril stereotypes depicted Chinese immigrants as a working-class horde, threatening to overrun US shores, take jobs from White men, and sleep with White women.[20] In this way, popular culture both reflected and created the political climate that made Chinese exclusion possible.

Laws barring Chinese immigrants from naturalization made it nearly impossible for Chinese Americans to challenge yellow peril stereotypes with a strategy of assimilation into White American norms.[21] After all, Whiteness and US citizenship were denied to Chinese immigrants by law.[22] Instead of challenging the perceived racial difference of Chinese immigrants through assimilation, Chinatown performances embraced difference, attempting to reframe it as a nonthreatening form from which certain Chinese Americans could profit.[23] Public performances for movie audiences and tourists challenged the meaning of race itself, shaping the way Asian Americans experienced race in the twentieth century.[24]

The scholarly consensus in the field of Asian American history holds that the US alliance with China during World War II caused a rapid shift in popular perceptions of Chinese Americans. Roger Daniels writes that this

FIGURE O.I. George Fredrick Keller's "A Statue for Our Harbor" from *The Wasp* (1881), depicting the Chinese laborer as "Filth," "Immorality," "Disease," and "Ruin to white labor." Bancroft Library, University of California, Berkeley.

alliance with China after Pearl Harbor had an "almost instantaneous" impact on Chinese Americans.[25] Similarly, Peter Kwong and Dušanka Miščević see wartime changes for Chinese America as happening "almost overnight."[26] Shelley Lee asserts that "wartime international realignments" caused a "sudden embrace" of Chinese Americans.[27] In these retellings, the geopolitical realignment in the Pacific, and specifically the US-China alliance during the war, led to a rapid increase in opportunities for Chinese Americans. *Performing Chinatown* complicates this narrative by foregrounding the preceding five decades of Chinatown performances as context for the transformations experienced by Chinese Americans during World War II.

Tracing the co-evolution of tourism and cinema as overlapping sites of racial formation, I demonstrate the ways in which movie extras, street performers, business owners, and others used Chinatown performances to reshape popular ideas about Chinese Americans.[28] I do not see this reshaping as the sudden or instantaneous result of the geopolitical realignment of World War II. Instead, I demonstrate how Chinese Americans utilized performance to configure popular ideas about Chinese people in the United States beginning in the late nineteenth century. World War II was not the catalyst for changing attitudes toward Chinese Americans. Rather, this period was the culmination of a process that had begun in the 1890s.

Against the long history of Chinatown performances, the 1930s and 1940s became a pivotal period in which the US negotiated popular conceptions of Chinese Americans. In 1934, Congress passed the Tydings-McDuffie Act, cutting off immigration to the United States from the Philippines and marking the final step in the curtailment of immigration from Asia that began with the restriction of Chinese immigration in the nineteenth century.[29] As David Palumbo-Liu has shown, American cultural producers in the 1930s then began to grapple with how to incorporate Asian people already in the United States into the nation's popular imagination.[30] I show that Chinatown performances in Los Angeles were among the most significant aspects of this process of incorporation. Rather than seeing geopolitical events of the war in the Pacific as the sole cause of shifting attitudes, I demonstrate that Chinatown performances used the changing geopolitical landscape of the 1930s and 1940s as a stage on which to shape the American public's understanding of Chinese Americans.

Of course, not all groups in the Chinese American community had equal access to Chinatown's metaphorical stage. Like broader American society, Chinese American ethnic enclaves were divided by class, gender, and even race.[31] Exclusion-era Los Angeles was home to many mixed-race Chinese Americans who often found themselves marginalized in Chinatown by their mixed-race background. The ability to perform for tourists and movie audiences determined who in the community had the greatest agency in shaping popular ideas of racial difference and who financially benefited the most from performances. The upwardly mobile merchants of New Chinatown had much greater control over Chinatown performances than did their more working-class compatriots in China City. In fact, many Chinese American merchants used Chinatown performances to seek their own incorporation into the city by defining themselves against working-class Chinese immigrants as well as against Japanese Americans and Black Americans. In this way, Chinatown performances became another site of social division both within the Chinese American community and between Chinese Americans and other racial and ethnic groups.

Across six chapters, *Performing Chinatown* demonstrates how different groups in the Chinese American community in Los Angeles used performance both as a means of economic subsistence and as a mechanism of inclusion. I divide the history of Chinatown performances into three parts: (1) Chinatown tourism, (2) Hollywood extras, and (3) wartime Los Angeles. Part I situates Los Angeles Chinatown in the history of North American Chinatowns as sites for the performance of race, gender, and nationality. I trace the rise of what I call Chinatown Pastiche, a cultural assemblage of food, architecture, clothing, postcards, and other cultural forms created by Chinese American merchants during the exclusion era. Chinatown Pastiche reimagined the geography of Chinatown as a nonthreatening space of tourism and theatricality compatible with the underlying tenants of American capitalism. Developed at the 1893 World's Columbian Exposition, Chinatown Pastiche reached its logical conclusion in 1938 in Los Angeles with the opening of New Chinatown.

Part II discusses how Chinese Americans found empowerment as extras and bit players in the Hollywood film industry during the 1930s. I show how they used increased demand for their services on MGM's *The Good Earth* to reshape pay and hiring practices. I then discuss the ways in which

Chinese Americans used protests and oppositional readings of Hollywood films to reimagine an alternative, more inclusive Hollywood.

Part III analyzes the ways in which Chinese Americans leveraged the heightened interest in China—brought on first by the Second Sino-Japanese War (1937–1945) and then by World War II (1939–1945)—to foreground Chinatown performances. I examine the agency of Chinese American performers in exploiting the shifting geopolitical landscape for their own benefit, at times at the expense of others, including Japanese Americans. I do this through a focus on Chinese American movie actors who played Japanese villains in World War II propaganda films. This section concludes with an examination of the China relief performances of the Los Angeles Mei Wah Girls' Drum Corps.

Whether on screen or for tourists, Chinatown performances shaped perceptions of race far beyond the Chinatown ethnic enclave. Writing about representations of Chinese Americans in Anglo-American literature, Elaine Kim observes that "many depictions of Chinese have been generalized to

FIGURE 0.2.   The Los Angeles Mei Wah Girls' Drum Corps in a "V" for victory formation during World War II. The representation of the corps contrasted markedly with earlier yellow peril stereotypes. Peter SooHoo Collection, Huntington Library, San Marino, California.

Asians, particularly since Westerners have found it difficult to distinguish among East Asian nationalities."[32] Building on Kim's observation, I contend that Chinatown performances not only influenced dominant understandings of Chinese American communities across the US but also shaped postwar perceptions of other Asian American communities as well. By placing Los Angeles Chinatown performances in the 1930s and 1940s in a longer history reaching back to the late nineteenth century, we see how the history of these performances helped transform the social standing of Asian Americans through the postwar period.

In making my argument, I focus on the ways in which New Chinatown merchants, China City business owners, movie extras, the Los Angeles Mei Wah Girls' Drum Corps, and others used the staging and restaging of Chinatown to shape popular understandings of Chinese Americans. *Performing Chinatown* complicates the mainstream historiographical argument that changing opinions of Chinese Americans during World War II were the result of geopolitical shifts alone. Instead, I place Chinatown performances in general, and Los Angeles Chinatown performances specifically, at the center of the history of Asian American racial formation.

PART I

Chinatown Tourism

CHAPTER I

Chinatown Pastiche

Surveying the parade as it passed by the reviewing stand and continued through the West Gate into New Chinatown, Peter SooHoo must have felt proud. That day, June 25, 1938, was the official opening of the newest Chinatown in the United States, and SooHoo was serving as master of ceremonies. A third-generation Californian, SooHoo was officially the English-language secretary for the Los Angeles Chinatown Project Association, but his role in the construction of New Chinatown was much more significant than his title implied.[1] Four years earlier, city leaders had announced that Old Chinatown would be torn down and its residents displaced to build the new Union Station. Since then, Peter SooHoo had acted as a liaison between the railways and Chinese American business owners. Over the past few years, as crews dismantled Old Chinatown block by block, Peter SooHoo worked tirelessly to forestall evictions. Because of his efforts, many Chinese Americans were able to remain in their old neighborhood much longer than they otherwise would have.[2]

The desire of city elites to destroy Old Chinatown should not have been a surprise. In the popular imagination, Chinatown had long been represented as an alien threat to the city.[3] For at least half a century, newspaper reporters, Hollywood film producers, and political leaders had portrayed Old Chinatown as a site of tong violence, illicit drug use, and prostitution. These stereotypes were rooted not only in perceived racial differences but also in perceived differences of gender and sexuality.[4] Popular

FIGURE I.I.   Governor Frank Miriam speaking at the New Chinatown opening on June 25, 1938 (Peter SooHoo at left). Chinese Historical Society of Southern California.

representations depicted the ethnic community as composed almost entirely of young "bachelors" living together in an all-male social world.[5] The few Chinese American women were usually depicted as prostitutes. In this context, many city residents associated Chinatown with deviant sexuality, and they often believed that the district and its residents challenged normative ideas of the White middle-class family united in Christian marriage.

The association of Chinatown with deviant sexuality extended to the neighborhood's built environment. Novels, newspapers, and films all told stories of an underground network of secret tunnels where Chinese men smoked opium and held White women in captivity. These stories perpetuated the idea that Chinatown lay outside the control of the visual and political authority of the city's White male power structure. In contrast, the opening of New Chinatown represented a way for upwardly mobile

Chinese American merchants to challenge representations of the imagined underground Chinatown while monetizing their own.

New Chinatown in Los Angeles represented the culmination of nearly five decades of work by Chinese American merchants across North America to redefine the place of Chinatown in the popular imagination. These efforts began with the Chinese Village at the World's Columbian Exposition in Chicago in 1893, continued through the reconstruction of San Francisco Chinatown after the 1906 earthquake and fire, and culminated in Los Angeles in 1938.[6] In tracing this history, I argue that the various sites were united by a distinctly Chinese American cultural form that I call "Chinatown Pastiche."[7] As a reaction to Chinese exclusion, Chinatown Pastiche redefined perceived Chinese racial differences through nonthreatening consumption, surface aesthetics, and theatrical performance. Incorporating food, architecture, clothing, postcards, and other cultural items, Chinatown Pastiche reimagined the geography of Chinatown as a space of tourism and theatricality compatible with the underlying ideology of US capitalism.[8] This cultural form represented Chinatown as ornamental, consumable, and thus consistent with emerging ideas of the United States as a melting pot of cultures.[9] At a moment when most of the Chinese American community was socially, economically, and legally excluded from much of American life, Chinatown merchants utilized Chinatown Pastiche to gain acceptance in White American society.

While Chinatown Pastiche was primarily how upwardly mobile Chinese Americans in New Chinatown shaped public opinion, its origins date to changes in popular culture sweeping the nation at the end of the nineteenth century. Chinatown Pastiche developed in conjunction with other forms of late nineteenth-century urban entertainment such as vaudeville, dime museums, zoos, and early cinema. Film historians have suggested that urbanization brought about a change in the nature of seeing that facilitated the rise of cinema and related urban entertainments.[10] These changes facilitated the rise of many new cultural forms, including Chinatown Pastiche.[11]

Through Chinatown Pastiche, Chinese American merchants lay claim to full personhood at a moment when Western scientific racism sought to deny humanity to the world's non-White people. In doing so, they sought to differentiate themselves from Chinese immigrant laborers by positioning themselves as future citizen-subjects of the United States willing to contribute to its commercial success. The claims these merchants staked to US national belonging through Chinatown Pastiche were conditional, gendered, and class based. This fraught cultural form was the foundation on which certain groups in the Chinese American community were eventually incorporated into the United States in the mid-twentieth century, but it also ensured that the incorporation of Chinese Americans remained tenuous and incomplete.

By the 1890s, Chinatowns had become an increasingly central part of mainstream American culture. From dime novels to plays to ever-present articles in the nation's press, White cultural producers increasingly portrayed urban Chinatowns as an extension of their imagined Orient.[12] Even after the start of the twentieth century, as US politicians moved their focus toward excluding immigrants from Japan, the Indian subcontinent, and the Philippines, these newer ethnic communities never supplanted Chinatowns in the popular imagination.[13] What explains this? Where did the popular image of Chinatown come from, and what accounts for the longevity of Chinatown's place in the national consciousness?[14] The answers lie in the profound social and cultural transformations under way in American cities at the moment when Chinese immigrants became an increasingly urban population.

In the nineteenth century, San Francisco was home to the largest Chinatown in the nation. Chinese immigrants began arriving in the US in significant numbers following the discovery of gold in the California foothills in 1848. By the 1850s, a small enclave of a few thousand immigrants lived and worked at the intersection of Sacramento and Dupont Streets in the center of the city. Most of them came from the Pearl River Delta region of southern China.[15] During this period, English-speaking residents referred to this neighborhood as "Little China."[16] In 1870, the 12,000 Chinese Americans living in San Francisco composed around 8 percent of the city's population.[17] Publications began referring to Sacramento and Dupont Streets as "China-Town."[18] Yet despite the size of San Francisco's Chinatown, Chinese Americans in the 1870s remained largely rural, with most working as miners, migrant farm laborers, and railroad workers.[19]

Then, in the closing decades of the nineteenth century, mob violence drove whole Chinatowns out of rural areas across the American West.[20] From Eureka, California, to Rock Springs, Wyoming, in rural towns small and large, White settlers boycotted, accosted, and threatened Chinese immigrants,[21] large numbers of whom sought refuge in cities with existing Chinese American populations. By 1900, 45 percent of the Chinese in California lived in San Francisco.[22] Mob violence pushed Chinese Americans into urban areas in large numbers at a moment when the forces of modernity were transforming the demographics of the nation's cities as well as the form and function of mass entertainment.[23] In the late nineteenth century, department stores, dime museums, zoos, and cinema emerged as popular leisure activities for the emerging White middle class. At the same time, magazines, postcards, and short silent films circulated images of urban life.[24]

The confluence of events—rapid urbanization of Chinatowns and new forms of mass culture—lodged images of urban Chinese enclaves in the national consciousness at a moment when the nation was debating the place of immigrants and immigration in US society. Had Chinese Americans been pushed into the nation's cities a few decades earlier or later, Chinatowns almost certainly would not have come to occupy the same place in the popular imagination. Their representations in mass culture drove increasing numbers of middle- and upper-middle-class tourists to visit the Chinatowns of San Francisco and New York.[25] In the closing decades of the nineteenth century, many tourists came to understand these Chinese American neighborhoods as sites of vice and danger but also as sites of leisure and performance.

Overlapping social, infrastructural, and cultural changes laid the groundwork for White visitors to see San Francisco's Chinese American neighborhood as an urban amusement. With the completion of the transcontinental railroad in 1869—enabled in part by the labor of Chinese immigrants—travelers from East Coast cities no longer had to cross the Great Plains by wagon or travel by ship around South America to reach California.[26] A trip from the East Coast to the Golden State that once took months now took about a week by rail. At the same time, entrepreneurs like George Pullman began catering to wealthy travelers. Trains added a range of amenities, including dining cars and sleeping cars, parlor cars, observation cars, and club cars with full bars. By the early twentieth century, some trains even included libraries, barbers, and bathtubs.[27] Cities also began to cater to affluent tourists.[28] San Francisco's Occidental Hotel opened in 1861; its Palace Hotel opened in 1875. The Cliff House overlooking Ocean Beach opened in 1863 as a destination for the city's wealthy.

The growth in tourism coincided with a transformation in middle- and upper-class thinking about the public sphere. In the early nineteenth century, wealthy elites often saw the world as divided into two spheres: the pubic and the private. They did not generally imagine urban public spaces as sites of leisure. When they did travel for pleasure, they vacationed in Europe where they appreciated art and architecture. In the second half of the nineteenth century, this conception of the public sphere began to shift.[29] Both the upper class and the growing middle class increasingly saw cityscapes as cultural products that could be visually consumed. By the mid-nineteenth century, the idea of the *flaneur*, the middle-class gentleman who strolled the city for pleasure, was circulating in US popular culture.[30] Soon, the emerging middle class came to see the city itself as a form of leisure.[31]

Of course, tourism and the ideologies of visuality and mobility that supported it, were not open to all Americans equally. It was able-bodied middle- and upper-middle-class White men for whom the city became a site of visual pleasure.[32] Social structures of race, class, and gender defined who circulated in the nation's cities and whose bodies became objects of the White male gaze. For example, before the 1880s White middle-class women moving about the city alone challenged the emerging social norms that governed middle-class life.[33] Because these norms of middle-class domesticity sought to place women inside the home, White women who moved about the city on their own risked being stereotyped as prostitutes by the middle-class men who had taken to roaming the city for fun.[34] And they were not the only city residents who had their movements curtailed.

Chinese immigrants also found their movements curtailed by the new visual regime. Even in a boomtown like San Francisco that attracted people from around the globe, Chinese people became objects of the White gaze as early as the 1850s. For example, an 1855 city guide described the early impression many White San Franciscans had of the Chinese residents: "The Chinese in San Francisco make an extraordinary feature of the city, and appeal very strongly to most organs of the stranger—to his eye, ear, and nose. They were seen in every street quietly passing along. The white immigrant, who may never before have met with specimens of the race involuntarily stops and gazes upon this particular people, whose features are so remarkable, and whose raiment is so strange, yet unpretending, plain and useful."[35]

In the mid-nineteenth century, the mere presence of a Chinese person on the streets of San Francisco was so arresting that White onlookers stopped and stared. While Chinese men did move around the nineteenth-century city, they could not enjoy the leisurely pace and detached observant position of the *flaneur.*

In succeeding decades, as the size of the Chinese immigrant population grew, the White gaze was increasingly transformed into violence. In San Francisco, Chinese American vegetable peddlers and others forced to travel outside of the ethnic enclave regularly encountered White violence.[36] White children in San Francisco often threw stones at newly arrived Chinese immigrants as they made the short trip from the docks to Chinatown.[37] One immigrant recalled the dangers of wandering the streets in the late nineteenth century: "The hoodlums, roughnecks, and young boys pull your queue, slap your face, throw all kinds of old vegetables and rotten eggs at you."[38] Not only were most Chinese bodies racially marked in a way that transformed them into objects of the White gaze, but beginning in the summer of 1893 the Geary Act, which renewed the Chinese Exclusion Act for ten years, heralded the emergence of a system of regulations that further limited the mobility of Chinese Americans. Chinese found moving about the city without photo identification risked arrest and deportation.

This combination of visual, legal, and bureaucratic mechanisms often led Chinese Americans in the late nineteenth century to live in or spend most of their leisure time in urban Chinatowns. Even those who lived and worked elsewhere in the city often traveled to Chinatown on Sundays seeking not only camaraderie but also the relative anonymity that only Chinatown could provide. In New York in the late nineteenth century, so many Chinese laundry workers and household servants surged into Chinatown on Sundays that, according to one estimate, the population of the community quadrupled.[39] These Chinese American men were able to remain relatively anonymous in Chinatown.

While Chinatown allowed Chinese American men to become lost in a crowd of their compatriots, it could not afford them freedom from the probing eyes of White visitors. By the late nineteenth century, the perceived racial and gendered differences of Chinatown attracted tourists in large numbers. The neighborhood became an attraction precisely because restrictions on Chinese American mobility rendered it racially and ethnically different. Chinese Americans were certainly not the only ethnic group that called these neighborhoods home, but they did constitute a majority of residents and businesses in most major urban Chinatowns.[40]

Perhaps more important, tourists often imagined Chinatown as a racially distinct space.[41] In 1886, the *San Francisco Chronicle* reported: "A part of the city that has life infused into it by the influx [of tourists] is Chinatown. The guides are busy every night, piloting parties through the devious ways of the quarter and in the day time the main thoroughfares of Chinatown are thronged with unguided tourists who benefit from the Mongol Merchant in the way of bric-a-brac purchases of small intrinsic and less artistic value, but well enough for souvenirs of our 'visit to California.'"[42] Daytime Chinatown with its merchant shops and throngs of tourists offered White visitors—including middle-class White women—a chance to become lost in the crowd while marveling at the spectacle of urban ethnic difference.

Merchants in Chinatown wanted to control the image that was presented to tourists, but the defining element of Chinatown for many visitors soon became the nighttime tour, which offered a different sort of visual pleasure. This was the allure of the unseen—the hidden tunnel, the opium den. Almost all guidebooks recommended that tourists see Chinatown by night. The travel guidebook *Seen by the Spectator* tells the reader: "It is in the evening, and preferably late at night that Chinatown must be seen . . . [when] opium joints, the theater, gambling-places, and the restaurants are the liveliest."[43] *Cosmopolitan* was more specific:

> Under the flickering gas-light, the grime that covers its buildings looks simply like the touch of time; squalid ruins transformed into picturesque decay; burning incense, many-colored lanterns, illuminate balconies, brilliantly-lighted shops, Rembrandt depths of shadow in narrow alleys—all these features the night brings forth.[44]

This was nighttime Chinatown as the ultimate urban visual scene.

Between 1870 and 1900, the nighttime tour of San Francisco Chinatown developed from an informal network of guides into a highly structured and regulated business. In the 1870s, visitors often had to seek out detectives by name or else venture to City Hall to find a policeman to escort them.[45] By the 1880s, guides could be found in the lobbies of some of the finest hotels.[46] Chinese Americans occasionally acted as guides, but most guides were former policemen or other White men who touted their knowledge of the community.[47] By the mid-1890s, tourism had become such big business that police officers began to abandon the job of watching the lobbies of fancy hotels for the more lucrative job of guiding tourists around Chinatown.[48] In 1897, San Francisco's board of supervisors began requiring all Chinatown guides to be licensed.[49] By the close of the nineteenth century, tour guides were leading paying visitors on tours of Mott Street in New York and Old Chinatown adjacent to the Plaza in Los Angeles. A few, like New York's Chuck Connors, became minor celebrities in their own right.[50] Chinatown had become a true urban attraction controlled primarily by White men.

Between the 1870s and the 1890s, elements of the new urban attraction became highly structured. In the 1890s, guidebooks like *Seen by the Spectator* described to their readers particular Chinatown sites that had to be seen on any visit. Key among these were the Chinese temple or joss house, the theater, the restaurant, and the underground opium den.[51] Publications rarely identified the name of the restaurant, temple, or theater, as such specifics were deemed unimportant. Rather, tour descriptions presented Chinatown as a series of archetypes standing in for unchanging cultural objects (The Chinese Restaurant, The Chinese Theater, etc.). These same sites appeared repeatedly in turn-of-the-century travel literature and were replicated in descriptions of visits to the Chinatowns of New York, Los Angeles, and San Francisco.

Among the archetypes, the opium den was often the central attraction of the Chinatown tour. According to the *San Francisco Chronicle*:

> Your party of exploration is guided into it by the faithful policeman, down steps slippery with accumulated filth and through an inner court whose pungent smells astonish by their novelty in spite of much previous experience of similar character. . . . On every shelf is a Yellow clay-skinned Chinaman in some degree of somnolent inebriety who stares at the intruders out of squinting oval eyes, and chatters faintly to neighbors regarding their presence. . . . It is only the novelty of a sight like this that prevents absolute disgust and sickness. It forms a fitting finale to the night's ramble in Chinatown. [52]

Written in the second person, this description places its reader at the center of a nighttime Chinatown tour. The opium den, the tour's finale, is described as a series of tropes at the center of yellow peril rhetoric: Chinatown as filthy, underground, crime-ridden, dangerous, and filled with illicit drug use.

At the same time, the article highlights the tour as a sensory experience. It describes underground Chinatown as a site where what is seen is augmented by what is felt (slippery steps), heard (faint chatter), and smelled (pungent odors). In the process, it becomes a novelty that elicits "disgust and sickness." Visitors often described Chinatown as engaging all the senses, unlike the cinema, which offered only moving images, and vaudeville, which offered images, sounds, and the occasional smell.[53]

Not only places in Chinatown were treated by visitors as archetypes; people were as well. A chapter in *Seen by the Spectator* opens with "Chinamen, like babies, are distinguishable—when you know them."[54] The writer describes a "small foot woman"[55] who "can be seen in a stuffy room at the head of a narrow flight of stairs, and her foot, what there is of it, is well worth the climb." After a discussion of a Chinese merchant, the writer states: "The guide has two trump cards, and he plays them last—his opium den and his leper." At the opium den, "one man, near the door, is awake, and after a monetary greeting, he smokes for the visitor and makes what the guide assures you is an opium inspiration of remarkable length. This man is always smoking when the parties arrive; unlike his fellows he is never overcome, and is always ready for exhibitions." Finally: "The leper lives on the same floor, and a pitiful object he is—an old man covered with a most revolting disease."[56]

In focusing on archetypical sites (the restaurant, the joss house, the theater, and the opium den) and people (the Chinese merchant, the woman with bound feet, the opium addict, the leper), the Chinatown tour reflected existing trends in nineteenth century entertainment.

Many nineteenth-century American cultural forms were defined by their conglomeration of elements or what film studies scholar Mark Rubin has called "aggregate forms" of entertainment. Dime museums, circuses, minstrel shows, vaudeville performances, and amusement parks were defined not by their narrative continuity but rather by their diverse elements. For example, Rubin describes the minstrel show as a "conglomeration of diverse parts in which each act was presented as a self-contained unit designed to stop the show."[57] He says that these elements came to define nineteenth-century American theater, where audiences became "more receptive to the concept of a theatrical show as a collection of powerful autonomous

THE COSMOPOLITAN.

JOSS HOUSE.

FIGURE 1.2. A joss house in Chinatown. *Cosmopolitan*, 1887.

moments and spectacular effects."[58] As aggregate entertainment, the purpose of the Chinatown tour was for visitors to experience a sequence of related spectacles, with each purportedly offering insight into a different aspect of Chinese American life. Tourists did not venture into Chinatown to interact with residents, stores, or restaurants in any meaningful way. Instead, tour guides and tourist literature positioned them to see Chinatown's archetypes as spectacles—individual manifestations of the Orient of the popular imagination.

The historian Raymond Rast argues that tourists in the late nineteenth century visited Chinatown out of the need to experience an authentic representation of Chinese American life. For Rast, Chinatown at the turn of the century was a place where both White tour guides and eventually Chinese American entrepreneurs drew in tourists with competing claims of authenticity. This authenticity was partly a result of a conception of Chinatown as existing outside of modernity. Rast writes of how bohemian writers and artists of the time "recast Chinatown as a vital preserve of authentic premodern culture, conveniently if curiously located amidst the swirl of modernity."[59] In the process, he argues, Chinatown became an "antimodern refuge" for many visitors. Given the ways in which modernity had come to define so much about the American city, Rast is most certainly correct in foregrounding authenticity in the Chinatown tourist experience. Authenticity, though, was not the only discourse at work in defining Chinatown for tourists.[60]

While visitors to Chinatown in the 1870s may have ventured into the neighborhood in the hope of experiencing an authentic representation of a pre-modern culture, by the turn of the century they were also coming to see Chinatown as a site of ethnographic performance, whose authenticity they were constantly doubting. One turn-of-the-century visitor, C. A. Kelley, described an underground den in Chinatown and an old man smoking opium: "It was sort of a fake, but gave us a very good idea of what those dens are like," but "whether it was real or not, it was a very good imitation, and answered the purpose just as well."[61] As far as Kelly was concerned, this performed authenticity functioned the same as the real thing. By the first decade of the twentieth century, short films like *Deceived Slumming Party* began to satirize the theatricality of Chinatown tours.[62]

With White city residents and visitors both in on the performance, Chinatown's theater of authenticity reached its logical conclusion the year before the 1906 earthquake. Chinese American merchants had worked diligently to get rid of the opium dens, and yet the underground was what tourists paid to see. As a result, the tour guides banded together and funded their own opium den, which the *San Francisco Chronicle* called the "municipal opium den" because it was known to city officials. The *Chronicle* reported: "[it] exists in Chinatown in the face of protests of the Chinese themselves, and for the sole profit of the Chinatown guides."[63] The transformation of Chinatown into a theatrical attraction was complete.

By this time, tourism in urban Chinatowns had become closely intertwined with theatricality. Performance studies scholars have shown that an actual theater is not a prerequisite for theatricality; rather, according to Josette Feral, theatricality occurs whenever the audience's gaze creates a "spatial cleft" between spectator and performer that allows illusion to emerge. As long as this spatial cleft is present, theatricality exists regardless of whether the subject of the gaze is consciously performing.[64] Similar to theater, Orientalist depictions of Chinatown led many tourists to believe that they were entering a world that was socially, spatially, and temporally distinct from the rest of the city. As a result, Orientalist understandings of urban Chinatowns created the spatial cleft that led visitors to regard urban Chinatowns as a theater in which both the neighborhood and its residents existed for their visual pleasure.

Visitors arrived in Chinatown hoping to witness the dangers they had read about and expecting these dangers to be performed for them. That is to say, many tourists entered Chinatown hoping to encounter not the actual yellow peril but a performance of the world they had long seen represented in popular culture. In this way, Chinatown tours came to be defined paradoxically by competing discourses of authenticity and theatricality. Visitors did not want to be put in actual danger. Like theatergoers, they wanted to suspend disbelief and be transported to an imaginary world—albeit one that provided what they believed to be "authentic" insights into Chinese life.

Given the ever-present theatricality of Chinatown, many Chinese American merchants wanted to stage their own productions for tourists.[65] The problem was that, for the most part, they did not control the mechanisms necessary to write and publish guidebooks that would reach a mass audience. By the 1890s, they were even marginalized as tour guides. What's more, in San Francisco and New York Chinese Americans merchants owned few of the buildings they occupied and had little control over the general atmosphere of the community. While some, such as restaurant owners and the occasional tour guide, found ways to profit off of tourists, for the most part Chinese American interactions with tourists occurred in the larger tourist industry controlled by White entrepreneurs.

There were sites during this period that offered Chinese American merchants a platform for their own representations to tens of thousands of enthralled visitors. These were the nation's world's fairs. It was on the Midway Plaisance of the World's Columbian Exposition held in Chicago in 1893 that

Chinese American entrepreneurs began to develop techniques that would eventually be used by Chinese merchants in urban Chinatowns to reshape the boundaries of race, gender, and nationality in ways more beneficial to themselves.

The Midway Plaisance sat between 59th and 60th Streets on the west side of the exposition.[66] Entering from Cottage Grove Avenue and walking east down the Midway toward the "White City" and the official grounds, tourists passed Sitting Bull Cabin, the Streets of Cairo, and the Panorama of Volcano Kilauea among other attractions. The Midway was a hybrid of popular anthropology, commercial spectacle, and urban amusement that placed all the world's people on a racist continuum from civilization to savagery.[67] Fighting for the attention of tourists was the Chinese Village. Like other attractions on the Midway, the Chinese Village was built to make a profit for its investors, and, like other ventures, it did this through the sale and performance of ethnic difference. Unlike most other attractions on the Midway, however, which were controlled by White entrepreneurs, the Chinese Village was established and run by Chinese Americans.

To build their Chinese Village, Gee Wo Chan, a Chinese herbalist from Omaha, Nebraska, and Hong Sling, a labor contractor from Ogden, Utah, along with Wong Kee, a Chicago grocer, founded a company that raised over $90,000 from investors in the Chinese American communities of Chicago, Kansas City, and San Francisco.[68] They named it the Wah Mee, or Chinese American, Exposition Company,[69] and hired the architectural firm of Wilson and Marble to build a joss house, a theater, a bazaar, and a café on the Midway.[70] So comprehensive was this attraction that Hubert Bancroft called it "the Chinatown of the Fair."[71]

Like all Chinatowns across the United States in 1893, the Chinese village welcomed visitors at a moment of profound precarity for the Chinese immigrant community.[72] The prior year, the federal government had passed the Geary Act, which renewed Chinese exclusion for another decade and required all Chinese immigrants to register for photo identification or risk deportation. The exposition in Chicago opened to the public on the first of May 1893, just four days before the federal deadline to register for an identification certificate.[73] The Chinese Village must be understood within the context of these restrictive immigration policies. Indeed, if it were not for the Geary Act, the Wah-Mee Company may never have been formed.

While countries across the globe built official exhibits on the main grounds, the Chinese government boycotted the exhibition to protest the passage of the Geary Act. This left Chinese American merchants to produce their own attraction on the midway beyond the official grounds.[74] The tension between the ostensibly "educational" aspects of the fair and the profit motive of the midway created a distinct space for Hong Sling, Gee Wo Chan, and Wong Kee to use the Chinese Village to challenge the anti-Chinese immigrant sentiments at the heart of the Geary Act.[75] Thus, the Chinese Village represented a challenge to the political rhetoric that undergirded Chinese exclusion.[76]

Far from being just a commercial venture, the Chinese Village provided an opportunity for the merchant class to assert a distinctly Chinese American identity at a time when they were actively fighting for civil rights and inclusion. The first use of "Chinese American" occurred with the launch of the bilingual newspaper *Chinese American* in 1893 in Chicago, published by Wong Chin Foo.[77] The first issue called for a national civil rights conference for Chinese Americans in Chicago: "You could come here for a double purpose, that of seeing one of the grandest sights of your life and inaugurating one of the greatest movements the Chinese ever had in this country. You will then have an opportunity to elect your own national leaders to fight for your own rights."[78]

The *Chinese American*'s call built on work done the year before, when 150 upwardly mobile Chinese Americans met in New York and founded the Chinese Equal Rights League. Wong Chin Foo was named secretary. The group formed with the broader mission of denouncing the Geary Act and advocating for expanded civil rights for Chinese Americans.[79] In challenging the act, the league stated: "We, therefore, appeal for an equal chance in the race of life in this our adopted home. . . . Chinese immigration, as well as Irish immigration, Italian and other immigration cannot be stopped by the persecution of our law-abiding citizens in the United States."[80] They declared the Geary Act "a monstrous and inhumane measure."

Yet in challenging the act, they also embraced a set of divisive stances that distanced Chinese American merchants from more working-class Chinese immigrant laborers. The members of the league wrote: "Treat us as men and we will do our duty as men and will aid you to stop this obnoxious evil that threatens the welfare of this Republic. We do not want any more Chinese here anymore than you do. The scarcer the Chinese here the better would be our condition among you." In making claims to their own equal rights as middle-class merchants, the members of the league embraced a respectability politics that perpetuated many of the darker elements of yellow peril stereotypes. Rather than challenge the stereotypes of Chinese laborers as an alien threat to the nation, the members of the Chinese Equal Rights League distanced themselves from their more working-class immigrant compatriots.

While not as explicit in its rhetoric, the *Chinese American* furthered the League's respectability politics through its profiles of Hong Sling, Gee Wo Chan, and Wong Kee, emphasizing their use of English, their western dress, and their economic investment in the United States. The paper introduced Hong Sling as a railroad contractor from Omaha, Nebraska, "who invested nearly all his money in this country."[81] Gee Wo Chan was a Chinese medicine practitioner who first came to the US in 1884 "and fell deeply in love with the country." Wong Kee was a grocer, "reported to be the richest" Chinese merchant in Chicago. Alongside the profiles, the paper ran illustrations of Gee Wo Chan and Hong Sling attired in western suits with their hair cut in a western style and missing the traditional Chinese queue. From other sources at the time, we know that Gee Wo Chan had recently married one of his former patients, Clara De Witt. Shortly after his marriage, he told the *Omaha Bee* that he expected to make Chicago his "permanent home."[82] We also know that Wong Kee was a member of the Chinese Equal Rights League.[83]

For the three controlling members of the Wah Mee Company, the exposition was the ideal place to construct counter-representations that supported their political demands of equal rights for the Chinese American elite. In the process, they chose the Chinatown tour as their mechanism to advance these counter-representations. Like other American Chinatowns, the Chinese Village functioned as an aggregate form of entertainment that allowed visitors to experience autonomous spectacles. These spectacles included a restaurant, a joss house, a bazaar, and a theater. Unlike the typical White-led Chinatown tour, the Chinese Village tour replaced yellow peril stereotypes with the new Chinatown Pastiche. By simultaneously drawing on White Americans' growing fascination with the Far East and assuaging dominant fears of an unassimilable yellow peril, Chinatown Pastiche transformed the imagined Orient of the West into a nonthreatening commodity that could be sold for the benefit of the Chinese American merchant class.

F I G U R E   1 . 3 .   The Chinese Theatre. *The Dream City: A Portfolio of Photographic Views of the World's Columbian Exposition*, 1893.

The *Chicago Tribune* described the Chinese Village on the Midway as "one of the most picturesque ornaments," highlighting its defining ornamental aesthetic.[84] Designed not by a Chinese architect or even by the merchants of the Wah Mee Company but rather by a Chicago-based architectural firm, the village was not so much an authentic representation of China as it was a Chinese American attraction, managed and performed by the Wah Mee Company explicitly for White visitors. The entrance was marked by two 80-foot pagoda-esque towers painted in what Hubert Bancroft described as "prismatic colors."[85] The towers featured six levels, each with a small ornamental balcony adorned with bells on its four corners. Atop one tower was an American flag. Between the two towers was a covered balcony and tiled roof, across which hung a sign that read "Wah Mee Exposition

Company." The colorful pagodas and flags contrasted explicitly with the underground Chinatown tours with their staged opium dens experienced under the cover of darkness.

The foregrounded ornamental aesthetic existed alongside the Chinatown performances. Visitors entered the village—not by passing through an opium den or underground chamber but by entering an expansive building that held most of the attractions. A band played Chinese musical instruments on the balcony above the entrance as visitors walked past two yellow wickerwork dragons and through the doors of the Temple of China, where they were greeted by a large indoor bazaar.[86] The size of the building, 15,000 square feet, was noted by Hubert Bancroft. The bazaar featured what Bancroft described as "silks and embroideries, toilet appliances and table ware, with other articles such as are offered for sale in Chinese stores of the better class."[87] Its size and openness were in direct contrast to the stereotypes of a dark underground Chinatown with cramped secret passages.

The musicians at the entrance of the Chinese Village were only one of its theatrical elements. The village also featured an actual theater where tourists could watch staged performances. The village was also defined by the numerous smaller rehearsed actions of its Chinese employees. For example, visitors to the bazaar encountered an old man who told them their fortunes for a fee of ten cents. An assistant sat at the fortune teller's side to translate for those who paid.[88] According to the *Chicago Tribune*, the fortunes were always positive.[89] Visitors paid not for an actual fortune but for the performance of one.

The connection between the village's Chinatown performances and its ornamental surface aesthetic was also present in the restaurant and tea garden. Here the Wah Mee Exposition Company once again challenged dominant representations of the Chinatown tours of the period. Toward the end of the nineteenth century, few White tourists ate in Chinatowns, which were often represented as a public health problem. A popular stereotype was that the Chinese ate rats.[90] In fact, Chinese restaurants serving White customers were so rare that the city directory of San Francisco for the years 1897 and 1898 showed not one among the 540 restaurants it listed.[91] This is not to say that tourists never ventured into Chinese restaurants during the 1880s and 1890s. Rather, they usually did so under the guidance of a White tour guide. In contrast, the Chinese Village offered its restaurant and tea garden for visitors to explore and enjoy at their own pace.

A few months before the opening of the village, Gee Wo Chan described his plans for the restaurant. It was to be furnished with "ebony tables and stools all artistically inlaid with pearls"[92] set in a room that was planned at 8,000 square feet. According to one guidebook, "the restaurant is conducted upon both the American and Mongolian plans, and fried chicken, ham sandwiches, etc., will alternate with Chinese fruits, preserves, shark's fins, bird's nest soup and similar delicacies."[93] It introduced elaborate Chinese dishes alongside foods recognizable to typical White visitors, who were welcome to stay as long as they liked, in an opulent environment. White-robed Chinese waiters interacted with visitors while taking their orders.[94] One report noted that the exposition company had educated its waiters to take orders in French and German in addition to English.[95] The cosmopolitanism displayed by the waitstaff directly challenged the common stereotype of Chinese immigrants as insular and unwilling to assimilate into broader American society.

The aspect of the attraction that best embodied the ornamental surface aesthetic was the joss house, which visitors paid an additional 10 cents to enter. Located above the bazaar, the joss house was not, as the name implied, an actual religious site. The term "joss" refers to a Chinese religious statue, but there was no religious significance to this joss house. Instead, the visitor encountered a room "crowded with Chinese curios that are rarely brought into this country," including a large carving entitled "Ten Courts of Justice In-Hell."[96] Lacking any actual religious significance, the joss house offered only its ornamental aesthetic appeal. Despite this, it was, according to the *Chicago Tribune*, "still worth a visit."[97] In assessing its worth, the *Tribune* mentioned not only the curios on display but also the presence of three people—a Chinese woman with two children—whom the Wah Mee Exposition Company presented to the White visiting public as attractions in their own right.

The woman and children were mentioned in two *Chicago Tribune* articles. The first described "a little Chinese mother who moves about very softly and does everything in a gentle way that must be soothing to the nerves of the two babies that everyone crowds up to see."[98] The second described "one of the few Chinese women who have ever been brought to America. She has with her two children a girl 2 and ½ of age and a boy of 11 months, who are alone worth the price of admission."[99] Neither article provided the names of the woman or the children. Instead, the paper treated them as just another attraction.[100]

FIGURE 1.4. The Chinese Joss House. *The Dream City: A Portfolio of Photographic Views of the World's Columbian Exposition*, 1893.

In her book *Ornamentalism*, Asian American Studies scholar Anne Anlin Cheng traces the gendered connection between the Oriental and the ornamental that has long defined Western cultural conceptions of Asian femininity. Cheng demonstrates the ways that the racialized and gendered Asian American female body has been conflated with ornamentation. She writes that ornamentalism "describes the peculiar process (legally, materially, imaginatively) whereby personhood is named or conceived through ornamental gestures, which speak through the minute, the sartorial, the prosthetic, and the decorative,"[101] and she describes how the "White, masculine, organic personhood of Western modernity" came to be defined in part against this understanding of "Ornamental personhood" as embodied in Western representations of Asian femininity.[102] With its focus on bright colors and surface aesthetics, and its display of the unnamed Chinese woman, the Chinese Village was suffused with ornamentalism.

One guidebook mentioned perhaps the only other Chinese woman on display at the fair, "The Chinese Beauty," in the International Costume

Exhibit on the Midway. According to *The Dream City*, "she was often seen fast asleep in her chair, oblivious to the indifference with which the male generation of Caucasians passed her on their way to Fatma's Sultanic bower at the end of the room."[103] The sleeping woman found her agency where she could, in this case by ignoring the many tourists.

Of course, sleeping in the face of visitors was only one way the two Chinese women on display at the Columbian Exposition could assert their agency. The other, most obvious, way was to return the gaze that looked upon them as little more than attractions. Writing about the agency of indigenous and other racialized people in ethnic villages at world's fairs, film studies scholar Fatimah Rony finds that a primary form of agency for racialized people was in the ever-present possibility of their turning their own gaze on the White spectator.[104] For many of those forced to be on display at world's fairs, returning the spectator's gaze was one of their most potent tools in asserting their humanity.

Gee Wo Chan, Wong Kee, and Hong Sling deployed Chinatown Pastiche in ways that laid claim to their place as future citizen-subjects of the United States, but they built their claim on a foundation riddled with contradictions. They may have sought entry into full personhood in the eyes of White Americans in part through the display of the Chinese woman and children. However, like the Chinese Equal Rights League, Chinatown Pastiche did not provide equal entry into the imagined community of the nation for all Chinese Americans. Rather, these Chinese American merchants based their claim for inclusion on a respectability politics that was gendered, class based, and marginalizing of many in their own community. The Chinese American women on display at the fair were the most obvious example. Chinatown Pastiche also did relatively little for the mass of Chinese immigrant laborers at the center of yellow peril rhetoric.

Despite attempts by Hong Sling, Gee Wo Chan, and Wong Kee, the Chinese Village was a financial failure, sending the Wah Mee Exposition Company into receivership before the summer was over.[105] The failure laid bare its financial troubles, splashing the company's problems across the pages of the nation's newspapers. By the fall of 1894, one of the two men who had been sent to China to recruit performers for the village found himself facing a lawsuit for embezzlement brought by Chinese American investors in the company.[106] The other recruiter refused to return from China.

A second suit was brought against the White agent who had secured the Midway property for the exhibit.[107] Hong Sling, the manager of the Chinese Village and one of its principal investors, lost more than $30,000 of his own money. According to the *Chicago Tribune*, he called the whole venture "a gigantic swindle."[108] From an economic standpoint, Wah Mee proved a complete disaster, but the cultural legacy of the Chinese Village on the Midway would be far-reaching.

In the decades that followed the World's Columbian Exposition, the vision of Chinese America first set out in the Chinese Village became a significant cultural counterpoint to yellow peril imagery. Two images of Chinatown now competed for dominance in the American popular imagination—underground Chinatown and Chinatown Pastiche. This cultural conflict would soon escape the confines of Chicago and head to San Francisco.

The destruction of most of San Francisco's Chinatown in the 1906 earthquake and fire provided an opportunity for its Chinese American merchants to replicate the strategies of the Chinese Village on much larger scale.[109] Among the leaders of these efforts was Look Tin Eli, the manager of the Sing Chong Bazaar, who was born in the coastal Northern California town of Mendocino and who played an important part in rebuilding Chinatown after the 1906 earthquake and fire. In 1907, he was a founder and the first president of the Bank of Canton in San Francisco, one of the first Chinese-owned banks in the nation.[110] But perhaps more important in the wake of the earthquake was that with other Chinese American leaders he pushed the merchant class to hire White firms to create a new architectural motif for the neighborhood that would appeal explicitly to tourists.[111]

Look Tin Eli hired the architect T. Patterson Ross and the engineer A. W. Burgren to redesign the Sing Chong Bazaar building in a more overtly ornamental style. The pair also redesigned the Sing Fat Company, which sat directly across the street. Ross and Burgren put pagoda-like towers atop each building and installed large expanses of glass on the ground floor of the bazaar as display windows. Designed in conjunction, the two buildings framed the intersection of California Street at Dupont Avenue (later renamed Grant Avenue) when approached from the east.[112] As was the case with most of Chinatown, the Sing Chong Bazaar was located on a lot owned by White landowners and leased to the Chinese. Despite not owning the land, Look

FIGURE 1.5.   The Sing Chong Building. *Architect and Engineer*, 1908.

Tin Eli, like so many other Chinese American merchants, pushed ahead with his plans. [113]

Tourists who visited the Sing Chong Bazaar after the earthquake were certainly taken in by it. In 1908, the magazine *Architect and Engineer* described the Bazaar as "one of the sites of San Francisco . . . truly the gateway to the Orient of the Golden Gate." After describing its Pagoda roofs and electric lights, the article stated: "The Sing Chong Bazaar is a startling but pleasing combination of flamboyant Far Eastern gaudiness of color and clear Yankee enterprise and up-to-dateness. Chinese clerks, speaking precise English, attend to customers with Oriental politeness." [114]

Despite the broader success of this venture, the image of Chinatown promoted by Look Tin Eli and his fellow merchants did not signal the end of the underground stereotypes. [115] Instead, at a moment when White guides found it increasingly difficult to lead tours that drew on yellow peril imagery, one vaudeville promoter found a way to revive the tours. Ironically, the destination of the new underground Chinatown tour was not Chinatown at all but rather the city's Panama Pacific International Exhibition of 1915. The promoter, Sid Grauman, a thirty-six-year-old Bay Area theater owner and vaudeville showman, chose the exhibition's midway area, known popularly as the "the Zone" for his attraction.[116]

Amid the showmen, animals, and mechanical amusements, Sid Grauman invested $12,000 to produce a walkthrough exhibit that he dubbed "Underground Chinatown" in the Zone's Chinese Village and Pagoda.[117] It combined elements of a Chinatown guided tour with vaudeville in an exhibit that reflected the worst yellow peril stereotypes. Visitors witnessed scenes featuring both wax figures and White actors in yellowface.[118] These included wax Chinese opium smokers along with actors playing Chinese prostitutes who would call out to White tourists. According to one contemporary account, the scenes changed depending on whether there were Chinese in the crowds. When none were present, there were scenes of Chinese men plotting to kidnap White women.[119]

The exhibit was met with outrage from the local Chinese American community. Different groups in the ethnic enclave wrote letters to the president of the exposition expressing their desire to see it closed. Only after the official head of the Chinese delegation added his voice to the protest did the president agree to close it.[120] Grauman stripped the exhibit of all mention of the Chinese and representations of Chinese characters in the show. He then reopened it with a new name, "Underground Slumming." As historian Abagail Markwyn has noted, the name change could not remove the association with the Chinese.[121] After all, Underground Slumming was still housed in the Chinese Village and Pagoda.

While it would be tempting to see Underground Chinatown's replacement by Underground Slumming as the end of yellow peril representations of Chinatown, this was hardly the case. The years 1918 and 1919 saw the mass production of a traveling carnival attraction,[122] which appeared in rural towns and large cities from Beatrice, Nebraska, to Coney Island and featured all the stereotypes of the underground Chinatown.[123] An advertisement described it as a walkthrough that faithfully reproduced "all the weird and interesting sights of San Francisco's Chinatown as it was before the great fire and days of reform,"[124] including "opium dens, gambling holes, joss house, secret tunnels, slave girls"—in short, all of the worst yellow peril stereotypes associated with San Francisco Chinatown before the earthquake.[125] Chinese Americans protested this traveling attraction, making its success short lived.[126]

Of course, by 1918 carnivals, urban tours, and vaudeville were being re-placed by motion pictures. Ever the showman, Sid Grauman recognized this. In the months following the opening of his exhibit at the Panama Pacific International Exposition, he signed a contract with Fox Studios for his Empress Theater in San Francisco to show movie serials. In 1918 Grauman moved to Hollywood to pursue movie exhibition full-time. In 1929 he opened what would become perhaps the world's most famous movie palace, Grauman's Chinese Theater. The Chinese American community would respond less than a decade later with New Chinatown.

Opened during the height of the Depression by Chinese American merchants, New Chinatown in Los Angeles drew on elements of Chinatown Pastiche that the merchants had been developing for nearly fifty years. Even as car culture began to dominate the city, New Chinatown was built in a way that required visitors to park and then walk through its central plaza. Both White visitors and Chinese Americans were now able to stroll through the district's streets, taking in the sights like the nineteenth-century *flaneur*. New Chinatown quickly became a meeting place for Chinese Americans and White tourists alike.

Entering New Chinatown from Castelar Street, visitors passed through one of two large Chinese gates.[127] To the left was the Yee Hung Guey restaurant; to the right, the Yee Sing Chong grocery store. As visitors walked east through the plaza, they passed Tin Hing Company Jewelry, the Man Jen Low restaurant and the Y. C Hong building, which housed Hong's law office on the second floor. Across from Man Jen Low was a wishing well based on the Seven Star Sacred Caverns in China and a willow tree donated by Paramount Studios in honor of Anna May Wong. Across from the wishing well was a stand where Charlie Chan sold fortunes to curious tourists.

As visitors continued through the district, they passed the large neon-lit "Chop Suey" sign that adorned the new Tuey Far Lowe restaurant.[128] The restaurant building also housed K. G. Louie Gifts and the Chinese Jade restaurant and cocktail lounge. Finally, on Broadway stood Chinatown's East Gate, which was sponsored by Chinatown founder, Y. C. Hong, and dedicated to the memory of his mother. All this existed on a privately owned outdoor mall.

FIGURE 1.6. Fortune teller Charlie Chan in New Chinatown in the late 1930s. *New York Daily News*, UCLA Library Special Collections, Copyright © 1935, Creative Commons, Attribution 4.0 International License.

Despite an opening-day speech by the Chinese consul of Los Angeles lauding the "traditional beauty of [the district's] Chinese architectural arts," New Chinatown's pagoda style and Chinese-themed roofs more closely reflected the motifs of the rebuilt San Francisco Chinatown than they did anything traditionally Chinese.[129] In fact, like the Chinese Village at the World's Columbian Exposition of 1893 or San Francisco Chinatown after the earthquake, the Los Angeles Chinatown Project Association hired White architects—in this case Erle Webster and Adrian Wilson. Early in the process, Y. C. Hong went so far as to send Erle Webster to San Francisco for ideas.[130] By the 1930s, San Francisco had come to represent the archetypal Chinatown in the minds of many visitors. It was the Chinatown Pastiche of San Francisco, and not the traditional aesthetics of China itself, that New Chinatown emulated.

With wide open boulevards and neon lighting, New Chinatown was the antithesis of the narrow alleyways and underground opium dens of the nineteenth-century Chinatown tour. In fact, a defining feature was its neon.

In 1948, ten years after the opening of New Chinatown, local resident Garding Lui described the district in *Inside Los Angeles Chinatown*:

> When trains from the north and the east enter Los Angeles at night, children out the west side of the coaches flatten their noses against the windowpanes and say, "Look at Fairland!" The last thing that is seen before the train gets into Union Depot, are the lights of New Chinatown. The electrical display, outlining these buildings and the prominent North Broadway location, put New Chinatown very prominently on the map. The grounds are spacious and future growth is anticipated.[131]

Thus New Chinatown eventually came to be associated in the minds of the public with wide-open, brightly lit boulevards in the same way that Old Chinatown had been associated with dark and narrow alleyways.

FIGURE 1.7.   New Chinatown, opening night in 1938. Photo by Harry Quillen, Harry Quillen Collection, Los Angeles Public Library.

New Chinatown mirrored many of the elements of the Chinese Village in Chicago at the turn of the century. The whole district was in many ways a visual attraction meant to capture the attention of tourists and encourage them to stay and spend money. It employed many of the same techniques that had been used in both Chicago and San Francisco: Chinese-themed architecture, bright colors, food, and even a fortune teller—all located in an outdoor mall owned by Chinese Americans. In Los Angeles, Chinatown Pastiche reached its logical conclusion with the opening of New Chinatown in 1938, one year before the outbreak of the Second World War.

CHAPTER 2

China City and New Chinatown on Broadway

On June 8, 1938, the front page of the *Los Angeles Times* announced: "China City Lures Crowd." The paper described the opening festivities the prior night: "cymbals crashed and great gongs thundered" while visitors took rickshaw rides "through narrow streets lighted by Chinese lanterns" and tourists "thronged cafes and shops." According to the *Times*, ten thousand people took part in the opening night celebration. They were greeted by "Chinese girls in flattering silks." They watched movies as part of "standing room only" crowds. "Even Mrs. Christine Sterling, founder and developer of both Olvera Street and China City, expressed her surprise," according to the *Times*.

Ms. Sterling should not have been surprised by the crowd. After all, her friends at the *Los Angeles Times* had been actively promoting her tourist attraction as it was being built over the prior six months. Earlier that week, *Times* columnist Ed Ainsworth had devoted a column to previewing Sterling's new tourist district.[1] In March, the *Times* had announced that China City had been given the film set from Paramount Pictures' *Bluebeard's Eighth Wife*.[2] Then, a day before opening, Dora Song appeared on the paper's front page grinning as she posed next to a dragon head that had once featured on the *Los Angeles Times* building. The accompanying headline announced: "Curtain Raised on City's Bit of Orient." An adjoining image featured Sterling eating in China City with *Times* publisher Harry Chandler.[3] From January through June of 1938, the paper bombarded its readers with stories about Sterling's new project. Readers could be forgiven for thinking that it was the only Chinatown opening in Los Angeles. Over the same period, the paper ran almost no stories about Peter SooHoo's competing New Chinatown project, which opened on June 25, 1938. Most of the city's papers gave the opening front-page coverage. A few even devoted an entire two-page spread. In contrast, the *Times* limited its coverage to one short story, without images, buried on page A3.[4]

For most of the early twentieth century, the city's newspapers had played a critical role in crafting an image of Los Angeles Chinatown as a dangerous slum populated with criminals and drug users, all the while selling Southern California as the suburban dreamland for middle-class White families. If Los Angeles was going to promote itself as a suburban dreamland, it needed a racialized, working-class urban community against which it could define itself.[5] The *Times* helped transform Chinatown—or at least its popular image—into that community.[6]

In their competition with Sterling, SooHoo and his Los Angeles Chinatown Project Association demonstrated a deft understanding of Chinatown's changing place in the local and national psyche. The group dubbed their project "Chinatown on Broadway," though most people would not refer to it that way.[7] SooHoo and his compatriots believed that New Chinatown should not explicitly reflect Hollywood's vision of Chinatown or China. Instead, they drew inspiration from the rebuilt San Francisco Chinatown. Explicitly rejecting the narrative of White paternalism so closely attached to Christine Sterling's China City, New Chinatown's founders presented an image of Chinese Americans as hardworking and civic-minded—an essential part of the city's new cosmopolitan image of itself. Implicit in this narrative was a deeply conservative celebration of self-sufficiency and individualism that rejected not only the White paternalism of China City but also the government support that so many in the community desperately needed during the Great Depression.

At a moment when Chinese immigrants were still legally considered "aliens ineligible for citizenship" and when Chinese laborers were still barred from entering the United States, the Los Angeles Chinatown Project Association used press releases, news coverage, and a highly choreographed opening to craft Chinatown as part of a new cosmopolitan understanding of Los Angeles. Challenging decades of coverage in the city papers depicting Old Chinatown as a yellow peril, the association sought to redefine its perceived differences as nonthreatening, consumable, and in line with conservative American understandings of individualism, merit, and unregulated free-market capitalism.

Certainly not all Chinese Americans could or would align themselves with the vision of progress advanced by the merchants behind Chinatown on Broadway. In fact, many would-be entrepreneurs priced out of New Chinatown rented space in the more affordable China City. It is easy to dismiss China City as "a site that articulated a domesticating form of White supremacy," as one scholar has done, but reading the district only through the ways in which it racialized Chinese Americans misses the opportunities China City provided for Chinese Americans who could not, or would not, buy into New Chinatown.[8] China City may have been defined by its Hollywood artifice and, at times, racist logics, but the bonds that Chinese Americans formed with one another in China City during the community's short existence were real.

Seen in this context, the Los Angeles Chinatown Project Association's greatest success was not that New Chinatown uplifted the entire community—it did not. Instead, the narrative advanced by Peter SooHoo and his fellow merchants accepted the premise of Chinese ethnic difference so ingrained in exclusion-era United States while seeking to reshape perceived differences to make them more compatible with American consumerism. The New Chinatown founders wanted to reshape the image of Los Angeles itself from one in which suburban Whiteness was defined against an imagined underground Chinatown to one in which the Chinese American business district—and its upwardly mobile merchants—were celebrated as a part of a burgeoning multiethnic metropolis.

In many ways, the city of Los Angeles was imagined into existence.[9] Following the completion of the Southern Pacific Railway in 1876 and the Santa Fe Railway in 1886, city leaders, boosters, and land speculators began transforming this former Mexican town into a major U.S. urban center. Railroads hired journalists to promote the area while newspapers publishers like Harrison Gray Otis used their power to sell a carefully crafted image of the city to the nation. These city boosters brought a demographic transformation to Southern California. The historian Carey McWilliams described the transformation as the "largest internal migration in United States history."[10] This characterization is certainly debatable, but rapid growth following the completion of the railways and the subsequent booster campaign was undeniable. Los Angeles proper grew from a town of 11,000 in 1880 to city of 100,000 by the turn of the century. By 1910, there were more than 300,000 people living there; in 1920, there were more than 575,000; and by 1930, there were more than a million. Rather than being drawn to any specific industry, the new transplants were often attracted by the image of a White family in a suburban-style home located in a region of temperate weather.

In selling Los Angeles, Progressive-era reformers and developers advanced the suburban single-family house as the antidote to urban overcrowding in older cities on the East Coast and in the Midwest.[11]

Private developers placed deed restrictions on lots forbidding owners to build anything but single-family dwellings. At the same time, city government designed parks, planned streets, built government buildings, and established building codes.[12] Even as Los Angeles grew rapidly over the first three decades of the twentieth century, its population remained smaller and more dispersed than the populations of Chicago or New York.[13] The 1920s alone saw the creation of 3,200 subdivisions and 250,000 homes.[14] Central to this expansion was the idea that the suburban home represented a refuge for the White middle-class family fleeing the multitudes of the city with its urban racial differences. In linking the home to the nation, one 1924 advertisement touting the Los Angeles area quoted President Coolidge: "The American home is the foundation of our national and individual well-being. Its steady improvement, at the same time, a test of our civilization and our ideals."[15]

Unlike Chicago or New York, which attracted large numbers of immigrants from Europe during this period, most people who settled in Los Angeles during the early twentieth century were US-born Whites. Between 1910 and 1930, Americans born outside of California made up three-quarters of those who moved there. In the 1910s alone, a full one-third of all Americans moving west of the Rockies settled in Los Angeles.[16] The Midwestern transplants established state societies to preserve their Kansas, Nebraska, and Iowa roots.[17] The influx of Anglo settlers was so great that in the decades before World War II, *Los Angeles Times* publisher Harry Chandler took to calling the city the nation's "white spot," an expression of rapid economic growth tinged with racial meaning.[18]

As the center of the suburban image of Los Angeles, the family home became the symbolic site where property, Whiteness, and normative notions of gender, sexuality, and family collided. The thirty-second edition of Harry

Los Angeles, A City of Homey Homes

FIGURE 2.1. "Los Angeles, A City of Homey Homes." Harry Ellington Brook in *Los Angeles California: The City and County*, 1921.

Ellington Brook's guidebook to Los Angeles, produced by the Los Angeles Chamber of Commerce in 1921, presented the Southern California home as a place of leisure whose benefits were available only to White homeowners. It declared: "After all is said, the chief attraction of Los Angeles to new arrivals lies in its beautiful homes. The rare beauty of the grounds surrounding

Just Southern California

FIGURE 2.2. "Just Southern California." Harry Ellington Brook in *Los Angeles, California: The City and County*, 1921.

the attractive homes of Los Angeles, Pasadena, Long Beach, and other Los Angeles County cities is a constant theme of admiration on the part of Eastern visitors."[19]

In this setting of power and privilege, some of the most interesting photos in the guidebook are those of White residents in the yards of single-family houses. In one, "Just Southern California," a young woman in a white dress stands smiling in her front yard. The yard is so overgrown that flowers engulf the entire front porch. The composition emphasizes this overgrowth. When contrasted against the guidebook's many images of banks, schools, and government buildings, "Just Southern California" represents the home as a garden sanctuary where middle-class White women can escape from the stresses of urban life and its racialized masses.

Other promotional materials were even more explicit in centering the White middle-class family. An advertisement for the new subdivision of Eagle Rock in 1925 sold the community as "The Homeland of the World." It showed a large home surrounded by trees with a woman in the doorway and a child running down to meet a suited man with a briefcase. The accompanying text states: "As you journey about Eagle Rock, enjoying immeasurably the ideal climate that is ours, you will observe that the residents are all of the White race—and you will note that building restrictions have prevented the construction of unsightly homes."[20] The ad explicitly connects a White supremacist logic with suburban aesthetics as a selling point.[21]

Beneath this vision of what Charles Fletcher Lummis called the "land of sunshine" lay a violent and exclusionary boosterism that was racialized from the start. Promoted primarily to middle-class Anglo-Saxon Protestants in the Midwest, this vision relied on legal and extra-legal means to marginalize people of color. No amount of advertising could mask the fact that people of color had been in Southern California well before boosters like Charles Lummis began their aggressive promotions. From the indigenous Tongva people whose native land this was, to the wealthy Mexican land-grant owners whom Anglo settlers encountered following the Mexican-American War, to the Chinese railroad workers who helped complete the Southern Pacific and Santa Fe railways—Los Angeles was composed of a vibrant mix of people. In the early twentieth century, race in Los Angeles did not function around a Black/White binary. Rather, as Natalia Molina

FIGURE 2.3. Racist advertisement. *Los Angeles Times*, 1925.

has observed, "in Los Angeles, people saw race differently."[22] Whiteness in Los Angeles was cast against a larger non-White category, with various non-White ethnic groups having differing access to power and privilege.[23]

Even as the population of Los Angeles grew, its cheerleaders recast the city's non-White residents in ways beneficial to the city's White majority. In 1880, 800 Chinese, Japanese, Mexicans, and Blacks lived in a town of little more than 11,000 people. By 1930, people of color made up more than 150,000 of the city's 1.2 million residents. In the case of Mexican Americans, city image-makers sought to incorporate this subpopulation into the image they were meticulously crafting. City leaders and boosters created what William Deverell has called a "usable ethnic past" that incorporated the Spanish and Mexican history of the region into a coherent story that matched what the promoters wanted to sell.[24] To do this, they reshaped the public perception of Mexican history into what Carey McWilliam's calls a "Spanish Fantasy heritage."[25] Examples include the revival of Spanish Colonial architecture in the closing decades of the twentieth century, the La Fiesta Festival held in the city in 1894, and Christine Sterling's refashioning of Olvera Street as a romanticized Mexican marketplace.[26] In this way, the Los Angeles's Spanish and Mexican past was incorporated into its racially White present. While less well documented, Chinese Americans, and Chinatown in particular, also played a defining role in the way the city was imagined.

For most of the nineteenth century, Los Angeles was not a welcoming place for Chinese Americans. The first Chinese woman to live in Los Angeles reportedly attempted suicide less than a month after her arrival in 1859.[27] Despite the inhospitality, by 1870 172 Chinese Americans called the city home.[28] They built a small Chinatown on a street known in Spanish as Calle de Los Negros. In the minds of nineteenth-century Anglo residents, anti-Blackness collided with Orientalism to shape the popular conception of the street. Local newspapers and many of the region's Anglo residents gave it a much more violently racist moniker: [N-word] Alley.[29] They saw the neighborhood as a den of vice, depravity, and racial Otherness that threatened the body politic. These feelings erupted into violence in 1871, when the death of a White man led an angry mob to lynch nineteen Chinese Angelenos in what would become known as the Chinese Massacre.[30]

By the turn of the century, the small Chinese American community had built a thriving ethnic neighborhood home to restaurants, curio shops, two Chinese temples, and a Chinese theater.[31] The Garnier Building on

Los Angeles Street housed the Chinese Consolidated Benevolent Association (CCBA). The community even supported a Chinese newspaper.[32] More than just businesses, Chinatown was a thriving community with its own understanding of homemaking. As historian Isabela Seong Leong Quintana has shown, Chinese American women often fashioned homes that were "quite different from the single, nuclear-family model that reformers and planners of the early twentieth century would have preferred."[33] Their homemaking occurred alongside, and at times in collaboration with, the adjoining Mexican American community. Together with French and Italian immigrants, the Chinese and the Mexicans formed the bustling multiethnic core of the city. At the same time, the city's press treated Chinatown as a pariah, as a den of filth, violence, and vice that threatened the city proper.

Chinatown occupied an outsized place in the popular imagination which did not seem warranted by its relatively small population. While Los Angeles was home to sizable Japanese American, Black, and Mexican American populations, Chinese Americans made up a less numerically significant portion of the city's residents. In 1900, the US census reported only 2,062 Chinese in a city of 102,479. By 1930, it listed 3,009 in a city of more than a million. This represented less than one-quarter of 1 percent. The three thousand or so Chinese in Los Angeles in 1930 were far less than the 21,081

TABLE 2.1.   Coverage of neighborhoods in the *Los Angeles Times*, 1900–1939.

Period	Chinatown	Sonoratown	Little Tokyo, Little Tokio, or Japantown	Little Manila or Filipinotown
1900–1909	1,581	170	8	0
1910–1919	803	57	8	0
1920–1920	1,028	76	7	0
1930–1939	1,180	14	215	6

Source: Proquest Historical Newspapers: *Los Angeles Times*, 1881–1999.
Note: This is a general estimate, not a definitive count, based on a 2023 search. The results varied slightly from a 2017 search. For example, in 2017 for the number of times "Chinatown" appeared in the *Los Angeles Times* between 1910 and 1919, Proquest returned 1,593 mentions. The same search in 2023 resulted in 1,581 mentions. These discrepancies appeared in a few results, which I attribute to a change in the software algorithm. In any case, whether 1,581 or 1,593, the *Los Angeles Times* devoted vastly more coverage to Chinatown in 1910-1919 than the district's small population seemed to warrant.

TABLE 2.2. Population of Los Angeles by race/ethnicity, 1900–1940.

Year	Black	Japanese	Chinese	Foreign-born Mexican	Total
1900	2,131	150	2,111	498	102,479
1910	5,101	4,238	1,594	5,632	319,198
1920	15,579	11,618	2,062	21,598	576,673
1930	38,894	21,081	3,009	97,116*	1,238,048
1940	63,774	23,321	4,736	36,840	1,504,277

Note: In 1930, the Census counted Mexicans as a distinct racial category that included Mexican-born immigrants and US citizens. Figures for the other years count only immigrants.

Japanese Americans or the 38,894 African Americans or even the estimated 4,000 Filipinos who lived in the city.[34]

Despite the relatively few Chinese Americans, the city's papers devoted an inordinate amount of coverage to Chinatown compared with other immigrant communities. Between 1910 and 1919, the *Los Angeles Times* mentioned Chinatown 803 times, while it mentioned Little Tokyo only 8 times, and Little Manila not at all. In the 1930s, Chinatown was mentioned 1,180 times and Little Tokyo 215 times. During this same decade, the paper used the phrase "Little Manila" or "Filipinotown" only half a dozen times.[35] Coverage of Chinatown also surpassed that of the Mexican American community near the Plaza, which White residents referred to as "Little Mexico" or "Sonoratown."

Driven by fear and fascination, the *Los Angeles Times* defined its coverage of Old Chinatown through a few unchanging themes: opium use, gambling, tong violence, and police raids, crowding out other, equally important themes of an ethnic enclave in the throes of a demographic transition.[36] In Los Angeles, a city that more than any other sold itself as the White middle-class home to the nation, Chinatown became an important foil against which city boosters constructed this White suburban image.

Grounded in this overt politics of White supremacy, the suburban dream of Los Angeles was often a nightmare for its Chinese American residents. Most designers of the dream had little interest in extending it to any of their non-White neighbors. Through restrictive covenants and homeowners' associations, White land developers, realtors, and city leaders segregated Chinese Americans into the city's central neighborhoods. Zoning laws ensured that these neighborhoods were adjacent to or in industrial districts. Most racially mixed neighborhoods in the central city had higher levels of industrial pollution and more multifamily dwellings, making them incongruent with the White suburban ideal. Yet even within the central core, by the start of the Depression Old Chinatown stood out for its general neglect by City leaders and land developers.

In 1933, Old Chinatown must have seemed to many like a throwback to another era. Taking up only a few square blocks in central Los Angeles directly off the Old Plaza, the boom times of the past few decades that had brought the accouterments of modern living to most of Los Angeles had largely passed the neighborhood by. Stretching east from Los Angeles Street, the area was crisscrossed by small, narrow streets and alleys that gave parts of the community an almost claustrophobic feel. Old red-brick buildings, many with wooden balconies, dotted the area.

Most residents lived in abject poverty, crowded into boarding houses or small, often windowless rooms behind their storefronts. Houses often lacked bathing facilities, forcing residents to use one of the community's Japanese-owned bathhouses. At night, the few streetlights left much of the neighborhood shrouded in darkness.[37] According to historian Mark Wild, Old Chinatown did not receive streetlights until 1913 and as late as 1922 it

FIGURE 2.4.   Quong Dui Kee Company, 1930s. Chinatown Remembered Project, Chinese Historical Society of Southern California.

had only two paved roads.[38] In part because much of the community was on private land, which most Chinese Americans occupied as renters, infra-structural improvements had been largely ignored. Many residents could not afford to move and so were forced to deal with conditions as best they could.

After decades of neglect by absentee landlords, conditions were so bad that even some Chinese Americans expressed their displeasure with the community. In the early 1930s, one youth put it this way: "The Chinatown here is terrible. I do not like to go there . . . except at times I hunger for food. I never go there. I feel sluggish when I go there. It is dirty and poor in appearance. They need great improvements in the buildings and the streets."[39] Peter SooHoo's own son, whom he took to the community as a youth every Sunday for family dinner, remembers the few streetlights: "I can recall only one overhead light in front of grandpa's store, which did not seem to illuminate the area very well. Also, the streets did not seem to be asphalt-covered, but bumpy with potholes. Despite this, people seemed to be very upbeat. They were a tight-knit group even though living under tenement conditions."[40]

Those who could afford to leave Chinatown did so. Beginning in the 1910s, large numbers of Chinese Americans decided to settle in the multi-ethnic neighborhood that surrounded the City Market—at the intersection of Ninth and San Pedro, which provided produce to the city's groceries and restaurants. Local Chinese Americans dubbed the area *Gui Gai*, or Ninth Street, in the local Toisanese (Taishanese) dialect.[41] By the 1930s, increasing numbers had also moved into the East Adams neighborhood, near the intersection of East Adams and San Pedro. With its detached single-family homes for sale, East Adams was a huge improvement on the rental proper-ties of Old Chinatown. By 1936, members of the Federal Writers Project estimated that only one-third of the city's Chinese Americans lived in and around Old Chinatown.[42]

Because of actual living conditions in Chinatown, along with its negative representations in the press, city leaders and boosters had long looked for a way to destroy the old neighborhood. In the mid-1920s, the opportunity to do so finally arose. Beginning in 1909, the major newspapers, the railroad companies, and the city started discussing a central "union station" for the numerous rail lines that terminated in Los Angeles.[43] In the fall of 1926, the City Council attempted to build momentum for a union station by putting it to a nonbinding vote. In a special municipal election, voters were asked to decide on two propositions: Proposition 8 asked if a rail station for all steam railroads should be built in Los Angeles; Proposition 9 asked whether the station should be built at the Plaza site.[44] No other options for location were offered. The Los Angeles Chamber of Commerce, along with Harry Chandler's *Los Angeles Times*, became the primary backers of a union station at the Plaza. In contrast, the three major railroads in Los Angeles—The Santa Fe, The Southern Pacific, and the Salt Lake—along with William Randolph Hearst's *Los Angeles Examiner*, opposed it.

Both newspapers drew on stereotypes of Chinatown as a yellow peril to make their case. The *Examiner* argued that, next to the Plaza, the new station would be adjacent to Old Chinatown.[45] An April 20 editorial argued: "If ever there is to be a Union Station, let it at least not be located between Chinatown and 'Little Mexico.'"[46] An April 24 editorial argued against "[a] passenger terminal on the Chinatown site." Through its comments on Chinatown and Little Mexico, the paper drew on the long-standing association of the area around the Plaza with racialized blight to convince readers to vote no. Their argument was that proximity would doom the station from the beginning.

In contrast, the *Los Angeles Times* argued that readers should vote yes because the Plaza location would doom Old Chinatown. The paper contended that the station should be seen as a harbinger of growth, renewal, and modernity. In a front-page story that ran the same day as the *Examiner* editorial, the *Times* reported: "As a matter of fact, the steam shovels are at work now creating the great civic center which will mark the passing of Chinatown and in its place will be the great city, county, state, and federal buildings and the Union depot."[47] Two days before the vote, a *Times* editorial again argued that a union station at the Plaza would "forever do away with Chinatown and its environs";[48] a vote for the project was a vote for the destruction of a community.

When the returns were counted, more than 70 percent of the city's voters approved a union station in Los Angeles. In contrast, they barely passed building the station on the Chinatown site next to the Plaza.[49] Within two weeks, the *Times* ran an article declaring that "the march of progress" would soon erase a district that was "once the city's most exotic attraction."[50] Yet even as it predicted Chinatown's demise, it asked, "Where will the Chinese go?" With the destruction seemingly imminent, the city began to lay the groundwork for a new Chinese-themed district whose image it could more easily control.

Demolition of Old Chinatown began three days before Christmas in 1933, when crews from the Whittier Wrecking Company began knocking down the Bong Hing Company building on the corner of Apablasa and Juan Streets.[51] Over the next few weeks, wrecking crews demolished the Chinese school, the Apablasa playground, where local children once played baseball, and the old Chinese vegetable market, with its community grill where the Chinese vegetable peddlers once gathered to eat. Not all the buildings in the construction zone were to be destroyed immediately, though. Only a few blocks away, life in what remained of Old Chinatown continued as best it could. Many of the major markets and restaurants were still open. Early estimates proclaimed that the razing of the old Chinese neighborhood would take only 30 days and that the train station "would be in operation

FIGURE 2.5. Peter SooHoo (center, seated) meeting with Los Angeles chief of police Joseph Taylor. *Los Angeles Times*, UCLA Library Special Collections, copyright © 1935, Creative Commons, Attribution 4.0 International License.

in a year and a half."[52] This was not to be. As a result of the efforts largely of one man, residents and businesses were allowed to remain in the community even as work progressed. That man was Peter SooHoo, and he would prove to be the leader that Chinese American merchants needed.

Peter SooHoo was born in Old Chinatown on September 6, 1899, the eldest son of nine children. His father, SooHoo Leung, emigrated from Kaiping (*Hoiping*) as a young boy in the 1870s. His mother, SooHoo Yee, was born in Ventura County just north of Los Angeles. After an arranged marriage, Peter SooHoo's father and mother eventually moved to Los Angeles, where they lived in Old Chinatown on Apablasa Street and ran the Sang Yuen Company store. SooHoo attended Los Angeles public schools and graduated from Polytechnic High School.[53] He went on to receive his BS in electrical engineering from the University of Southern California.

Peter SooHoo reflected the changing demographics in the Chinese American community. By 1930, more than 40 percent of Chinese Americans had been born in the United States.[54] While many were able to attend college, they often faced White racism as they tried to enter the workforce. In 1931, one of SooHoo's contemporaries recounted her experiences with American racism after finding it difficult to secure a job despite her college degree: "I am beginning to realize more and more that I am in a 'white country,' and what chance have we in this country? Sometimes I am so disgusted. The future seems so uncompromising."[55] Many in this generation became so fed up with the racism of White Americans that they left the country of their birth for China.[56]

After graduating from college, SooHoo encountered the same discrimination that many in his peer group did. In 1925, he told a sociological researcher of the difficulties he faced as a recent college graduate: "I am an American-born Chinese and have spent all my life in America. . . . I have tried to get positions with several of the local public service corporations but have been unable to do so. I have been told by several men that they could not employ me because I was Chinese. I have not given up yet. . . . I expect to stand up for my rights as an American citizen."[57] Despite living in a period of rampant racial discrimination, SooHoo eventually landed a city job with the Department of Water and Power, where he worked as topographical drafter in the underground engineering section. He was the first Chinese American to be hired.

From a young age, SooHoo fought for the civil rights of Chinese Americans. At twenty-one, he joined the Chinese American Citizens Alliance, an organization of US-born citizens of Chinese descent.[58] While still in his twenties, he participated in the alliance's national campaign to overturn a law that barred Chinese Americans from bringing foreign-born wives into the United States. SooHoo and several other alliance members, including the lawyer Y. C. Hong, journeyed to Washington to testify before a congressional subcommittee hearing on the issue.[59]

Given his educational background and US citizenship, SooHoo often acted as a broker between the larger Chinese American community and White society. Before his untimely death at the age of 45, he served as president of the citizens alliance (1937–1940). During World War II, he was a captain in the Chinese American State Militia. Believing that US-born Chinese Americans should exercise their rights as citizens, he helped the local Republican Party register Chinese American voters.[60] At the same time, he joined a few largely White organizations, including the Shriners, reportedly becoming the first Chinese American Mason in Southern California.[61] He also served as president of the China Society of Southern California, a largely White organization focused on Chinese history and culture.[62]

As Old Chinatown found itself under threat of destruction, Peter SooHoo was able to negotiate more time for businesses and residents to remain in the community. At an arranged meeting with Mr. Barclay, the project engineer, he was able to forestall the destruction of what was left of his neighborhood. The station would continue collecting rent, and the residents would not have to move until their part of the construction zone was needed.[63] At the same time, a small section of Old Chinatown lay outside the construction zone and was to remain untouched. Thus Chinese American businesses along Los Angeles Street, such as the Soochow restaurant and the T. See On Company, were not physically threatened.[64] Despite the continued existence of this section of the neighborhood, the *Los Angeles Times* and local White business owners threw a "farewell fete" for Old Chinatown in 1934, declaring its premature end.[65]

The *Times* might have wanted to announce Old Chinatown's early demise, but this was certainly not in the best interest of the Chinese American business owners who relied on tourism to stay afloat. In December of 1934, Peter SooHoo issued a press release reminding potential White customers

Figure 2.6. Billboard in Old Chinatown. *Los Angeles Daily News*, UCLA Library Special Collections, copyright © 1938, Creative Commons, Attribution 4.0 International License.

that Old Chinatown was in fact still open: "Only a small section of the Chinese quarter has been affected by the construction. The remaining stores along Alameda and Ferguson Alley will continue to do business for years to come."[66] SooHoo sought to have this information included in tourist guidebooks. In one, he said, "Chinatown has not been torn down and has not moved to any new quarters."[67] The Chinese merchants on Los Angeles Street would eventually erect a giant billboard declaring that they were still open for business.

Peter SooHoo understood the importance of publicity to the neighborhood's livelihood, but he also had to know that press releases, comments in local guidebooks, or even a large billboard could challenge the *Times*-backed narrative about the neighborhood's demise. Chinese Americans needed to create and control their own counter-narrative. Looking for support, SooHoo turned to Christine Sterling, a White philanthropist who only a few years earlier had opened Olvera Street. By 1935, she had already begun fashioning her own plans for a new district.[68]

In many ways, Christine Sterling would seem like the ideal person to help SooHoo realize his goal of a new, centralized Chinatown. A master of publicity who, in launching Olvera Street, had proven that she could turn a neighborhood into an ethnic-themed tourist destination, she was eager to lend her vision to this goal. With Olvera Street, Sterling sought to repackage the city's Spanish and Mexican past in a way that could be easily digested by White tourists. Olvera Street was not the Plaza as it had actually existed under Spanish or Mexican rule; as the historian William Estrada has shown, it was a selective reimagining of that history in a way that "celebrated a mythic preindustrial past that was both appealing and useful to Anglos while at the same time obscuring the contemporary reality of Mexicans in Los Angeles."[69] Despite its historical inaccuracies, Olvera Street was a rousing success.

Sterling had proven her business acumen, and her concept for a Chinese-themed district was economically viable. At the level of vision though, she and Peter SooHoo found themselves in disagreement. Sterling's conception of China City drew on the long history of theatricality in North American Chinatowns and on the recent Hollywood fascination with China in films like *The Good Earth*. She hoped to capitalize on this trend by creating a Chinese village that would give the impression of visiting a Hollywood film set. She aimed to attract Chinese American businesses with reasonable rents on stands and small storefronts in China City, but with the understanding that owners would contribute to her vision.

While SooHoo's project was not as blatant in its embrace of theatricality, his group did seek to perform their own vision of Chinese American life for visitors and the city at large. In contrast to Sterling's project, he felt that first and foremost Chinatown needed to be developed and controlled by Chinese Americans. He would publicly express these views, two years after the aborted Sterling partnership, in a speech to the Los Angeles Chamber of Commerce, "It takes a Chinese heart to feel the needs of the people; it requires a Chinese mind to understand their needs, and it demands a sense of public responsibility and service from those who seek to administer such needs."[70] SooHoo and Sterling's partnership never came to fruition. Instead, the two would become competitors.

By 1937, the Chinese American community was divided on how to proceed. A few major restaurant owners like Woo Fon Lee of Man Jen Low and Quon S. Doon of Tuey Far Low remained in the construction zone, even as their businesses faced imminent removal. A handful of merchants reestablished their businesses on various sections of North Spring Street. Others moved to the neighborhood surrounding the City Market at Ninth and San Pedro.[71] The Chinese Consolidated Benevolent Association along with the major family and district associations remained on Los Angeles Street in the safe section of Old Chinatown. In heated meetings at the CCBA offices on Los Angeles Street, diverging groups expressed their opinions on how to proceed. The CCBA remained hopelessly deadlocked and unable to lead the way forward.[72]

In February of 1937, a group of merchants decided to venture out on their own without the backing of the CCBA. In addition to Peter SooHoo, the group included Quon S. Doon, owner of the Tuey Far Low restaurant, Woo Fon Lee, owner of the Man Jen Low restaurant; Dr. John Lum, former president of the Chinese Chamber of Commerce; Lee Wah Shew, proprietor of the Yee Sing Chong grocery; and the San Francisco-born lawyer Y. C. Hong, reportedly the first Chinese American to pass the California bar. They formed the nucleus of the Los Angeles Chinatown Project Association. They knew they had to act fast. Construction of Union Station's main terminal was scheduled to start at the beginning of May, and the remaining section of Chinatown east of Alameda Street would, by necessity, be demolished shortly thereafter. The management of the station project had referred SooHoo to Herbert Lapham, a land agent for the Santa Fe Railroad, which owned the property he was eyeing. Lapham would play a pivotal role in the realization of his plan. In April the members of the Los Angeles Chinatown Project Association met with Lapham at Tuey Far Lowe to lay the groundwork for what would become New Chinatown.

As a novel idea for control, the association formed a California corporation, with the intent of buying the lot for their new Chinatown from the railway company. While US-born citizens like Peter SooHoo were free to purchase land, many of the owners of established businesses were Chinese immigrants. In the 1930s, the US government still labeled them "aliens ineligible for citizenship" and California barred them from purchasing land directly in the state. The corporate ownership structure of New Chinatown would ensure that it was controlled completely by the merchants. The corporation would buy the land, and the merchants would rent lots. By August, the Los Angeles Chinatown Project Association had raised $40,000 and had grown from twenty-eight members to thirty-three.[73] Ownership, control, and vision would remain in their hands. The association soon hired architects Erle Webster and Adrian Wilson to realize their vision.[74]

FIGURE 2.7. Sketch of New Chinatown by architects Erle Webster and Adrian Wilson. *Los Angeles Daily News*, UCLA Library Special Collections, copyright © 1938, Creative Commons, Attribution 4.0 International License.

Peter SooHoo understood that the competition with Sterling was not simply over whose project would be finished first. Chinatown was an idea as much as it was a place, and the struggle over who would control its image was as important, if not more so, than the creation of a physical space. Over the coming months, SooHoo tracked the coverage of both the New Chinatown project and China City, clipping articles from the city's papers. He would save these articles in a three-ringed tabbed binder, devoting a section to "Sterling's Walled China City." On August 11, 1937, Sterling announced the commencement of her project in a front-page article in the *Los Angeles Times*, "Chinatown to Rise Again," featuring an illustration of the "proposed picturesque city center" sketched by a *Times* staff artist. Sterling was quoted: "Los Angeles is under obligation to hundreds of Chinese, many of them early residents here, who have been uprooted from the place where they have made their homes for years and years. . . . The new China City will give these Chinese new opportunities to preserve their racial and cultural integrity by bringing them together in one district. As it is now, the Chinese are being dispersed over all the city. Under a continuance of such a widespread distribution of the Chinese population they would lose their unity." As if speaking to Sterling, SooHoo wrote in his binder: "Suddenly Mrs. Sterling popped up to announce her building of a 'Chinatown.'" He surrounded the word in quotes.[75]

While many local papers devoted space to both projects, Harry Chandler and the *Los Angeles Times* threw their full support behind China City. Chandler was a friend of Sterling's and had supported her work since before the launch of Olvera Street. Their partnership had long proven fruitful. Sterling did not try to hide the link between the *Times* and China City, going so far as to name the main gate after recently deceased *Times* columnist Harry Carr.[76] In the following year, the paper ran story after story promoting China City while essentially ignoring the Los Angeles Chinatown Project Association and its work. Having spent the last few years attempting to shape the public narrative around Old Chinatown's purported demise, the *Times* now began to craft a narrative of China City as the only legitimate replacement for the old neighborhood, holding it up as Sterling's gift to the struggling Chinese American community.

The Los Angeles Chinatown Project Association rejected this narrative of White paternalism and went to work crafting its own narrative about New Chinatown. On August 16, the leadership—Quon S. Doon, Walter Yip, and Lee Wah Shew—held a press conference in a Chinatown grocery, where they issued a statement and presented a rendering of New Chinatown.[77] Their statement read: "We are no longer willing to do business in old rodent-infested buildings or something similar gotten up for us. . . . We are able to pay our own way and stand on our own feet." Responding to allegations that their project ignored Chinese Americans in poverty, the group said, "To care for the poor Chinese people is not the problem. The Chinese are self-reliant."[78] They also emphasized: "We want to be given the chance to relocate in proper quarters and have an opportunity to prosper in accordance with our contribution to the American community. We want our Chinatown to be a credit to our community and our race. . . . Now, with the final notice being served to vacate, the Chinese merchants have come to the realization that they must first help themselves before they can expect help from anyone else."[79]

That same day, Peter SooHoo gave a speech to the city's Chamber of Commerce in which he expanded on the association's vision: "We Chinese must contribute to the civic progress of Los Angeles by giving up our old quarter and building a new and more representative Chinatown similar to the world famous Chinese community of San Francisco."[80] He explained how his vision fit into the larger vision of Los Angeles as a global city. The Chinese merchants wanted "proper stores where they may present to people from all over the world the various natural products of far away China." In conclusion, he emphasized Chinese American self-sufficiency: "[Chinese merchants] are not asking for donations, but rather for a loan to be paid back at a fair and reasonable rate of interest in the course of years by these Chinese themselves." While SooHoo was clear that San Francisco Chinatown would be the model for New Chinatown, he emphasized that he and the other members of the Los Angeles Chinatown Project Association saw their plan as a contribution to "the civic progress of Los Angeles." The members wanted their district to be seen as part of a modern, cosmopolitan image of the city.

In demanding to be included in the imagined community of Los Angeles, the Los Angeles Chinatown Project Association cast Chinese American merchants as self-reliant, law-abiding business owners, who were building New Chinatown through their own individualism and hard work. This was meant to push back against the narrative of gifted indebtedness that Christine Sterling advanced with China City; however, a bootstrap narrative of success at the height of the Great Depression produced its own problems. If the Depression had proven anything, it was the dangers of a purely laissez-faire capitalism without enough government regulation. It had laid bare the need for a social safety net for all people living in America. The mutual aid provided by the local district and family associations had proven far from sufficient to support Chinese Americans in need. Structural inequalities and a global depression produced by unregulated free markets were only part of the problem. Racism was deeply embedded in the everyday structures of American society: in 1938, Chinese immigrants were still barred from buying land in California, and they could not become naturalized citizens; as such they were barred from voting and limited in political power. This narrative of Chinese American uplift deflected attention away from needed structural changes in a racist American society.

In a *Daily News* article that covered the association's press conference, Sterling responded to the vision presented by her competitors: "What do they want? . . . an Oriental Westwood Village? Let them build it if they think they can get away with it, but I think it will fail."[81] Sterling mocked the idea: "What the Chinese want is prosperity. The investment will be $300,000 and they won't be able to pay for it out of profits."[82] She repeated her criticism that the association's plan would be well out of reach for many residents of old Chinatown.

Despite ongoing denials by Chinese American leaders, Sterling's allegations were not without basis. Participation in the district proposed by the Los Angeles Chinatown Project Association required investors to purchase stock in the project, a luxury that many Chinese Americans could not afford during the Depression, even though rents would be reasonable, based on rents in Old Chinatown. The relatively high bar for entry was reflected in an early list of participants in the project that Peter SooHoo drew up in late 1937 or early 1938.[83] The list included the Man Jen Low and Tuey Far Low restaurants, the Yee Sing Chong grocery, the Chew Yuen Company, and the Dun Wo Hong drugstore. All these businesses had been in Los Angeles for more than fifty years. They represented some of the most well-established firms in the entire city.

In contrast, China City provided a home for Chinese Americans who for one reason or another fell outside of the traditional circles of power that had long defined life in the Chinese American ethnic enclaves of the West Coast. For example, the man who would become the leader of the China City Merchants Association was Tsin Nan Ling, an itinerant merchant who had spent most of the 1930s selling carved stones from his home province of Chekiang (*Zhejiang*). By the time China City opened in 1938, Ling and his family had sold these so-called scholar's stones at World's Fair's exhibitions in Chicago, Cleveland, and San Diego.[84] Given that he was not from the Pearl River Delta region of China and did not share linguistic or cultural similarities with people from there, Ling would have found it difficult if not impossible to take a leadership position in New Chinatown. China City also became home to the Chan family. Thomas Chan was a US-born Chinese American who had performed frequently in vaudeville in San Francisco before his marriage to Jomac Potter, a White woman. Like many in China City, he had come to Los Angeles looking for work in Hollywood and ended up working for Tom Gubbins. Thomas and Jomac's daughter Camille would find regular work as a stand-in for Hollywood stars like

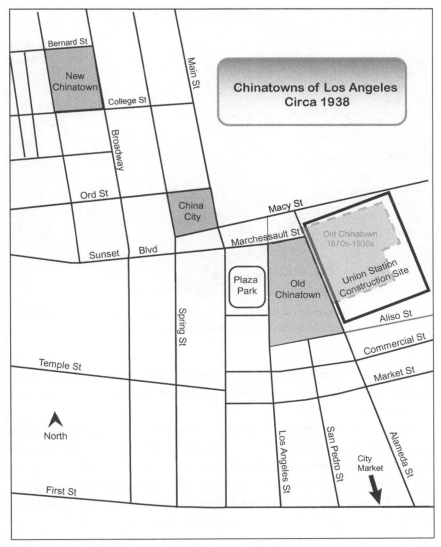

MAP 2.1. Old Chinatown construction zone. (by author.)

Virginia Wielder.[85] Then there was Dorothy Siu, a circus performer and the sister of Dr. Margaret Chung.[86] She married Jake Siu, a mixed-race Chinese American, and together they joined the Al G. Barnes Circus. After traveling with the circus for more than half a decade, the couple eventually settled in Los Angeles, where they ran a flower shop in China City, which they called the *Eurasian* after Jake's mixed-race heritage.[87] In short, those who opened

FIGURE 2.8. Roland and Gilbert Siu playing in front of the House of Wang set in China City. Chinese Historical Society of Southern California.

businesses in China City differed not only in economic class from those in New Chinatown but also often in profession, place of origin, and even racial identity.

China City also offered reasonable rents that were accessible to more Chinese Americans than rents in Chinatown on Broadway. In part because it was not run by the established Chinatown elite, China City became a real community for those who did not feel at home with the traditional circles that had run Los Angeles Chinatown for more than half a century. Of course, the trade-off was that those who invested or worked in China City had to conform to Sterling's vision of a Chinatown shaped by White paternalism and an obsession with Hollywood representations.

While theatricality was not completely missing in New Chinatown— the Charlie Chan fortune teller being the most obvious holdover—all of China City seemed to be defined first and foremost by its theatrical elements. From stage shows to rickshaw rides to fortune telling, visitors were constantly made aware of its overtly performative nature. Drawing on a timeless imagined Orient promoted in contemporary Hollywood films alongside overt references to the project's backing by the city's booster class, China City sold itself not as an authentic representation of East Asia as it had once been but rather as a simulacrum.[88] It was an assemblage of media images of China that circulated in the Western imagination. Celebrating its theatricality and selling its connections to Hollywood film, China City was a theme park for central Los Angeles built decades before Walt Disney built his park in Orange County.[89]

To celebrate the opening of New Chinatown on June 25, Peter SooHoo and the other members of the Los Angeles Chinatown Project Association created a contrasting media event with its own distinct narrative. Rather than presenting New Chinatown as an extension of Hollywood's imagined Orient, they presented New Chinatown as a distinctly Chinese American venture that blended Chinese cultural traits with American values while celebrating the immigrant history of Chinese Americans. Unlike China City, which played up an Orientalist film-set aesthetic, this new Chinatown embraced the sensibilities of the American-born generation, like Peter SooHoo and Y. C Hong.

The gala celebrating the opening of New Chinatown flew both Republic of China and US flags. A parade featured four hundred members of the Federation of Chinese Clubs, most of whom were American-born youth who had banded together to raise financial support for China following the outbreak of the Sino-Japanese War in 1937.[90] A military veterans band played the Chinese and American national anthems. In complex and overlapping ways, the opening celebration positioned New Chinatown as distinctly Chinese *American*, reflecting the increasingly US-born demographics of the nation's Chinese American community.

In keeping with the theme of Chinese American inclusion in the national polity, the leadership of the Los Angeles Chinatown Project Association invited prominent state and local officials to participate in the festivities. Peter SooHoo used his position as president of the Los Angeles branch of the Chinese American Citizens Alliance (CACA) to entice politicians to attend. In a 1942 interview, Y. C. Hong, the association's lawyer, explained how the alliance leveraged its vote: "We look after the voters, prepare their ballots, and fine them if they don't vote. We vote as a block."[91] In 1938, the Republican governor of California, Frank Merriam, was mired in a difficult re-election campaign and wanted to lock in the state's small but not insignificant Chinese American vote. He agreed to speak at the New Chinatown opening, and in return the alliance agreed to support his reelection bid.[92] The presence of officials like Governor Merriam and Los Angeles Mayor Frank L. Shaw furthered the narrative of the Chinese Americans as part of the social fabric of the city. If their presence did not highlight this narrative clearly enough, Governor Merriam dedicated a plaque at the opening to the "Chinese pioneers who participated in the constructive history of California."[93]

Notes from the speech that Peter SooHoo gave on opening day show that he also emphasized the long history of Chinese Americans in the state:

> We are dedicating our gate to commemorate the great spirit of those tens of thousands of Chinese pioneers who braved four thousand miles of open seas to reach these Western shores to lend a helping hand in the winning of the Great West, the result of which is the Great and Glorious state of California. As their posterity, we hope to exemplify their spirit of co-operation in order to continue their contribution to the constructive history of this State and Nation.[94]

He was positioning Chinese immigrants as contributing to the "winning of the Great West." His rhetoric drew on long-standing stereotypes of Native peoples as savage and White settlers as civilized. With his speech, SooHoo cast Chinese immigrants as occupying a position similar to that of European colonists.

Yet even as New Chinatown founders embraced an idea of themselves as part of the settler colonial experience, many still felt the need to perform ethnic difference for tourists. Interviewed in 1980, resident Allan Mock recalled the fake Chinese accents that some storeowners put on for their White customers:

> Well, the American people come to Chinatown to be entertained. They come to Chinatown to buy things that are Chinese. They almost expect you to speak with a Chinese sing song . . . some of them are great actors. They put it on, and they put it on thick. Just to please the customers but it was really unnecessary, but I guess it was part of the Chinese flavor when you go to Chinatown.[95]

This was the paradox at the heart of New Chinatown in the late 1930s. On the one hand, the Chinese American merchants sought incorporation into the social fabric of the city by claiming inclusion in national myths of European settlement. On the other hand, they sought entry into this imagined community by selling commodifiable forms of Chinese difference that marked them as ethnically distinct. Nearly all New Chinatown businesses depended on this selling of difference, even if many leaders promoted the district as definitively American.

If representations of Old Chinatown as a yellow peril became the site against which the dream of a racialized White suburb was produced, New Chinatown became the vehicle through which a small segment of the city's Chinese American middle class sought to gain acceptance as part of a new cosmopolitan image. They did this not by challenging ideas of Chinese ethnic difference but rather by commercializing this difference and thus making it compatible with American capitalism. Of course, Chinatown was not the only site through which Chinese Americans performed racial difference for predominantly White audiences. Hollywood provided an opportunity to perform on a much larger stage. Even more so than in Chinatown, Chinese Americans in the movie industry faced the challenge of controlling the reception and profits of their own performances.

PART II

Hollywood Extras

CHAPTER 3

Chinese American Extras During the Great Depression

By August of 1936, the demolition of Old Chinatown was well under way. In what had once been the center of the neighborhood, construction crews were at work on the new Union Station. Even as the Great Depression ravaged the city, hundreds of Chinese Americans had already been evicted from the area. Those who remained faced an uncertain future. That summer the *Los Angeles Times* columnist Lee Shippey visited the construction site and described his impressions to his readers. Shippey noted the baggage, mail, and express units nearing completion. A few yards away, he observed the Chinese American merchants on Apablasa Street going about their lives as best they could in the face of imminent eviction. Of Chinatown's presence in the middle of a construction site, Shippey wrote: "A walk down Apablasa Street gives one who knew old Chinatown something of a shock. It is cut off as abruptly as a movie set, and modern America is very busy on ground from which transplanted China had been rudely sliced."[1] Shippey's conflation of Chinatown with a movie set reflected the long-standing relationship between Old Chinatown and Hollywood, a relationship that was much more complex than visitors like Shippey ever understood.

At the very moment that Shippey made his comparison, thirty miles north, in the foothills of the San Fernando Valley, MGM Studios were constructing a replica Chinese village. Built on a 500-acre lot in Chatsworth, the village was part of an elaborate set for MGM's production of Pearl Buck's novel *The Good Earth*.[2] It featured water buffalo, rice fields, and more than 200 buildings, many imported directly from China.[3] In part to populate it, MGM reportedly employed more than a thousand background extras, most from the Los Angeles area.[4] The producers had passed over Anna May Wong for the lead, hiring the German actress Luise Rainer to appear alongside Paul Muni as the characters of Wang Lung and O-Lan. Still, the film did feature an unprecedented number of Asian American performers in speaking roles. Prior to *The Good Earth*'s 1937 release, the national press publicized the verisimilitude of the Chinese Americans, but highlighted the fact that the studio only cast those who "spoke perfect English."[5] In the midst of the worst economic downturn the nation had ever seen, the replica Chinese village became a site of performance, labor, and economic subsistence for large numbers of Chinese Americans displaced by the construction of Union Station.[6]

As civil unrest and then war swept Asia, Hollywood studios began producing films that employed many Chinese American extras from the Los Angeles area. These included *Shanghai Express* (1932), *The Bitter Tea of General Yen* (1933), and *The General Died at Dawn* (1936). Garding Lui, who in the 1940s published one of the few English-language guidebooks to Los Angeles Chinatown, estimated that one in every fourteen people in the Chinese American community worked in the Hollywood film industry.[7] If anything, Lui's estimate was too low. *The Good Earth* alone claimed to have hired more than a thousand. In 1930, the US Census counted 3,009 Chinese Americans living in Los Angeles proper. If MGM employed even half that number, this film alone would have featured one out of every six Chinese Americans, a much greater proportion than Garding Lui proposed for the entire industry.

Performance studies scholar Esther Lee Kim argues that *The Good Earth*'s casting "was a setback for Asian American actors such as Anna May Wong."[8] There is no doubt that the film was a setback for Wong and other potential Asian American leading performers, and yet when seen through the eyes of Chinese American extras, *The Good Earth* represented a transformative moment in Hollywood history. Its production shaped both the labor conditions of Chinese American extras and the representation of their labor in the press. Far from being passive, with no influence over their working conditions, they leveraged the increased demand for their services brought about by *The Good Earth* to organize against the exploitative labor practices that had left them one of the few groups not covered by the protections of Central Casting—the primary organization in charge of hiring extras for Hollywood films.[9]

The transformations in Hollywood that *The Good Earth* brought to Chinese American extras were both material and symbolic. The film became the vehicle through which they secured additional labor rights in the film industry. At the same time, the coverage of the film in the press facilitated their inclusion in Hollywood cinema. This in turn brought about their incorporation into the social imagination of the city and the nation. The increased inclusion of Chinese Americans in Hollywood allowed everyday residents of Los Angeles Chinatown to continue doing extra work throughout World War II and well into the postwar period.[10] For these reasons, it would be wrong to see *The Good Earth* as a setback for all Chinese American performers. Rather, the fight over labor rights by its background players and the subsequent media coverage of its production and release generally improved the economic and political realities of Chinese Americans in Los Angeles in the 1930s and beyond.

Chinese Americans in Southern California began securing background roles shortly after the emergence of the film industry around the 1910s. High-profile silent films such as *Red Lantern* (1919), *Broken Blossoms* (1919), and *Wing Toy* (1921) featured scores if not hundreds of Los Angeles Chinatown residents. These roles provided income to a small group of Chinese Americans. However, their overall economic influence on the ethnic enclave was marginal. Furthermore, they were all but ignored by the entertainment press.

In the 1910s, Hollywood studios began to develop an intricate system for recruiting extras. Prospective performers arrived at the studios everyday hoping to be included, but hiring decisions fell to the whims of White male casting directors and producers.[11] The studio producer Thomas Ince recalled keeping cards listing extras' height, weight, and even whether they had missing teeth or visible physical disabilities.[12] In 1922, the casting director for Paramount Studios told the *Los Angeles Times* that Paramount had hired 12,306 extras in the prior year. The majority were the three thousand or so "society" extras hired to provide "well-dressed atmosphere."[13] In this way, gender, body type, and physical attributes influenced which performers could secure regular work.

The standard system of background casting worked well enough when studios were casting the White society extras, but when studios needed large numbers of what they called "types," they used advertisements or specialized recruiters. The *Los Angeles Times* described the recruitment process in 1914: "When types are desired, of course, other methods are chosen. For instance, in the case of types needed in the Selig productions of *The Adventures of Kathlyn*, Hindus were searched out by special agents." The article said that Black actors were "advertised for" and Irish types were "carefully selected."[14]

Chinese Americans were among the extras recruited by special agents. In the silent era, only a limited number of recruiters worked with Chinese Americans. The 1919 film *Red Lantern* employed a local actor named James Wang to recruit hundreds from Chinatown for the film's crowd scenes. Wang, who had arrived in the United States more than three decades earlier, was a former Baptist minister who had left the ministry to pursue an acting career. He played minor roles in several silent films, including *Broken Blossoms* (1919).[15] Among those whom Wang recruited for *Red Lantern* was Anna May Wong, then a fourteen-year-old high school student with no acting experience.[16] In the mid-1930s, she recounted the experience to the *Los Angeles Times*:

> One day I happened to see a movie in which was a Chinese actor. I ran around to an old Chinese who helped out the movies by getting Chinese actors for them. He looked me over critically. "Well," he said, "you have big eyes; you will do." I felt flattered until I learned that he had an order for 600 actors in a hurry and hadn't been able to find but fifty. [17]

The difficulty in securing the extras that Anna May Wong referred to was real. The 1920 census listed only 2,062 Chinese American residents in the city of Los Angeles, so 600 extras represented more than a quarter of the population. In this system, recruiters like James Wang were the most likely Chinese Americans to be featured in the press.[18] The newspapers all but ignored the individual stories of the 600.

The press did not ignore all background performers. To the contrary, during the silent era both the industry and audiences became increasingly obsessed with the so-called extra girl. Imagined as a young White woman recently arrived in Hollywood from the Midwest, the extra girl was a constant presence in popular press and film industry coverage of the 1910s and 1920s.[19] Silent films like the aptly titled *Extra Girl* (1923) and *Show People* (1928) were fictional narratives about young White women trying to become movie stars in Hollywood.

The extra girl catered to the expanding demographic of young White women who were film fans. As Denise McKenna has shown, this "discovery

FIGURE 3.1. Advertisement for *The Extra Girl. Motion Picture News,* 1924.

narrative," in which a young female came to Hollywood, found work in the film industry, and went on to become a film star, became prominent in the popular press during the industry's first decade in Los Angeles.[20] In the popular imagination, extra work soon came to be associated with White women even though in reality White men were as likely, if not more so, to be extras.[21] Men were sometimes included in the discovery narrative, but the press most commonly featured the discovery of White women.[22]

Given these racialized and gendered representations of extra work, it should come as little surprise that labor practices for most Hollywood extras changed in part because of the real threat of exploitation young White women faced from Hollywood producers. The Fatty Arbuckle case in the early 1920s, in which Arbuckle was tried for the murder of the actress and model Virginia Rappe, brought national attention to this exploitation.[23] The press coverage of the trial was in stark contrast to the attention paid to less public forms of abuse that so many extras faced on a daily basis. Not only was the association of extra work with White women a narrative of discovery and stardom; it also often functioned as an extension of the narrative of White women in peril.[24] This threat spurred the industry to act.

By 1925, state labor authorities had received so many complaints of abuse of film extras that the California Industrial Welfare Commission decided to investigate. Allegations included women being forced to work overtime without overtime pay and being asked to arrive at the studio hours earlier than they were needed on set but not being paid for their waiting time.[25] As a result of its investigation, the commission issued regulations governing the employment of women and children—but not men—as extras. In addition to mandating overtime pay, under the new regulations either women had to be allowed to leave early enough to take public transportation home or the studio had to furnish transportation. At the same time, the California State Labor Commissioner urged state lawmakers to make it illegal for employment agencies, middlemen, and contractors who placed extras to collect the 7 to 10 percent commission that they had been charging.

In response to the commission's regulations, the Hollywood studios agreed to eliminate the worst labor abuses in the industry and to apply the new standards to all extras regardless of gender or background. By December of 1925, The Motion Picture Producers Association had finalized plans for the formation of a Central Casting Bureau to begin registering extras in 1926.[26] The new organization had four main goals: (1) eliminating high fees charged by private employment agencies; (2) ending payment violations; (3) discouraging the "increasing influx of persons as extras"; and (4) maintaining a list of extras "who would be called upon frequently and who would be able to derive a decent living from their employment. . . ."[27]

In many ways, Central Casting was an immediate success. In the first six months of 1926, it placed 113,837 background performers in Hollywood films. Of these, roughly 75,000 were men and 35,000 were women.[28] According to the Bureau of Labor Statistics, by the end of 1926 90 percent of all extras were recruited through Central Casting.[29]

Despite Central Casting's goal of becoming a clearinghouse for all background performers, the ethnic differences and social standing of various groups played an important role in determining which performers had access to the bureau's services. Well into the early 1930s, many non-White performers were forced to use outside recruiters. While Central Casting made a concerted effort to hire African American extras directly, other so-called racial or ethnic types were not so lucky.[30] In 1932, *Variety* reported: "Besides [the] Central Casting Bureau there are a number of small casting agencies who supply extras for studios. . . . Jamiel Hanson handles nothing but Arabs. . . . Nick Koblainsky, president of the Russian-American club and Alexis Davidoff handle all the Russians. . . . Hawaiians and Filipinos are hustled by Alessandro Gambo. Mexicans report for work to John Eiberts."[31] For nearly a decade after the formation of Central Casting, Chinese Americans were among those who found employment through this older system of individual labor recruitment.

By the 1930s, US newspapers were awash with stories of the Japanese drive for empire in the Pacific. Between the mid-nineteenth and early twentieth centuries, Japan transitioned from an insular nation to an emerging military power whose colonial expansion challenged the hegemony of Great Britain, the US, and other Western powers in East Asia. By the end of World War I, Japan had colonized portions of Sakhalin Island, the Korean peninsula, and the island of Taiwan. Its invasion of Manchuria in 1931 thrust the region into the popular consciousness of many Americans in ways that earlier incursions had not.[32] As headlines about East Asia covered the nation's front pages, Hollywood saw financial opportunity. Cinematic depictions of Chinatown as a yellow peril would soon be replaced by big-budget films about China.

Throughout the 1930s, the cycle of Chinese-themed films brought economic opportunities to Chinese American performers. At the start of the 1930s, Anna May Wong was probably the only Chinese American actor who made her living as a full-time performer in the movie industry. By the time the United States entered the Second World War in 1941, a handful of Chinese American supporting players were achieving limited success in Hollywood. These included most prominently Keye Luke, Victor Sen Yung, and Richard Loo. A handful of bit players also found increasing success, including Moy Ming, Roland Got, Chester Gan, Willie Fung, Lotus Liu, and Soo Yung. While many had minor speaking roles, often little more than a line or two, the most profound economic impact was not on the bit players or supporting actors but on the extras.

In June of 1932, the *Los Angeles Times* ran a story entitled "Warfare in Orient Brings Film Gold to Chinatown." In it the writer stated: "Front page news of China has inspired Hollywood studios to produce more big oriental pictures this year than ever before."[33] According to the article, Hollywood studios planned to provide 30,000 days of work for Chinese extras in 1932. Three films—Columbia Pictures' *War Correspondent* (1932), RKO's *Roar of the Dragon* (1932), and Paramount's *Shanghai Express* (1932)—had already provided 20,000 days of work for Chinese Americans. The average Chinese American performer earned $7.50 a day for a nonspeaking role while those who landed speaking parts earned between $10 and $15 a day. In total, according to the story, between $200,000 and $250,000 would be divided among Chinese American performers employed on these films.

The economic windfall came at a time of great social and political precarity in the Chinese American community in Los Angeles. In the fall of 1933, the Union Pacific, Central Pacific, and Santa Fe railroads finally agreed to build a passenger station on top of Old Chinatown. The agreement ended a twenty-two-year battle with the city which followed an election and involved local, state, and national agencies as well as litigation all the way to the US Supreme Court.[34] With the railroads acquiescing to the city's demands, the fate of Old Chinatown was set. Most of the neighborhood would be demolished. Even as Chinatown residents begged for more time, those living on the future construction site were told to vacate their properties by the end of November.[35] In December, the first demolition crews arrived. Some residents were still removing their belongings as crews began to demolish their homes.[36]

The demolition of most of Old Chinatown and the subsequent eviction of most the neighborhood's residents occurred against the backdrop of the Great Depression. American racism rendered Chinese Americans especially vulnerable to the Depression's economic effects. Simultaneously excluded

FIGURE 3.2. Workers demolishing Old Chinatown. *Los Angeles Times*, UCLA Library Special Collections, copyright © 1938, Creative Commons, Attribution 4.0 International License.

from most organized labor unions by the long-standing racist policies of the unions and kept out of many white-collar professions by a similar, if albeit less overtly confrontational, structure of White supremacy, most found themselves relegated to work in the nation's Chinatowns or else in certain segments of the service economy such as restaurant, domestic, or laundry work.

Barred from many New Deal programs as "aliens ineligible for citizenship," many in the nation's Chinatowns turned inward. Some Chinese Americans relied on the generosity of relatives. Los Angeles resident Walter Chung remembered visiting restaurants owned by relatives and eating food that patrons did not finish.[37] Others relied on district or family associations. Lew Kay, a resident of Seattle's Chinatown, described how mutual aid worked in the Northeast in 1933: "When a Chinese has exhausted his savings he appeals to clansmen. They may not necessarily be relatives; they may be very distant relatives. Maybe they are related in name only but a clan is sort of a family. His clansmen take care of him or his wife and children. They may not take him into their homes, but they'll see he has a place to stay and something to eat and a little something to do."[38] This support did not mean that the Chinese refused to seek out public assistance. On September 21, 1933, the *Los Angeles Times* reported that eight elderly Chinese men had applied to the County Welfare Department for help paying to have their bones sent back to China once they passed away: "Because of scarcity of money, the county cannot, this year, like in the past, repatriate elderly Chinese so they could be buried in their native soil." Even in death, Chinese immigrants were denied the support of the state.

Like other Americans, most Chinese Americans tried to survive on whatever work they could find. Yet even in the restaurant industry, where they found moderate success, their pay remained significantly less than the wages for White workers. Heather Lee has estimated that Chinese restaurant workers in New York City in the 1930s made on average 30% less than the national average. The average partner at a Chinese restaurant took home about $100 a month; cooks earned between $60 and $70 a month, and the lowest paid waiter made only $50 a month even with tips.[39] Those in other positions fared little better. According to the US Bureau of Agricultural Economics, the average farm worker, which many Chinese Americans in Southern California still were, made an average of $1.11 a day in 1933 if they worked without board.[40]

With this dearth of economic opportunities, Chinese Americans turned toward extra work to support themselves. In 1934, the *Chicago Tribune* reported that "most Los Angeles Chinese are on the ragged edge of penury. An occasional few days' of work in the studios as part of oriental mob scenes bridges the gap between near starvation and comparative affluence."[41] By 1934 wages for extras ranged between $5 a day for crowd scenes to $25 for extras who spoke "atmospheric words."[42] If the average Chinese cook made around $60 a month, he could earn this amount in twelve days working at the rate of the lowest paid extras.[43] Given this reality, the decision by Hollywood to produce films about China could not have come at a better time for Chinese Americans in Los Angeles.

Oral history interviews with community members who grew up in Chinatown and worked in Hollywood in the 1930s show the importance of work as extras to Chinese American families. Esther Lee recalled the difficult times her family faced in the Depression: "We didn't go out to buy shoes. We didn't have three, four, five pairs of shoes. We have one pair for school and that was it, and we didn't have Sunday shoes or tennis shoes to play. I give credit to my parents for raising us right to make us hard workers."[44] Esther Lee's first film was *The Good Earth* at the age of 8. Hers was far from the only family in Chinatown who encouraged its children to work as film extras to help support the family. Lilly Mu and her brothers were born in Old Chinatown on Marchessault Street. All of them appeared in Hollywood films during the 1930s. She appeared in her first film when she was still a baby. As an infant, Lilly Mu along with her family would have made much more than older performers. The rates for infants were $75 a day for babies under thirty days old, $50 a day for those between one month and three months, and $25 for those three to six months.[45] Mu continued appearing in films as a girl through the end of elementary school, including playing a small part alongside Clark Gable in *Too Hot to Handle* (1938). There was still some stigma in Chinatown about appearing in films in the mid-1930s, she said, but her family needed the money and so they encouraged the children to perform.[46]

Whereas silent film labor recruiters competed to place Chinese Americans in Hollywood films, by 1930 nearly all recruitment of Chinese Americans, fell under the control of one man: local casting agent and Chinatown resident Tom Gubbins. Raised in Hong Kong, where he learned to speak Cantonese fluently, Gubbins immigrated to the West Coast and worked in San Francisco before relocating to Los Angeles in 1916 at the age of 37.[47] He began work as one of several recruiters of Chinese American talent for silent motion pictures. The height of his influence came between the end of the silent period in the mid-1920s and the production of *The Good Earth* in mid-1930, when he served as the sole recruiter of Chinese American talent in Hollywood. Gubbins's influence in Hollywood would continue in some capacity through the end of World War II.

Over the course of his long career, Gubbins occupied several positions in the Hollywood studio system in addition to labor recruiter. He ran a store on North Los Angeles Street in Old Chinatown called Asiatic Costumes, which supplied Chinese costumes and props to studios. He served as a technical advisor on numerous China-themed films, responsible for ensuring their authenticity. He also served as an informal translator on set between Chinese background performers who spoke limited English and directors and other creative personnel.[48] An advertisement for Asiatic Costumes

FIGURE 3.3. Lilly Mu with Clark Gable on the set of *Too Hot to Handle*. Chinese Historical Society of Southern California.

The man who put ease in Chin-ese pictures for you
Let him dress your Chinese sets, select your types, and assist you in directing
Chinese scenes. He knows. He speaks the language. 10 years in China.
Ask Emmett Flynn, Tod Browning, Joe DeGrasse, Colin Campbell
Tom Forman and Raoul Walsh about his work

"P. S.: Do you know that Tom Gubbins has a retail department at the
same address where he sells silks, Chinese suits, jades, in fact everything
Chinese?" Special discount to professional people. Open evenings.

Tom Gubbins' Asiatic Costume Co.
Chinese props and costumes sold and rented
522 North Los Angeles Street (Chinatown)   VA ndike 2983

FIGURE 3.4. Advertisement for Tom Gubbins's Asiatic Costume Company.
Standard Casting Directory, 1925.

that Gubbins ran in a casting directory in 1925 gives an idea of the ways
in which he sold his services to Hollywood studios. It read: "The man
who put ease in Chin-ese pictures for you. Let him dress your Chinese
sets, select your types, and assist in directing Chinese scenes. He knows,
He speaks the language, 10 years in China."[49] Gubbins's expertise and experience in China along with his connections in the Chinatown community helped him build a successful business in the 1920s and positioned
him for the surge in Chinese-themed films that began appearing in the
early 1930s.

Many Chinese Americans who grew up in Los Angeles during the 1930s
remember Gubbins. Swan Yee was a teenager when he arrived in Chinatown in 1931. Gubbins took him in and gave him a job in his store, Asiatic
Costumes. He paid Yee $20 a month and gave him room and board. "Tom
Gubbins is a very nice fellow, very kindhearted," Yee said many years later.[50]
Soon, with Gubbins's help, Yee began supplementing his income by working as an extra: "He puts me in the motion pictures. The first picture I
work on was the *Hatchet Man* (1932). . . . My dream came true. So I began
to work as an extra here. He made an agreement. He said if I make more
than twenty dollars. I take it. If not he pays me." Regardless of whether Yee
found extra work, Gubbins guaranteed him $20 a month. He was only one
of many Chinatown residents that Gubbins helped. In fact, Gubbins was
known for the regular dinners he hosted for Chinese American extras in
the area.

Because Gubbins controlled nearly all casting opportunities available to
Chinatown residents, he became a controversial figure in the community.

FIGURE 3.5.   Swan Yee in a rickshaw. Chinese Historical Society of Southern California.

As Swan Yee recalled, "lot of people don't like him [Gubbins] because people say he favors certain person. . . . Naturally he is going to call the people he thinks are dependable. He makes a lot of enemies as you call it. . . . Some people are jealous because some people maybe need the money." But other Chinatown residents suggested that Gubbins's position was controversial for more than whom he decided to cast. According to Jennie Lee, who worked as an extra on *The Good Earth*, "there was Tom Gubbins. He used to cast Chinese people for the movies, and he rented out costumes and everything. . . . If they needed any extras, he'd take a cut . . . and he made himself a rich man doing that."[51] Future Hollywood animator Tyrus Wong agreed: "After we get paid, we have to pay two dollars to Tom Gubbins. . . . He's one man I don't care for."[52] Part-time performers like Jennie Lee and Tyrus Wong saw quite clearly the structure of Gubbins' business model and how he profited from the employment of Chinese American extras. Gubbins continued to take a portion of the extras' pay well after the Central Casting Bureau made efforts to eliminate the practice.

Regardless of how individual Chinatown residents saw Tom Gubbins, the very fact that he was able to monopolize the recruitment of Chinese American extras demonstrated the extent to which Chinatown residents remained socially and economically segregated from much of the Los Angeles economy. Because of this segregation, Gubbins was able to maintain his influence over Chinese American background performers even after the creation of Central Casting in 1926. In many ways, he represented the perfect broker in the eyes of Hollywood film producers. Not only did he grow up in China and speak Cantonese fluently but he was also of Irish descent.[53] For this reason alone, many White studio producers must have preferred working with him to working with brokers like James Wang. Despite his racial advantages, Gubbins did not retain his control over Chinese American extras for much longer. By the 1930s, shifting local, national, and global factors were challenging Gubbins as the extras' sole recruiter.

No single Hollywood film had a greater influence on the material conditions or representational politics of Chinese American extras than *The Good Earth*. With MGM studios going to great lengths to appease the Chinese government's demands, *The Good Earth* became in many ways an international production. In part because of its global publicity, the film provided the perfect vehicle for Chinese American background performers in Los Angeles to challenge long-standing discriminatory employment practices. They were able to demand changes in part because of the increased interest of the Chinese government in Hollywood representations of China in general and in the production of *The Good Earth* in particular.

While many Chinese American extras during the Depression were happy to have any work in Hollywood, the Chinese Nationalist government was displeased with the cinematic representations of China that Hollywood was producing during the period. Shaping the representation of China in *The Good Earth* soon became its priority. Once it was decided that MGM's film would be shot entirely in Southern California and not in China, the government in Nanking (*Nanjing*) sent General Ting-shu Tu (*Du Tingxiu*) to California to oversee its production. The general arrived in Los Angeles in the summer of 1935 and was present for the casting of the film's leads, Paul Muni and Luise Rainer, as well as most of the supporting players. He was also there in December of 1935 when the studio passed over Anna May Wong, leaving *The Good Earth* without the world's most recognized Chinese American actor.[54] In the new year, Wong embarked on an eight-month trip to China, where she expressed doubts to the Chinese press that the film would ever be completed successfully.[55]

Even though MGM decided not to cast Wong, the studio did make the decision to cast Chinese American performers in all background and bit parts as well as many supporting roles. In November, Reuters ran a story announcing that "Chinese who can talk perfect English" were being sought.[56] Paul Muni, General Tu, and other representatives of the film embarked on a tour of the West Coast to identify Chinese Americans to play supporting roles. In San Francisco, the *Associated Press* reported that the tour brought out, "hundreds of holiday-garbed Chinese from doddering septuagenarians to babbling infants . . . bent on crashing filmdom's gate."[57]

The November trip to San Francisco garnered roles for Ching Wah Lee, a Chinatown tour guide and publisher of the *Chinese Digest*, along with William Law, a merchant and president of the Chinese Consolidated Benevolent Association in San Francisco.[58] Other supporting roles went to established bit players such as Keye Luke and Soo Yung. In all, *The Good Earth* included 68 nonprincipal speaking parts.[59] What's more, it represented an unprecedented economic opportunity for Chinese Americans extras in Los Angeles.

The number of Chinese American extras required for the film, along with the heightened international interest in the production, challenged Tom Gubbins's monopoly over the hiring of Chinese American background performers. For years the studios had turned to him as the local voice of authority on all matters Chinese. Studios hired Gubbins to ensure authenticity, but when *Shanghai Express* was banned in China, despite his guidance as the film's technical advisor, the studios began to question his cultural authority. His position was further weakened when the Chinese government established a consular office in Los Angeles in 1932 and appointed twenty-four-year-old Yi-seng Kiang (*Jiang Yang-sheng*), as the its first vice consul.

The government in Nanking declared Kiang the "Chinese representative in Hollywood" that studios could go to for advice.[60]

Shortly after arriving, Kiang made his displeasure with Gubbins clear without directly mentioning him by name. In an interview with the *Illustrated Daily News*, the vice consul first identified *Shanghai Express* as having caused China "much trouble. . . . The beauty of the Chinese life has been unjustifiably marred by the overdrawn presentations on screen due to a few unscrupulous people who have, for mercenary purposes, inculcated in the minds of the producers such ideas and knowledge which they claim to possess, yet which are disastrously misinformed and misinterpreted."[61] In the vice consul, the studios now had an official of the Chinese government whose favor they could court. They no longer had to rely exclusively on Gubbins.

Gubbins's influence in Hollywood came under increasing threat. As early as 1933, Kiang began floating names of alternative technical directors. He suggested Jimmie Lee, a drama student at the University of Southern California and part-time bit player, as technical advisor for *The Good Earth*.[62] The studio did not follow the vice consul's advice. Then, in 1934, with preproduction under way, Tom Gubbins was fired from MGM's Greta Garbo film, *The Painted Veil* (1934). The vice consul pressured MGM to hire Dr. George Lew Chee as his replacement. The *Chicago Tribune* said of Dr. Chee's appointment: "Metro-Goldwyn-Mayer has the favor of the Chinese government to think about, for when its current Garbo picture is complete, the same studio is to film Pearl Buck's *The Good Earth* and each film represents a studio outlay of close to a half million.[63] . . . Each film may need more background scenes shot in China, and the cooperation which vice-consul Yi-seng Kiang, and the government might extend or withhold from future movie expeditions makes the vice-consul's friend Lew Chee, important to the studio."[64]

The Painted Veil was not the only film Dr. Chee worked on in 1934. He also served as Mandarin coach on Harold Lloyd's film *The Cat's Paw*, after the vice-consul urged that the film use Mandarin rather than Cantonese for all background scenes set in China.[65] Mandarin was a language the Hong Kong–raised Gubbins did not speak. With the production of *The Good Earth* set to begin, Dr. Chee opened his own rival casting agency on North Main Street called the Chinese-American Cinema Service.

By the start of 1935, there were two casting agencies in Chinatown, both operating without the labor protections offered by Central Casting. One agency was Dr. Chee's; the other was Tom Gubbins's. Each had its own loyal performers. Actors loyal to Gubbins, including Frank Tang, Walter Wong, and Wong Chong, began to express their displeasure with the vice consul's role in Hollywood productions. In a press release, they said, "We believe that the vice consul has demanded the right to censor Chinese sequences in script form and has, thereby, made himself obnoxious to motion picture producers. . . . He wants all Chinese characters pictured as high-minded gentlemen. There are bums in China as well as Los Angeles." In response, the vice consul told the *Illustrated Daily News* that he wanted to "eliminate from the American screen everything that is objectionable to the Chinese people. So far as Tom Gubbins is concerned, I know that the Chinese government is likely to suspect any picture with which he had been connected."[66]

Lurking behind the debate over screen representations were the material conditions of labor in Hollywood and the ability of particular actors to land roles in Chinese-themed pictures. Spencer Chan, a performer from the period, recalled this as "the battle of the Oriental agencies."[67] Chan, who became a labor organizer in Hollywood, recalled: "You work for an agent. You don't get a job directly from the boss. The idea being, which was a disadvantage to us [the performers], to get on the good side of an agent. If we don't, then we don't get the job. The agent will hire his own people. You won't get a job." Dr. Lew Chee's untimely death in March of 1935 meant that Tom Gubbins's primacy as a technical expert would continue.[68] Nonetheless, because he lacked the support of the vice consul, he continued to find himself under threat. On December 1, 1935, *The Los Angeles Times* ran an article declaring: "*Good Earth* Casting Stirs Feud Among Chinese Actors."[69] It quoted an MGM representative who said that the studio did not care who supplied the performers: "Anyone who can supply what we want will certainly get a hearing."[70]

With demand for Chinese background performers at unprecedented levels, a group of actors in Chinatown challenged Gubbins as the gatekeeper to Chinese American talent. In mid-December of 1935, dozens of performers, including Bessie Loo and her husband Richard, complained to the new vice consul about the additional fees that Tom Gubbins charged. Kiang filed a complaint on the performers' behalf with the California State Labor Commission. *Variety* reported: "More than 50 Chinese complained that they must pay the 10%, plus an extra charge for costumes, whenever furnished by Gubbins, reducing their net below figure on studio payroll."[71]

Years later, in an interview with the Chinese Historical Society of Southern California, Bessie Loo described the system of extra recruitment without naming Gubbins: "There was a man there who was a runner, by that I mean that he hired all of the Chinese people to work in the pictures. . . . He got paid by the studios, and he got a kickback from all of us. We were paid only five dollars. Each five dollars we had to give him a dollar, so he was making money both ways."[72] Two days of hearings attended by State Labor Commissioner Thomas Barker and Campbell MacCulloch of Central Casting were held in the offices of the Motion Picture Producers Association. By Christmas the charges had been dropped and a settlement reached. Tom Gubbins would become a runner for Central Casting, which would pay his commission. On Christmas Day, *Variety* reported: "Chinese extras hereafter will get their cues from Central Casting Bureau. And, free of charge."[73] In 1939, Central Casting hired Bessie Loo as the primary recruiter of Chinese American performers. Chinese American performers

FIGURE 3.6. Bessie Loo, Hayward SooHoo, and Ching Wah Lee on the set of *The Good Earth*. Chinese Historical Society of Southern California.

had successfully demanded their incorporation into Central Casting's for-mal hiring system.

The Good Earth did more than change the material conditions of labor for Chinese American movie extras.[74] It also transformed the ways that Chinese American bit players and extras were portrayed in the popular press. For much of the decade, Los Angeles newspapers followed the story of *The Good Earth*'s production with intense interest. They reported the crew's trip to China to shoot exteriors, tracked the studio's struggle to cast the leads, and described the 500-acre plot of land in San Fernando Valley on which MGM built its Chinese village. Bridging the period between the release of Pearl S. Buck's novel in 1931 and the release of MGM's film in 1937, the narrative that the national press put forth became a significant part of audiences' understanding of China and the Chinese people.

A portion of that narrative focused on the experiences of Chinese Ameri-can performers. As Janette Roan has argued, this focus was in part about the studio's claims that the film authentically represented China,[75] but it was also in part about Chinese American inclusion in the Hollywood system. The press began moving away from portraying Chinese American bit players and extras as an inassimilable mass that could only be understood through intermediaries like Tom Gubbins. For perhaps the first time in Hollywood history, the press portrayed Chinese American performers as individuals with lives and goals of their own, who, like their White counterparts, could be discovered by Hollywood. The papers reported the story of Lotus Liu, discovered by a casting director on a city bus;[76] San Francisco merchant Wil-liam Law, hired for a lead role after helping to cast extras in San Francisco;[77] and Mary Wong, discovered by Paul Muni "in a San Francisco bazaar."[78] We learn that "They sent for a doctor because one of the Chinese girls was ill in *The Good Earth* production and discovered an actor, Samuel Yen Eng. He was tested for the role of son of Wang."[79] The Hollywood columnist for the *New York Times* explained: "Hollywood has never used Chinese actors for anything but atmosphere. Because of this no record has been kept of Orien-tals capable of enacting important roles. With the search for talent for *Good Earth* Metro has accumulated the first comprehensive list for picture work, a roll that embraces men and women on the Coast."[80]

In their rush to tell these stories, newspapers often did not always take the time to determine ethnicity or even properly record names. For example, the *Los Angeles Times* ran two stories about a performer they called Philson On. One story, entitled "College Student Awarded Role in *The Good Earth*," began: "At 2:30 in the afternoon, Philson On was a divinity student. At 3:30 he was a cinematic thief . . . . On, son of a San Francisco merchant lives in Berkeley where he graduated from high school. Tall and athletic, he was chosen for the role from among a large number who were tested for the production. He is in his junior year in theology at Stanford"[81]—a Bay Area boy given a chance to appear in a Hollywood film. The problem was that Philson On was actually Philson Ahn, a Korean American.

On the bus, at the bazaar, while on call—passing references to bit players in the newspaper columns firmly extended the Hollywood narrative of discovery to Chinese Americans for the first time. In identifying performers by name, the press provided them visibility. Visibility was the first step toward acceptance as fully formed subjects—people with names, histories, and aspirations of their own. Between 1934 and 1937, at least thirty-nine articles in the *Los Angeles Times* mentioned a Chinese American extra by name. This coverage brought a sustained public focus to the large English-speaking, US-born Chinese American population on the West Coast. In this way, it aided the inclusion of Chinese Americans in US society in the coming decade.

This is not to say that the press completely embraced Chinese Americans as members of the acting profession. After all, they were kept out of all lead roles. The press did not portray them as skilled professionals able to carry a motion picture. Leads were reserved for White performers in yellowface, while Chinese Americans were relegated to background and bit roles. This ongoing racist practice did not keep Hollywood or its supporters in the press from lavishing praise on their own policies, which they imagined as inclusive. Short articles about Chinese American actors in *The Good Earth* made Hollywood producers feel good without their having to give any leads to the small handful trying to make a living. Hollywood simultaneously celebrated these small acts of diversity and maintained the racist structure that denied Chinese Americans control over the film's representations and its starring roles. But as we shall see, the fact that these performers were relegated to extra and bit roles did not stop Chinese American audiences from imagining a different Hollywood future.

CHAPTER 4

Oppositional Spectatorship and *The Good Earth*

One Friday evening in January of 1937, a crowd of onlookers gathered at the Carthay Circle Theatre on Wilshire Boulevard in Los Angeles for the world premiere of *The Good Earth*. MGM studios had spared no expense on the night's festivities. An entire city block was cordoned off. In the days leading up to the opening, Harry Oliver, the film's associate art director, transformed the forecourt of the theater into a Chinese village.[1] By opening night, the display stretched from the theater's entrance to Wilshire and included a fishpond, urns, Chinese flags, a row of giant bronze statues of Buddha, sampan boats, and two live water buffalos.[2]

A who's-who of Hollywood stars and political luminaries attended. The film's leading actors, Paul Muni and Luise Rainer, were there, along with Fay Wray, Joan Crawford, California governor Frank Merriam, and Chinese consul general Chao Chin Huang.[3] Thirty-two radio stations across the United States, Canada, and Mexico broadcast the event live, with an additional seventy-two stations rebroadcasting it.[4] *The Good Earth* was the first film premier to receive a national radio broadcast in US history.[5] The *New York Times*, the *Washington Post*, and the *Los Angeles Times* covered it. In this way the opening itself became a media event.

Since the release of Pearl S. Buck's novel in 1931, *The Good Earth* had become a cultural phenomenon that reached deep into the national imagination. The novel sold more than half a million copies in its first year alone and was translated into thirty languages.[6] Buck won the Pulitzer Prize in literature. Even as the novel garnered critical acclaim and positioned Buck as one of the nation's foremost experts on China, MGM's film reached a greater audience. Some 23 million Americans and another 42 million people around the world watched it during its original release.[7] It was nominated for five Academy Awards, including Best Picture, Best Director, and Best Cinematography. Luise Rainer won the award for Best Actress.

The cultural influence of the film reached beyond the screen images. Long before its release, the press ran stories on nearly every aspect of its production. In Los Angeles, the city where publicity for the film was the greatest, audiences encountered *The Good Earth* in more material ways. The Chinese exhibit at the Carthay Circle Theatre remained in place for the entirety of the film's Los Angeles run. More than ten thousand visitors viewed it in its first week.[8] In a first for the city, the superintendent of Los Angeles public schools approved the use of district buses to transport students "engaged in the study of the Orient" to the theater.[9] Thus the film united related texts—the novel and radio and newspaper coverage—with the exhibit at the theater to present a new vision of China and the Chinese people to American audiences at a moment when events in Asia had thrust the region into the national imagination.

Scholars have long credited *The Good Earth* with shifting American attitudes toward China and the Chinese people. The book was released shortly after the Japanese invasion of Manchuria in 1931, and the film began screening in theaters before the start of the Second Sino-Japanese war in the summer of 1937. According to political science scholar Harold Isaacs,

> Book and film together, *The Good Earth*, almost singlehandedly replaced the fantasy images of China and Chinese held by most Americans with a somewhat more realistic picture of what the China was like and a new more appealing picture of the Chinese themselves. Indeed, *The Good Earth* accomplished this feat of providing faces for the faceless.[10]

While scholars have debated the idea that *The Good Earth* "almost singlehandedly" transformed notions of the Chinese people, its impact on popular notions of Asia and the Asian people in the United States cannot be denied.

In recent years, both popular critics and academics have justifiably critiqued the racist casting of White actors in yellowface as the film's leading performers.[11] In her book *Made Up Asians: Yellowface During the Exclusion Era*, theater studies scholar Esther Lee Kim describes *The Good Earth* as "the most ambitious yellowface project a Hollywood studio had undertaken to that time."[12] Both stars were European immigrants. As a result of these casting decisions, critics today almost universally dismiss the film. Film scholars Ella Shoat and Robert Stam remind us that the casting of White actors as characters of color is a triple insult to communities of color because it implies "(a) you are unworthy of your own self-representation; (b) no one from your community is capable of representing you; and (c) we, the producers of the film, care little about your offended sensibilities."[13] The casting of White actors as the leads in *The Good Earth* was undoubtedly racist and modern audiences are right to find it offensive.

Yet in reflexively dismissing the entire film, modern critics miss its broader representational significance to the Los Angeles Chinese American community in the 1930s. The film was not exceptional because Louis Rainer and Paul Muni appeared in yellowface—yellowface was common in Classical Hollywood cinema.[14] Instead, it was exceptional because of more than a dozen Chinese American actors in speaking roles who appeared alongside Muni and Rainer. These bit players were supported by hundreds of Chinese American background extras, a significant number of whom had been recruited in Los Angeles. The stars may have been White, but the vast majority of "the faces of the faceless" were residents of Los Angeles Chinatown.

For this reason, it is overly simplistic to assert that the only reading of *The Good Earth* is as a work of racist cinema.[15] Only focusing on the yellowface performances risks overlooking the many ways that Chinese American audiences in the 1930s created their own understandings of the film. One might assert that *The Good Earth* erases the subjectivity of Asian Americans and make Asian Americans "objects in their own stories," as one recent media studies scholar has argued, but in the 1930s most Chinese Americans in Los Angeles did not view the film in this way at all.[16] Instead, they created their own oppositional readings, finding their own empowerment in a film that appeared at first glance to be nothing more than another example of racist yellowface casting.[17]

As this chapter will show, the Chinese Nationalist government, White American viewers, and US-born Chinese Americans viewed *The Good Earth* in different ways.[18] The Chinese government was most concerned with whether the film provided an "authentic" representation of China. In contrast, White Americans were positioned to see the film as a neo-Chinatown tour providing insight into a country increasingly in the national news.

Finally, Chinese Americans in Los Angeles in the 1930s were more likely to laud the film than criticize it. By choosing not to focus on the White actors in yellowface and focusing instead on the background and bit players, they reimagined their own place in the film industry—and by extension in American society—by celebrating the Chinese American performers as the film's actual stars.

By the late nineteenth century, US popular audiences had become obsessed with stories about the nation's Chinatowns. Fueled by twin motives of fear and fascination, audiences across the US consumed books, plays, and eventually films set in these ethnic enclaves.[19] Far from being ancillary to immigration exclusion and restriction, popular representations both reflected and created mainstream sentiments about Chinese immigrants that supported ongoing exclusion legislation. They helped transform the United States into a gatekeeping nation by portraying these immigrants and Chinatowns as threats to White American society.[20] Driven by an overt ideology of White supremacy, the nation's political leaders relied on cultural representations to buttress their arguments for curtailing immigration, first from China and then from other countries in Asia.

From the beginning of Hollywood, Chinese Americans had protested its racist images. What modern critics of *The Good Earth* miss is that many Chinese saw it as an improvement on earlier representations of Chinese people, and that the representations of China in *The Good Earth* were in a part a product of protests led by members of the Chinese American community that stretched back decades. In fact, most Chinese Americans in the 1930s considered *The Good Earth* to be a step forward, even with its yellowface performers. Indeed, the perceived improvement was a result of MGM's desire to avoid public outcry over the ways Hollywood had long represented Chinese people.

Chinese Americans were neither the first nor the only group to protest the film industry's racist practices. Over the first three decades of the twentieth century, Hollywood was awash in racist imagery, which viewers of color protested. Led by the NAACP, Black audiences across the nation protested the release of *Birth of Nation* (1915)—a film that portrayed the Ku Klux Klan as the saviors of the South following the Civil War. The same year that *Birth of Nation* was released, Japanese Americans protested the release of *The Cheat* (1915), which told the story of a villainous Japanese art dealer and his relationship with a White socialite, whom he assaults and attempts to brand.[21] As Denise Khor has shown, Japanese Americans in the 1910s "increasingly recognized the possibilities of cinema as a surface for representing race and charting a future in the United States."[22] This understanding fueled their protests. In 1917, the Japanese Photoplayers' Club of Los Angeles was established with the goal of organizing protests of silent films with racist imagery. Chinese Americans were far from alone in their protesting.

In the early twentieth century, Chinese Americans were most likely to protest portrayals of Chinatown as a den of vice. Throughout the silent film era and into the early years of sound in the 1930s, Hollywood producers depicted Chinatowns as riddled with underground lairs, where working-class Chinese men smoked opium and White women were constantly under sexual threat by Chinese bachelors. Even after the Chinese American merchants of San Francisco rebuilt that city's Chinatown into a modern tourist attraction, underground Chinatowns threatening White society continued to be a popular theme in Hollywood.[23]

Related to representations of an underground Chinatown as a yellow peril was the figure of Fu Manchu. As Ruth Myer tells us, we should regard Fu Manchu as a figure, not a character. Characters appear in "a closed fictional universe."[24] In contrast, figures are "more loosely connected by means of their status as cultural icons or stereotypes yet move across media and medial forms." Fu Manchu the figure would be a presence in film, radio, television, and print from the 1910s through the 1970s.[25]

Created by Sax Rohmer, Fu Manchu first appeared in the 1913 novel *The Mystery of Fu Manchu*. This was the first of at least thirteen novels to feature him. In 1923, the British film company Stoll Pictures produced *The Mystery of Dr. Fu Manchu*—the first time the archetypical Chinese villain appeared on screen. But even before then, this figure showed up in various silent serials. These included *The Exploits of Elaine* (1914) starring Pauline White, which featured the villain Wong Long Sin. Wong Long Sin's most notable feature was the drooping mustache that would later define Fu Manchu.[26] Wong Long Sin was followed by the character Wu Fang, this time in the serial *The New Exploits of Elaine* (1915).[27] A third character, Ali Singh, appeared in *The Yellow Menace* (1916), also embodying the characteristics of Fu Manchu. Film studies scholar Eugene Wong describes the figure that united these characters as "the monstrous

FIGURE 4.1. Advertisement for *The Exploits of Elaine: The Clutching Hand.*
Moving Picture World, 1914.

Mandarin . . . a Chinese character of the most demonic proportions, playing upon the American fascination of Yellow Peril."[28]

While these silent serials remain the best-known yellow peril depictions from the early twentieth century, they were not the only fictional accounts to represent Asian immigrants as a threat. The film industry in Los Angeles played a foundational role in perpetuating stereotypes of a threatening underground Chinatown. By the late 1910s, the bulk of the nation's Chinatown films were being shot in and around Los Angeles, even though many were set in San Francisco. Early Chinatown films produced in Southern California included *The Hop Smugglers* (1914), *The Highbinders* (1916), *The Chinatown Villains* (1916), *The Flower of Doom* (1916), and *The Midnight Patrol* (1919). Often filmed quickly on cheap studio sets for a mass audience, they relied on tropes such as underground tunnels and opium dens, and often featured stock characters such as the nefarious Tong leader, the White woman in distress, and the White male savior.[29]

The theme of the White woman in peril was a central element of many early Chinatown films. In 1915's *The Highbinders*, Ah Woo, the mixed-race daughter of a Chinese shop owner and a White mother, is captured by a local Tong leader and held in "the Third Circle, the lowest of the underground passageways in Chinatown" until she is rescued by Jack Donovan, a local saloon owner.[30] In 1916's *Flower of Doom*, a White dancer is kidnapped and held in a secret room in a Chinatown store before being rescued at the film's conclusion.[31] In Thomas Inces's *The Midnight Patrol* (1919), the Tong leader Wu Fang kidnaps a local settlement house worker named Patsy O'Connell. The sergeant of the Chinese vice squad kills Wu Fang and frees her. The movie ends with the sergeant and Pasty agreeing to marry.

Film studies scholar Gina Marchetti foregrounds the central role that narratives of captivity played in yellow peril discourse. Writing of cinematic depictions in which Asian men threatened White women, Marchetti states: "These fantasies tend to link together national-cultural and personal fears, so that the rape of the White woman becomes a metaphor for the threat posed to Western culture as well as a racialization for Euro-American imperial ventures in Asia."[32] Melodramatic narratives of captivity became increasingly popular during a period when the growth of the White middle-class was reshaping understandings of gender roles. Women were becoming the primary consumers in many middle-class households and they were charged with ensuring that the family maintained its status through consumption. As a result, Marchetti argues, captivity narratives were defined by a contradiction: they offered White women "a promised release from Victorian constraints and an implicit permission to indulge oneself sensually through the consumption of exquisitely exotic commodities."[33]

Throughout the silent film era of the 1910s and 1920s, many Chinese Americans protested cinematic representations of an underground Chinatown. One of the earliest films to elicit protest was *The Chinatown Trunk Mystery* (1911), which depicted the kidnapping and murder of a White woman by Chinese men. The film was based on one of the biggest news stories of 1909. Elsie Siegel was a White woman who worked with Chinese immigrants at a missionary school in New York. She was found murdered in 1909, and her death was blamed on Leon Ling, a former student. The murder garnered national news coverage,[34] which constructed a narrative of long-standing White fears about Chinese men raping or murdering White women. When a film of Elsie's death based on the news stories was released in 1911, Chinese up and down the West Coast protested. The Chinese consul in San Francisco was able to keep the film from being screened in that city. Protests also occurred in Los Angeles. *Moving Picture World* reported that Los Angeles Chinatown "had been flooded with yellow posters advertising the show at a local theater." Several prominent Chinese Americans in Los Angeles complained to the chief of police because they felt the film would reflect poorly on the character of Chinese people.[35] According to *Moving Picture World*, the police chief agreed to "prevent the screening of the film if he found it to be improper."

Protests were held not only after a film was released. In Los Angeles, when the 1921 film *Shame* was being produced, Chinese American actors refused to appear in a scene they found exploitative and degrading. Tom Gubbins, who was the on-set technical expert, recalled the reaction of the performers asked to appear in a series of opium den scenes: "Do you think the Chinese would appear in those scenes? Not on your life! When they found out what was to be filmed they began moving away. Called to go on set, they would not budge. . . . I was called and had to take great pains to explain that though the scene showed an opium den, the action would teach a splendid moral lesson and that it was their duty to help teach that lesson."[36] Gubbins eventually convinced the Chinese American actors to perform in the scene but not without much hesitation.[37]

Chinatown residents also protested during film production. On at least two occasions, one in New York and one in Los Angeles, they attempted to stop film crews from shooting exterior scenes in their communities.[38] One protest occurred in 1923, when the actor Thomas Meighan brought his cast and crew to New York Chinatown to film a scene for *Pied Piper of Malone* (1924) without asking permission of the residents. According to the Associated Press, the crew was met with "a shower of lamps, old furniture, and the ingredients of chop suey."[39]

> A Chinatown merchant tonight pointed out that virtually every motion picture showing scenes of Chinatown portrayed the section as being made up of "dives and disreputable places," with "murder and shooting matches rife." Such an impression, he declared, was false and acted against all the law-abiding persons who lived there.[40]

According to Tom Gubbins, the main complaint of the New York Chinese Americans was that the film depicted Chinese people smoking opium.[41]

A similar protest occurred in 1926 in Los Angeles Chinatown, when George Melford and his crew attempted to film scenes for *Going Crooked*. According to *Motion Picture News*,

> Everything was "set" and Melford had taken long shots of a taxi driving to the door of a Chinese shop when he noticed a crowd assembling at the entrance of the alley . . . . The crowd suddenly began to close in around the camera. The younger Chinese began hooting and yelling at the actors in Chinese, blocking the camera and holding up the action.[42]

Residents of the nation's Chinatowns were often quite angry about racist representations, and they expressed those sentiments by interrupting filming in their communities.

While these protests garnered limited attention in the nation's press, the one that sparked the most change in Hollywood was held not in the United States but in China over 1929's *Welcome Danger*. The film starred Harold Lloyd, one of the biggest stars of the silent era, and it was produced at a moment when Hollywood was transitioning between silent and sound. Lloyd targeted the film for wide international release at a time when a significant number of theaters had not made the transition. As a result, he produced two versions: one silent and the other with synchronized dialogue. While it received mixed reviews, *Welcome Danger* became one of Lloyd's most commercially successful films, with fans lining up to hear his voice for the first time.[43]

Like so many films about Chinatown, *Welcome Danger* is set in San Francisco. Nonetheless, the studio shot exterior scenes in and around Los Angeles, including in Old Chinatown. Like many Chinatown films, *Welcome Danger* involves the kidnapping of the main character, who is lured into underground Chinatown. Unlike many Chinatown films, the victim is a Chinese man, not a White woman. In the final half hour, Lloyd and a police officer enter the kidnappers' underground lair through a hidden door in a flower shop. After navigating successive tunnels, each lower than the next, he and his partner are chased by undifferentiated Chinese villains with much slapstick and physical humor. In the process, the film's stereotypes about underground Chinatown lay the groundwork for its visual and verbal jokes.

In late February of 1930, MGM released *Welcome Danger* at the Grand and Capitol Theaters in the Shanghai International Settlement. The movie attracted a mix of Chinese and international residents. A speech by Hung Sung, a local university professor and screenwriter who trained at Harvard, sparked a protest.[44] A former resident of the United States, Sung was aware of the racist ways that Hollywood film represented Chinese immigrants. At a five o'clock showing, he stood up and announced that the film degraded Chinese people. He led a crowd of more than three hundred people to the box office to demand their money back. In the chaos that ensued, the manager of the theater, who was a White resident of Shanghai, injured his neck.[45] The International Settlement police were called. Hung Sung was arrested and held for a few hours as settlement police officers attempted to convince him that the film was a comedy and not meant to offend.[46]

Following this protest, the Chinese government took an increased interest in *Welcome Danger*. The film censorship committee in Shanghai, which was controlled by the Nationalist government, ordered local papers to stop carrying advertisements of the two theaters until they apologized and agreed to submit all future films for review. It also banned the screening of Harold Lloyd films throughout China until Lloyd apologized.[47] Lloyd eventually wrote a formal letter of apology to the Chinese consulate in San Francisco, in which he said that he saw *Welcome Danger* as nothing more than, "an innocent bit of fun" and that he was a "great admirer of your people, civilization, and culture."[48] The Grand and Capitol Theaters also eventually apologized, though the loss of revenue from the protests forced the Grand to close shortly thereafter.[49]

The protests over *Welcome Danger* initiated by Hung Sung shaped the future of Hollywood representations of China. Producers became more aware of the power of the Nationalist government in China and tailored their stories to garner its support. In this context, *The Good Earth* soon became a contested site through which representatives of the Chinese government, White audiences, Chinese American residents of Los Angeles, and others engaged the place of Chinese people in America's popular imagination.

MGM's decision to produce *The Good Earth* quickly drew the attention of the Nationalist government. Chinese censors urged the studio to create a film that celebrated the Chinese people, and warned that if it wanted the cooperation of the Nationalist government—and thus access to Chinese audiences and markets—it needed to heed the input of Nanking. In order to shoot exterior shots in China, the government pressured MGM to agree to having its representative supervise the film and to "present a truthful picture of China and her people."[50] Wanting to avoid the international outcry that surrounded Harold Lloyd's picture a few years earlier, MGM became obsessed with demonstrating to audiences in both China and the US that the film was "authentic." The question was what exactly constituted authenticity. And who would play the lead roles authentically.

Soon after consolidating power in 1927, the Nationalists under Chiang Kai-shek (*Jiang Jieshi*) began to take an increased interest in the film industry. Prior to 1927, censorship had been left to local police departments. By November of 1930, the Motion Picture Censorship Law brought it under the control of the government,[51] and censors in Nanking began monitoring film scripts. The government also shut down fourteen film studios in the mid-1930s[52] and soon turned its attention to Hollywood films. In 1931, it passed a law mandating that all films screened in China be approved by the National Board of Film Censors before it could be shown.[53] By the summer of 1932, censors had already rejected twenty-six films produced in the United States, most because they were found to be "derogatory to the dignity of the Chinese race."[54]

According to film scholar Hye Seung Chung, in the 1930s Chinese government censorship was much different from censorship in the United States. "The Chinese government saw cinema as a medium of nationalist 'uplift' that served public purposes."[55] Chinese censors did not object to representations that would anger most film audiences today, such as Hollywood stars of the 1930s performing in yellowface. Instead, Chung shows, their "attention was focused on broader themes, narrative elements, and characterizations . . . that in their eyes, were contrary to national interests and damaging to China's standing on the world stage."[56]

Given this focus on "national uplift," it is hardly surprising that the Nationalist government would be interested in *The Good Earth*, which had already become one of the most high-profile novels focused on China ever produced in English. It was first translated into Chinese in 1932, and there would be no less than eight different translations by the end of the 1940s. Chinese interest was driven more by curiosity over how Americans represented China than appreciation for the novel itself. As historian Zhiwei Xiao has noted, the first translator of the novel in China saw it as a disgraceful representation of the nation.[57]

Because of China's concerns, when MGM sent a crew to shoot background footage in China in 1933, Nanking forced it to obtain permission first. The government was hesitant to allow the crew in the country—in part because many Chinese found the novel's depiction of their nation offensive—but they eventually acquiesced. In return, MGM agreed to truthfully represent China; they also allowed a Chinese representative to supervise the film's production; and they committed to an entirely Chinese cast.[58]

MGM did make a good-faith effort to employ an all-Chinese cast for the film. In November of 1934, The *Los Angeles Times* reported that this was "not beyond the horizon of possibilities."[59] Citing the precedent set by a 1933 MGM film about the lives of Alaska Natives—shot in Alaska in the Inupiaq language with English intertitles—released to critical acclaim, the reporter Edwin Shallert suggested that the story of *The Good Earth*, "would be told in action as far as possible and that the native flavor preserved by having characters talk Chinese."[60] But whereas in this earlier film, MGM cast a Chinese American as a lead performer and asked her to memorize her lines in Inupiaq verbatim, for *The Good Earth* they considered casting exclusively Mandarin-speaking Chinese actors from China.[61] In December of 1934, advertisements were run in Chinese papers seeking actors between twenty-four and twenty-six years of age who spoke both Mandarin and English for the lead roles.[62] The studio conducted at least fifteen screen and voice tests with Chinese actors.[63] Despite these efforts, the Chinese-language version of the film was never made.

As casting calls were being held in China, the government was sending its representative, General Ting-hsiu Tu (*Du Tingxiu*) of the Chinese National Army, to Hollywood to oversee production. MGM had already begun testing White actors for the leads.[64] By October of 1935, it had cast the Austrian actor Paul Muni as the peasant Wang.[65] In November, it cast German actress Luise Rainer as O-lan.

The casting of Muni and Rainer followed a long tradition in Hollywood. Since the silent film era, Chinese-themed films had been popular in Hollywood. Generally, though, European immigrants played the most prominent Chinese roles. These included the Russian American actor Richard Barthelmess, who had played Cheng Huang in *Broken Blossoms*, and the Swedish American actor Warner Oland who had played in *Mandarin's Gold* (1919), *East Is West* (1922), and *The Fighting American* (1924), and later played Fu Manchu and Charlie Chan. During the silent era, Chinese Americans in supporting roles was so rare that when a Chinese American landed a minor one in the 1922 film *East Is West*, the *Sacramento Union* reported with surprise that "a real Chinaman, Jim Wang, will portray the proprietor of the Love Boat."[66] Because MGM's casting of Muni and Rainer seemed to contradict its purported goal of truthful representations of Chinese people, the studio cast Chinese American supporting players to bolster its claims of authenticity.[67] Reporting on MGM's open casting call in San Francisco in early November of 1935, the Associated Press stated: "About 500 Chinese will be chosen from the local population, Maj-Gen. Tingshu [sic] Tu of the Chinese army, in charge of recruiting native talent, declared."

In addition to promoting Chinese Americans as the film's bit players and extras, the studio and its supporters in the press constructed a public narrative of the lead actors' authentic performances. The *Los Angeles Times* published a series of articles that described Muni working to transform his body to resemble that of a Chinese farmer. One explained how Muni tanned himself for a "half an hour daily."[68] Another described how he did the work of a Chinese farmer when he spent five hours on a primitive treadmill to pump water on location."[69] There was also a column discussing Muni and Rainer's use of "Chinese mannerisms."[70] Between 1935 and 1937, the *Times* ran eleven articles extolling the authenticity of the Chinese village set in Chatsworth, going so far as a headline claiming "Location So Realistic Swallows Build

Nests There: Crops Grow, Grain Ripens in Transplanted Chinese Villages as Cameras Continue to Roll on 'The Good Earth.'"[71]

MGM perpetuated the narrative of authenticity based on Chinese American background performers, the elaborate set in Chatsworth, and the efforts by Muni and Rainer to prepare for their roles.[72] While no one ever said that an Austrian actor working out on a treadmill could somehow make the film more authentic, the press narrative demonstrated how malleable and historically rooted the concept of authenticity was. No doubt there were aspects of the Chinese village that reflected actual conditions in China at some point in time, but in many ways the extent to which the film was authentic did not matter. Rather than ask whether the film authentically represented some aspect of Chinese culture or life, a more a more productive line of inquiry is in what ways the narrative of authenticity shaped the film's reception by White audiences.

When White American audiences entered theaters to watch *The Good Earth* in 1937, they had been primed by the press to see it as an authentic representation of China and the Chinese people at a moment when China was increasingly becoming a topic of conversation. At the same time, Muni and Rainer in yellowface constantly reminded audiences that the film was an elaborate performance. In such ways, *The Good Earth* ended up appealing to the same desires for authenticity and theatricality that had sent White visitors on Chinatown tours for more than half a century.

The press was rapturous in its praise, buttressing the film's claims of authenticity. The *New York Herald Tribune* stated: "*The Good Earth* is a powerful notable translation of a novel that has probably done more than anything else to acquaint us with China."[73] According to the *Los Angeles Evening News*, "It hardly seems a thing of fiction it is so full of scenes and moments of stirring reality—like photographs of actual events in China's present history."[74] The *Los Angeles Times* called it "one of the truly great films of the era."[75]

The press had bombarded readers for two years with stories about Muni and Rainer's immersion in their roles as Chinese peasants, highlighting the film's theatricality. Rather than claiming that their yellowface performances detracted from the film, the critics claimed that the transformation of their bodies was further proof of their dedication to their craft. Frank Nugent of the *New York Times* wrote: "Luise Rainer's portrayal of O-lan, wife of

Wang Lung the farmer, establishes her beyond doubt as one of the truly great actresses of our day."[76] Of Muni he wrote: "Mr. Muni as Wang Lung is flawless." Philip Scheuer of the *Los Angeles Times* wrote: "I have seen their Wang and O-lan several times now and am moved anew by their fidelity of interpretation."[77]

Of course, no amount of tanning, "Chinese mannerisms," Chinese American background players, or water buffalos in Chatsworth could transform Muni and Rainer into actual Chinese people, but this was not their purpose. White filmgoers never had to believe that the actors were Chinese peasants. All that was required was their own willing immersion in the world of the film. The discourse of authenticity promoted by MGM and entertainment press gave audiences permission to suspend disbelief while in the theater. Just as turn-of-the-century San Francisco tourists suspended disbelief in their visits to the city's fake municipal opium den, White viewers of *The Good Earth* suspended their disbelief in watching two White actors in yellowface pretend to be Chinese peasants. In the process, the press presented Rainer and Muni as the perfect guides for this journey. In multiple ways, *The Good Earth* drew on the same desires of its viewers that Chinatown tours of the later nineteenth century did.

While *The Good Earth* may have functioned in many ways like a Chinatown tour, MGM's cinematic tour of its Chatsworth set promoted different racial and ethnic understandings. Turn-of-the-century Chinatown tours recited a narrative of Chinese people as a yellow peril, which *The Good Earth* explicitly challenged. In the opening third of the film, we follow the peasant Wang as he travels to the great house in the village to meet his wife O-lan for the first time. Wang's father has arranged their marriage. O-lan works beside her husband in the fields, cooks, cleans, and takes care of the home while supporting both Wang and her father in-law. During a particularly bad rainstorm, O-lan goes into labor and returns to the couple's simple home, where she gives birth to a healthy boy. Wang throws a celebration with neighbors and relatives.

In both content and form, the first part of the film functions as a rejoinder to long-standing representations of urban Chinatowns as dens of depravity, vice, and violence. Featuring recurring images of the Chinese countryside while foregrounding a monogamous peasant couple, the imagery and themes of *The Good Earth* contrast with those of Chinatown tours and Chinatown films. Both were defined by the trope of the underground lair and the imagined threat of sexual violence against White women. At the heart of this trope was the fear of miscegenation, in which an illicit relationship between a Chinese man and White woman and the mixed-race children who would come from that relationship were an existential threat to the White, heterosexual, middle-class family in their suburban home. Popular representations of Chinatown were defined by a perceived deviant sexuality, specifically that of the Chinese bachelor's desire for White women.[78]

In contrast, the relationship between O-lan and Wang—at least in the first half of the film—is portrayed as the embodiment of a patriarchal, heterosexual relationship. O-lan is a caricature of the submissive Asian housewife. She dutifully serves her husband and father-in-law, cleaning, cooking, working the fields, pausing only briefly to give birth, putting the needs of her husband, father-in-law, and children before hers. Wang is portrayed as loyal to O-lan until he marries his second wife. Even as the introduction of a polygamous relationship injects the film with a subtext of deviant sexuality, the deviance is nonthreatening to White American audiences. Unlike nineteenth-century representations of young Chinese immigrant men threatening White womanhood or Chinese prostitutes preying on White men and boys, the deviance of the polygamous Chinese family in *The Good Earth* is tempered by the concluding scene of O-lan on her death bed, in which Wang reassures the audience of his devotion to her, his first wife.

In this cinematic response to the underground Chinatown tour, Luise Rainer and Paul Muni became tour guides to movie viewers on their journey through MGM's China. Rather than ethnic depravity, their tour was of a community hyper-devoted to heteronormative ideals. Thus the film fulfilled both the Nationalist government's challenging of cinematic representations like that seen in Harold Loyd's *Welcome Danger* and White American audiences' desire to believe that they were watching a film celebrating China. At the same time, Chinese American viewers in Los Angeles experienced a very different movie.

While White viewers were positioned to see the film as a neo-Chinatown tour, many Chinese Americans saw it as a celebration of the Los Angeles Chinatown community. Not only did the film reject yellow peril stereotypes but for the first time a major studio film featured more than a dozen Chinese Americans in speaking roles. With the glaring exception of Anna May

Wong, *The Good Earth* featured nearly every Chinese American regularly working in Hollywood. These supporting players were surrounded by more than a thousand extras, many of whom were Chinese Americans from the greater Los Angeles area. From performers like Bessie Loo and Keye Luke in bit roles to extras like Lilly Mu, Esther Lee, and Jennie Lee in the background, the film featured a diversity of local Chinese American talent.

This cinematic celebration of the Los Angeles Chinatown community could not have come at a more opportune time. In 1933, crews began the slow destruction of Old Chinatown to make way for Union Station. In part due to Peter SooHoo, whose advocacy allowed residents to stay in the area as long as possible, the destruction occurred slowly, block by block, over a period of years. By the time *The Good Earth* began recruiting extras in 1935, Old Chinatown was no longer the thriving center of the community that it had been only a few years earlier. Those who could afford to move had already relocated to other Chinese American neighborhoods near Ninth Street or in the East Adams area.[79]

The loss of Old Chinatown brought about not just economic pain but also the end of a community. At the very moment that the neighborhood was being dismantled and its residents dispersed, cinematic images of the Chinese village set in Chatsworth provided a space for members of the ethnic enclave to see their friends, neighbors, and family members on screen, in a film that celebrated rather than denigrated Chinese people.

The Good Earth also gave Chinese Americans a chance to reimagine their relationship with this most quintessential form of American entertainment. Whereas White audiences in the US and Chinese audiences in China saw a film about a nation, Chinese Americans in Los Angeles saw a film about the possibilities of big-screen Hollywood representation. For no group was this truer than for the US-born Chinese Americans then coming of age in Los Angeles. Having grown up attending movies in downtown Los Angeles, they saw their parents and aunties, friends and neighbors, classmates and co-workers, represented in a medium that the younger generation had embraced. They also saw performers who had long struggled in Hollywood land small speaking parts. In the same way that later Asian American audiences would embrace movies like *Flower Drum Song*, *Joy Luck Club*, and *Crazy Rich Asians* as their own, *The Good Earth* became a celebration of Chinese American representation in Hollywood for a generation of Chinese American moviegoers.[80]

The excitement that Chinese American youth felt is palatable in the film's coverage in the *Chinese Digest*, one of the earliest English-language newspapers published in the Chinese American community. Thomas Chinn and Ching Wah Lee founded the paper in San Francisco in 1935, a few months before MGM began casting *The Good Earth*. Both US-born, Chinn served as editor while Lee served as one of two associate editors and went on to finance much of the paper's production from the money he earned appearing in *The Good Earth*.[81] As a San Francisco expert on Chinese art, he had worked as a technical advisor on Hollywood films. MGM reached out to him to recruit extras in the San Francisco area, and he eventually became a supporting player.

The *Chinese Digest*'s coverage of the film began in 1936. Unlike mainstream reportage, it devoted almost no space to convincing readers of the authenticity of Muni's and Rainer's performances. Instead, it focused on the Chinese American actors and crew. In short, the magazine celebrated *The Good Earth* as a work of community representation, presenting the bit players and supporting actors as stars of the film and Muni and Rainer as performing a needed function in bringing the film to the screen. Most of its coverage was written by Ching Wah Lee. As a supporting player, he was featured in the *Los Angeles Times*. His picture even appeared in the paper.[82] In many ways, Lee's presence helps explain why his publication devoted so much space to *The Good Earth*.[83]

The *Chinese Digest* targeted a Chinese American audience that was US-born, urban, and growing. By 1930, the demographics of the Chinese American community had begun to shift drastically from only 10 percent US-born in 1900 to 41.2 percent US-born in 1930.[84] Thus the paper's readers had a keen interest in seeing others with life experiences like theirs represented. The paper's run was short, folding in 1940, and it never broke a thousand subscribers, but despite this limited reach it keenly reflected the sentiments of this growing portion of the Chinese American community.[85] Nearly all of its writers were US-born, and its volunteers wrote columns from Chinese American communities across the West Coast, including not just San Francisco but Portland, Seattle, and Los Angeles.

In March of 1936, the *Digest* began its extensive coverage of *The Good Earth*. This coverage continued for one full year, until the release of a special edition published in March of 1937.[86] Over the course of this period, the paper devoted at least nineteen articles to the film. Two were about the

March, 1937   CHINESE DIGEST   Page 9

HOLLYWOOD REVIEW

**WHO'S WHO
AMONG THE CHINESE IN
"THE GOOD EARTH"**

Soo Yong is an A.B. from the University of Hawaii and an M.A. from Columbia University. Her major is botany, and she has taught in high schools. She made her bow to America when she served as curtain raiser for Mei Lan Fang, and America is still loud in praise of her fine English diction—"better than the best among the English and the American." She made history again when she appeared as a Manchu princess in the picture, "Painted Veil." After that performance M-G-M chained her by a "Good Earth" contract to play both the ancient Mistress and the sloppy sharp-tongued aunt.

Mary Wong is the prettiest Chinese girl appearing in "The Good Earth." In

Some of the Chinese players and technical staff of "The Good Earth." Left to right are Roland Lui (Got), Caroline Chew, Chingwah Lee, Mary Wong, James Z. M. Lee, Soo Yong, William Law, Lotus Liu and Frank Tang.

FIGURE 4.2.   "Who's Who Among the Chinese in *The Good Earth.*" *Chinese Digest*, 1937.

Chinese government's involvement in its production, two were about the Chinese village set in Chatsworth, and only one was about the White cast's attempts to portray themselves as authentically Chinese. In contrast, six articles were about the Asian American cast and one was about a Chinese American who worked behind the scenes. Unlike the *Los Angeles Times*, which by 1936 was increasingly focused on Muni and Rainer, the *Chinese Digest* remained focused on the Asian American supporting players. In the process, it emphasized the film as a vehicle of Chinese American visibility. The most telling of the *Digest*'s articles was "Who's Who Among the Chinese in 'The Good Earth'" in the 1937 special edition.

The article covered a full page and half, including a picture of nine of the Chinese Americans who worked on the film and short biographies of each of them. While similar bios for some of the actors appeared in the *Los Angeles Times* and the *New York Times*, they were published over the course of three years, scattered in various columns along with other information about Hollywood. In the *Digest*, these Chinese Americans were highlighted as a collective and a case was made for them as the real stars.

Unlike many of the biographies in the *Los Angeles Times* that provided only occupational backgrounds, the *Chinese Digest* was invested in its readers seeing the performers as professionals. Readers learned that Roland Lui "received a year's training at the Motion Picture Academy (with pay) before participating in *The Good Earth*" and that Caroline Chew "studied dancing under both European and Oriental masters and has given many concerts here and in the East." It was reported that Mary Wong "radiated so much charm as the Little Bride that no cutting of even an inch from her acting was possible without removing something of the uniqueness from the picture." The paper wrote that William Law "was on the Orpheum Circuit in the good old days before the depression."[87]

The same issue ran an article devoted to the authenticity of the film, but even here Chinese American contributions to it were foregrounded. Lim Lee interviewed art technician Frank Tang, introducing him as having spent "something like 15 years in the motion picture mecca, beginning as a screen extra and working up to his present position. He is one of the very, very few Chinese who know all the intricate and complicated machinery which is necessary in making of pictures."[88] Tang talked about the set, the musical score, and his colleagues in the art department. He also discussed the possibility of Chinese Americans making films in Hollywood one day:

> The Chinese could organize their own companies," he answered, "and employ Hollywood technicians to advise and guide them in their productions, but the Chinese must produce English speaking picture in order to make money. The market for Cantonese picture is too small. If Chinese utilize American talent and technical skills and produce English speaking pictures, they can increase their box office receipts.[89]

Tang used his work on *The Good Earth* to imagine an independent Asian American cinema, one in which Chinese Americans owned their own film companies, drew on the advice of non-Chinese, and produced films in English.

The *Chinese Digest's* overwhelmingly positive coverage reflected a widespread embrace of the film by local Chinese Americans. It was replicated in interviews conducted by the Chinese Historical Society of Southern California between 1979 and 1982 about life in Los Angeles Chinatown before the Second World War. Many community members recalled seeing the movie in the theaters as youth, and they spoke of it with fondness. Ida Lee said she enjoyed *The Good Earth*.[90] Margaret K. Lee agreed, but contrasted the film's performances with the roles that Anna May Wong was forced to take, which she found more negative.[91] Alice Hum said *The Good Earth* was "as fair as they can get."[92] Frank York Lee said it was one of the films that began to change representations of Chinese people for the better. Before this, he noted, "the Chinese [had] the prototype of smoking opium or owning laundries or being vicious individuals."[93] Indeed, none of the Los Angeles Chinese Americans interviewed had anything negative to say.

It was not just Chinese American audiences who thought the film was positive. Chinese American performers who appeared in it, like Bessie Loo, who had a contracted role in a kitchen scene, and Keye Luke, who landed perhaps the most high-profile role as elder son, had every reason to resent the racist casting that kept them and others from major roles. Nonetheless, both saw representations of the Chinese people as overwhelmingly positive. Loo believed that the Chinese characters were portrayed in a truer manner than in previous films. [94] Luke was even more complimentary, recalling his time in *The Good Earth* with nothing but fondness: "I was very happy that I was in it because it was one of the best pictures that was produced here in Hollywood. It was a classic."[95] While certainly not the headlining roles they would have preferred, both Bessie Loo and Keye Luke saw *The Good Earth* as a platform for numerous Chinese American performers to land speaking roles in a major Hollywood film.

Even as Chinese American viewers celebrated *The Good Earth*, they still approached it aware of the structural barriers that so many Chinese American performers faced in Hollywood. For no actor were these barriers more explicit than Anna May Wong—whom MGM had passed over for the role of O-lan. As film scholar Celine Parreñas Shimizu has noted, not only was Wong typecast throughout her career but her early roles in *Toll of the Sea* (1922) and *Thief of Bagdad* (1924) together became the origin of two long-standing stereotypes of Asian American women on screen: the Lotus Blossom and the Dragon Lady.[96]

Having experienced racism in their daily lives, Chinese Americans in Los Angeles approached Wong's career in general, and her absence from *The Good Earth* specifically, with a more nuanced perspective on the movie's casting decisions than their counterparts in China.

Whereas viewers in China overwhelming dismissed Anna May Wong's performances as degrading to the Chinese people, US-born Chinese Americans appreciated the complex barriers the actress faced as the only Chinese American woman regularly appearing in Hollywood films.[97] Oral histories of Chinese Americans who grew up in Los Angeles in the 1930s watching her performances appreciated Wong's ability to negotiate the film industry as a

F IGURE 4.3.   Anna May Wong in an early role representing the Dragon Lady stereotype. *The Thief of Bagdad*, United Artists, 1924.

Chinese American woman even as they acknowledged the limitations of her portrayals.[98] Herbert Leong recalled that many Chinese Americans admired Anna May Wong and Keye Luke for their ability to find work in the film industry even though they often saw the roles they played as stereotypical.[99] Actor Ching Wah Lee recalled: "She's a remarkable girl, considering what the Chinese faced, with all the prejudice she was able to break through."[100] Jennie Lee, who worked as an extra on *The Good Earth* more explicitly ac- knowledged the reasons Wong ended up in the roles she did: "She didn't get treated right by the studio. They didn't give her a chance to play what she really wanted to be. Not one of these sinister mean women. . . . I mean give her a chance to play a good person. But they didn't want to do it, and that's not right."[101] While none of the oral histories addressed Wong's ab- sence from *The Good Earth* specifically, their general comments point to a more sophisticated understanding than that of viewers in China of the ways that Anna May Wong was forced to negotiate race, gender, and sexuality in her career in Hollywood.

Because the representations of Chinese people in *The Good Earth* were not one-sided caricatures, as was the case of Fu Manchu, and because the film provided a platform for so many Chinese American extras and bit play-ers to appear on screen, *The Good Earth* was lauded by many in Los An-geles Chinatown as a positive step forward. Despite the rejection of Anna May Wong by MGM, Chinese American viewers used the *Chinese Digest* to imagine a different Hollywood than the one they had been subjected to their entire lives. Only a few short months after the release of *The Good Earth*, war across the Pacific would expand the landscape in which Chinese Americans in Los Angeles performed.

PART III

Wartime Los Angeles

CHAPTER 5

Performing Japanese Villains in Wartime Hollywood

As a young girl, Bessie Loo wanted to be a performer. Born Bessie Sue in 1902, she grew up above her father's store in the Central Valley town of Hanford, California. Hanford had a small but bustling Chinatown that supported the Chinese American farm workers who for decades had been a pivotal part of the labor force in the state's agricultural heartland.[1] By the time Bessie Loo was born, the city's shrinking Chinese American population worked alongside a growing number of Mexican American laborers picking the region's crops. The town's white elite often discriminated against their Chinese American and Mexican American neighbors. When Bessie Loo and her Chinese American friends attended movies in Hanford, they were told to sit in the outer rows with Mexican Americans so that White patrons could have the center seats.[2]

As a girl, Bessie longed to leave the agricultural town and become a performer. Like so many American youth of the period, Hollywood captured her imagination. At Hanford Union High School, she appeared on stage in her senior play.[3] As a college student, she performed as one of eight background singers for the Chinese tenor Jude Fong.[4] Despite her dreams of stardom, growing up in a small farming town in California's Central Valley she never envisioned one day becoming one of the most influential Chinese American women in the film industry.

In the 1930s, as Chinese-themed films were becoming Hollywood's newest obsession, Bessie Loo was living with her husband Richard in Los Angeles. She was cast in a small speaking role in *The Good Earth,* but she would not make her name in Hollywood as an actress.[5] As her husband landed bit and supporting roles in wartime films, she was hired as a recruiter for Central Casting, where she focused on Chinese American performers. At the time, she was the only woman casting agent in Hollywood.[6] Working out of her home, which allowed her to raise her twin daughters, Bessie Loo remained busy throughout the war.

Because the US government had forced all Japanese Americans on the West Coast into incarceration camps, Hollywood had to recruit extras and bit players for the roles of Japanese characters in Hollywood war films. Studios cast Korean Americans and Filipinos in some of these roles, but Chinese Americans were given the bulk of them. Actors like Keye Luke, Victor Sen Yung, and Benson Fong found new visibility in wartime propaganda films. During the war, Hollywood studios also increased their demand for Chinese American background players, and Bessie Loo secured roles for most of them.

While many Chinese American performers played Japanese characters, Richard Loo, more so than any of his compatriots, become the face of the Japanese enemy for American movie audiences. Dubbed by film scholar Hye Seung Chung as one of the "Big Three" Asian male actors of Hollywood's classical period, Richard appeared as a Japanese character in no less than twenty-five films during the 1940s.[7] His breakout performance was in the 1944 film *The Purple Heart*. American newspapers such as the *Los Angeles Times* and the *Chicago Tribune* published his stills from the film and featured him in advertisements seen across the country. In earlier films, like *Little Tokyo USA*, studios generally cast white actors as Japanese villains, but *The Purple Heart,* at the urging of the film's director Lewis Milestone, cast only Asian Americans in the film's Asian roles. Altogether, thirty-one Asian characters appeared in the film, twenty-three of whom were played by Chinese Americans.[8] For the first time in many of their careers, these actors played characters who were not Chinese or Chinese American. In the role of the Japanese General Mitsubi, Richard was the film's lead antagonist.

Although the film provided a breakthrough for Chinese American performers in Hollywood, *The Purple Heart* had social ramifications far beyond the silver screen. Roles as Japanese villains in wartime propaganda films often stereotyped all people of Japanese descent as the enemy, seeing little difference between members of the Japanese military and second- and third-generation Japanese Americans.[9] In choosing to take these roles, Chinese

American performers launched their careers in ways that contributed to rising anti–Japanese American sentiments across the nation. As Japanese Americans began to return to the West Coast from US government-run incarceration camps after the war, they faced heightened prejudice and violence often at the hands of white neighbors. The wartime actions of Chinese Americans who worked on these propaganda films contributed to anti-Japanese sentiments.

Using the wartime careers of Richard and Bessie Loo as entry points, this chapter examines the contradiction at the heart of Chinese American inclusion in Hollywood during World War II. The film industry had long relegated Chinese Americans to stereotypical bit and background roles portraying peasants, restaurant workers, or Tong members. Now, for the first time in many of their careers, actors like Richard Loo, Victor Sen Young, and Benson Fong were given roles with multiple lines and backstories playing Japanese wartime villains. Chinese Americans justified these roles by claiming that they were patriotic contributions to the war effort. Benson Fong was even able to avoid the draft thanks to his Hollywood work.[10] These Chinese American performers thus found success in a racist industry that had long marginalized them, but in taking such roles, they contributed to heightened animosity toward and Japanese Americans.

The success of the Loos and other Chinese Americans in Hollywood during the war years was mirrored in other parts of society as well. Not just actors but merchants, restaurant owners, and others, found professional success at the expense of incarcerated Japanese Americans. In this way, Chinese American wartime inclusion was shaped in many ways by Japanese American exclusion. After the war, Richard Loo became a well-known character actor with a decades-long career in Hollywood; Bessie Loo launched the Bessie Loo Talent Agency focused on Asian American performers. Undoubtedly the post-war professional success of the Loos was built upon the choices they made as war swept the Pacific.

In 1936, Richard and Bessie Loo moved to Los Angeles from San Francisco so that Richard could manage a Chinese import shop on Wilcox Avenue.[11] Bessie stayed at home with the couple's newborn twins while Richard designed silk items to sell.[12] He used Chinese silk to create everything from pajamas to tennis shorts, which he sold to the limited few who could afford silk sleep and exercise wear amid the Depression.[13] He supplemented his income by working as a background performer and bit player.[14] Richard made good money selling silk lounge wear to wealthy Angelinos, but he aspired to be more. He wanted to be a performer himself. He held these aspirations of stardom even though there had never been a male Chinese American movie star in Hollywood.

By the early 1930s, the only Chinese American to come close to true Hollywood stardom was Anna May Wong. After dropping out of Los Angeles High School in 1921 to pursue acting, Wong landed her first leading role at the age of 17 in the 1922 film *Toll of the Sea*. She played Lotus Flower, a Chinese woman who falls in love with a white American man only to commit suicide when her love is not requited. This role laid the foundation for Hollywood's Lotus Blossom stereotype. Two years later, in 1924, she appeared with Douglas Fairbanks in *The Thief of Bagdad*, where she was relegated to playing the scantily clad Mongol slave, which became the foundation for Hollywood's Dragon Lady stereotype. By the end of the 1920s, Wong was so unhappy with the roles offered her that she crossed the Atlantic to pursue her career in Europe.[15] For young Asian American moviegoers, the barriers to becoming a Chinese American actor in Hollywood must have seemed insurmountable.

Despite these institutional barriers, Richard Loo was willing to take any role he could obtain; he simply loved performing. He earned his first theatrical role as a rickshaw boy in the musical *Hit the Deck* while working at an import-export house in San Francisco.[16] This led to other stage work and eventually to an uncredited part in the 1931 film *Dirigible*.[17] Richard no doubt won the part of a rickshaw boy because he *was* Chinese, and yet like many other third-generation Chinese Americans, he could not *speak* Chinese. According to a later report, when the director who cast him asked him to speak Chinese, Loo simply recited phrases from the menu of a local Chinese restaurant.[18]

Richard and Bessie Loo were part of a small cadre of young US-born Asian Americans trying to break into Hollywood in the 1930s. This group included Victor Sen Yung, Benson Fong, and Roland Got as well as Korean American Philip Ahn. Many of these performers were college-educated. Richard Loo and Victor Sen Yung had both graduated from the University of California, Berkeley.[19] Bessie Loo trained to become a teacher at San Francisco State. Sacramento-born Benson Fong moved to China to attend college. This generation of performers came of age in the US having the same interests as others their age. They played basketball, baseball, and tennis. They read magazines like *Life*, *Popular Mechanics*, and the *Saturday Evening Post*. They liked radio comedians like Eddie Cantor and Jack Benny. Of course, like everyone in their generation, they regularly attended movies.[20] Unlike their white peers, though, they rarely saw actors who looked like them on screen.

US-born and college educated, Bessie and Richard Loo had heard the promise of the American dream their entire lives but against this rhetoric of equality they also witnessed first-hand the reality of American racism. Bessie recalled going to movie theaters as a young girl in Hanford, California: "In those days, the prejudice is still there. In those days, we felt it. . . . At home in Hanford when I was a young girl every Saturday we went to a matinée. We always sat on the side we never sat in the middle. . . . All of the Chicanos and all of us sat on the side."[21] Other Chinese Americans who worked in Hollywood during the decade, like the animator Tyrus Wong, tell similar stories of being barred from the prime theater seats because of their race.[22] Even in movie theaters, white Americans pushed Chinese Americans to the margins.

Not only did Chinese Americans face racism from white Americans but they often faced pressure from their parents not to pursue careers in Hollywood. Bessie Loo's parents were outraged when they learned that she had begun performing as an extra. They felt that their daughter was wasting her college education on a profession that was illegitimate.[23] They were not alone in feeling that acting was not a desirable way to earn a living. Many in the older immigrant generation felt similarly.

Had global events in the 1930s not sparked Hollywood's interest in Chinese-themed films, societal barriers may very well have kept performers like Bessie and Richard Loo out of Hollywood altogether. As China found its way onto the front pages of the nation's papers, however, studios began producing a cycle of films set in China or Chinatown. *The Bitter Tea of General Yen* (1932), *The General Died at Dawn* (1936), and *the Good Earth* (1937) employed numerous local Chinese Americans as background performers; white movie stars in yellowface took all the lead roles. With Hollywood's newfound interest in Chinese storylines, Richard and Bessie Loo began to secure sporadic work in the industry.

While stardom may have seemed out of reach, Richard and Bessie Loo could still aspire to become full-time Hollywood actors. By the 1930s, demand for Chinese-themed films led studios to offer a handful of Chinese American performers contracts, which provided them with enough to support themselves. One of the few to secure a contract was Victor Sen Young. He earned $250 a week with a guarantee of forty weeks of work per year for Fox Studios.[24] He landed his first contract in the late 1930s through a combination of luck and initiative. After graduating from Berkeley, he worked in Tom Gubbins's Hollywood supply store, Asiatic Costumes. He landed his first role as an extra in the locust scene of *The Good Earth*. He also did stunt work in Hollywood. His father was eventually able to secure him a position at the Royal Chemical Company selling flame proofing, but Victor had other plans. After reading in a gossip column that Fox Studios was testing for roles in the Charlie Chan series, he decided to audition. He landed the part. This was his first speaking role. Yung recalls: "They could use me for anything, any shows, any parts, but primarily they just used me for the Charlie Chan series." The money was unlike anything else he had made before, so he decided to switch careers: "I started in at Fox and I decided, well, I better learn this business because you know I am getting paid for it."[25] Most Chinese American performers in the late 1930s were not as lucky as the future *Bonanza* star; instead, they settled for irregular extra work. Victor Sen Yung would go on to play roles as Japanese characters in *Behind the Rising Sun* (1943), *Destination Tokyo* (1943), *Up in Arms* (1944), *Secret Agent X-9* (1945), and *First Yank into Tokyo* (1945).

While the Loos did not have the same immediate success as Victor Sen Young, they had small speaking roles in the 1930s. Bessie recalls the first bit role her husband landed in 1936: "They were calling for *The General Died at Dawn*. They wanted Chinese to work in it. . . . We thought it would be fun,"[26] so both Bessie and Richard tried out. Richard immediately stood out to the casting director. As Bessie later recalled: "They saw my husband, tall and all, they approached him, and asked him to do a part instead of being an extra."[27] After that, Richard secured roles in *Captured in Chinatown* (1935), *Shadow of Chinatown* (1936), *Outlaws of the Orient* (1937), *Torchy Blane in Chinatown* (1939), and *Daughter of the Tong* (1939). A few of these, like Mr. Cheng in *West of Shanghai* (1937) and Fong in *Shadows over Shanghai* (1938), were bit parts with speaking lines. Bessie Loo did not have to wait long to secure a bit role of her own. She was one of four Chinese Americans in *The Good Earth* to be offered short-term studio contracts. She landed a small speaking role in *Mr. Wong in Chinatown* (1939).

Chinese American actors found even bit roles with single lines hard to come by, and when they did find them, they were often stereotypical. Bessie Loo recalled her role in *The Good Earth*: "My opportunities were only as an extra or a maid. Even in *The Good Earth*, I was stuck in the kitchen! Roles for Orientals were very limited as well as stereotyped. Maybe other actors didn't look upon the roles that way back then, but I did."[28] Richard Loo's roles were not much better. They included a Geisha customer in *Student Tour* (1934), a Chinese peasant in *The Painted Veil* (1935), and a Tong leader in *Mr. Wong in Chinatown* (1939). Not only were they stereotypical; these roles were sporadic and did not supply the type of consistent salary needed to support a family. In 1940, despite having appeared in least 21 roles in Hollywood films over the past decade, Richard Loo still told the census taker that his occupation was "salesman."[29]

Relegated to either background or bit roles of stereotypical characters, Chinese Americans were forced to create their own starring roles. In 1938, a group of Chinese American performers, including Richard and Bessie Loo, formed the Chinese Drama League to stage a performance of the play *Yellow Jacket*.[30] The group practiced for over ten weeks before their debut at the Wilshire Ebell Theater on June 3 and June 4. The cast featured nearly thirty Chinese American performers, including Beale Wong and Spencer Chan. The leads went to Bessie Loo and Roland Got. The play was so well received that the performers took the show on tour playing two days in San Francisco and three in Santa Barbara before playing the Bovard Auditorium at the University of Southern California.[31]

In 1939, Bessie began her career with Central Casting.[32] Richard had reached a point where he had constant work as actor even if most of his roles were the same stereotypical portrayals Hollywood had turned out for decades. Shortly after the US entered World War II, Richard and Bessie Loo would become the most influential Asian American couple working in Hollywood. The newfound success that Chinese Americans like Richard and Bessie found during the war came at a steep cost, not to the performers directly but to their Japanese American friends, colleagues, and neighbors.

The decision by Chinese Americans to take roles in wartime propaganda films cannot be understood outside the context of Chinese and Japanese American interethnic relationships in Los Angeles. When Richard and Bessie Loo relocated to Southern California, Los Angeles had the largest

FIGURE 5.1.   Roland Got and Kwai On performing on stage in Los Angeles. *Los Angeles Daily News*, UCLA Library Special Collections, copyright © 1939, Creative Commons, Attribution 4.0 International License.

Japanese American population of any city in the continental United States. Restrictive housing covenants forced residents of color into the same parts of the city. East Adams, the neighborhood where the Loo family lived in the 1940s, was one of the city's most multiethnic communities. In the confines of East Adams, Chinese and Japanese Americans became friends, colleagues, spouses, and neighbors.

In 1940, Richard and Bessie Loo, along with their eight-year-old twin girls, lived in a small house at 740 East 20th Street.[33] Unlike tenement housing and cramped living quarters behind storefronts that defined Old Chinatown, the homes in the East Adams were detached single family houses with all the amenities of modern life. The house that the Loo's bought was a prime example. Like many others on their block, the Loo home had a small porch that opened onto a small front yard. Built in 1908, it included running hot and cold water, a gas stove, electric lighting, a refrigerator, and an attached garage.[34] While the homes in East Adams may have resembled those in other suburban-style communities, the community itself was much more ethnically diverse. Chinese Americans, African Americans, ethnic European immigrants, and Japanese Americans lived side by side on residential blocks with porches and front lawns.

For approximately thirty years, from the mid-1930s until the 1960s, the vibrant neighborhood of East Adams was one of the centers of Chinese American life in Los Angeles. In 1920, less than a dozen Chinese Americans called it home.[35] By 1940, nearly two hundred did. Thus almost 10 percent of Chinese Americans in Los Angeles lived in this seven square-block neighborhood. The Chinese American community that developed in East Adams beginning in the 1930s was anchored by three institutions: The CFO Gas Station, the Chinese Presbyterian Church, and the Kwong Hing Lung market.[36] By the end of the war, the neighborhood also supported Chinese American businesses, including Tom's Radio Shop and Appliance, Frank's Key Shop, and James W. Ginn's photo shop.[37] East Adams also featured its own Chinese American youth basketball team, The Guardsmen, who played against other Chinese American and Japanese American youth teams in Los Angeles.[38]

On East 20th Street, Richard and Bessie Loo lived alongside numerous Chinese American and Japanese American families. Their neighbors on one side were the Louies. This Chinese American family had three children under the age of eight and ran a Chinese art store. Down the block lived Lem Fong, his wife, Sing Kwan, and their three children. Lem worked as a salesman for a Chinese wholesale produce stall, most likely at the City Market on Ninth Street. Directly across from the Loos lived the Sugimoto family. Kuno Sugimoto was born in Japan; his three adult children were all US citizens born in California. The oldest adult son worked as a clerk and his two adult sisters worked as waitresses. In addition to the Sugimoto family, Koichi Hata, his wife Kikuyo, and their three young children lived two houses down from the Loos. Their youngest daughter Masako likely attended school with the Loo twins. Further down the block lived Hiro and Jennie Yasuda, a married couple in their twenties. Both were US-born Japanese Americans. Hiro worked as a salesman for a wholesale produce dealer. Altogether, five Japanese American families lived on the 700 block of East 20th Street in 1940. Of the twenty-five Japanese Americans living on the block, sixteen were US citizens. Including the Loo family, there were five Chinese families. Of the twenty-five Chinese Americans, fourteen were born in the United States. There were also four Mexican American families, one Black family, one White man and a White woman, both living as lodgers.[39]

That Richard and Bessie Loo's neighbors Hiro Yasuda and Lem Fong worked as salesmen in wholesale produce is unsurprising, in part because of the neighborhood's proximity to the City Market, which stretched from Ninth Street to 11th Street and housed numerous wholesale produce stands. City Market had been founded through join financing by the Chinese American and Japanese American communities. Community historian Gilbert Hom describes this interethnic collaboration as a "strategic partnership" born of collaboration between Japanese American farmers and Chinese American merchants.[40] When the market incorporated in 1909, there were 158 Chinese American shareholders, 65 Japanese American shareholders, and 19 white shareholders.[41]

Despite living and working side-by-side, tensions between Japanese Americans and Chinese Americans in Los Angeles heightened following the outbreak of the Second Sino-Japanese war in 1937. As Chinese Americans fundraised in the community for war relief, at least one fight broke out between a Chinese American fundraiser and a Japanese American neighbor.[42] Against this backdrop of war in Asia, there remained a distinct generational divide in the way Chinese Americans looked at their Japanese American neighbors.[43]

Many younger Chinese Americans had close Japanese American friends. Dorothy Hom, who lived next to the City Market, remembers hosting interethnic dances: "We lived in a Victorian-type house, you know, where the living room ran directly into the dining room. So, we had the whole damn place and whatever furniture was allowed to be there. There was a sofa pushed to one side and a couple of big chairs pushed to one side. The dining room table was pushed all the way back and there was just a wide old place you can dance."[44] They danced the Jitterbug listening to Count Basie or Glenn Miller. Dorothy recalls that it was common before the war for Chinese Americans and Japanese Americans to date: "All the Japanese boys had Chinese girlfriends; all the Chinese boys had Japanese girls."

Younger Chinese Americans might have seen their Japanese American classmates as friends, older Chinese Americans often saw little difference between Japanese Americans and Japanese in Asia. Charlie Quon, who attended the Chinese school in East Adams, recalls: "Well, we never had any animosity with the Japanese people. We had real, real close friends with the Japanese people. Of course, my dad, the older generation, the first generation that came over here, they didn't want anything to do with the Japanese people. . . . They're very, very prejudiced about that."[45] Ben Fong, who in 1935, at the age of fourteen, moved from Sacramento to East Adams, recalls a similar dynamic in his family: "My mother she sort of despised them [the Japanese] because they are sort of the bullies of the Orient at that point in time."[46]

Richard and Bessie Loo straddled the two generations. Richard was born in in Hawai'i. Bessie was born in California. As such, they shared many cultural sensibilities with younger US-born Chinese Americans, but at the same time they were separated from them by age. When the US entered World War II in 1941, both were in their late 30s. Most of their contemporaries in the Chinese American community were immigrants who shared the anti–Japanese American sentiments expressed by the parents of Ben Fong, Abe Chin, and Charlie Quon. Regardless of their personal feelings, the lives of Richard and Bessie would be forever changed by the US entry into the war and the incarceration of the local Japanese American community.

In the months following Pearl Harbor, violence and harassment toward Japanese Americans surged. Many White Americans did not differentiate between Japanese and Chinese Americans, so Chinese Americans were accosted by the police, bullied at school, and found themselves the object of suspicious stares of the larger public. They had to decide how they would respond to increasing acts of anti-Asian violence. While a handful took principled stands in solidarity with their Japanese American friends and neighbors, the majority opted to distinguish themselves by performing their ethnic and national identities for the American public. With lapel buttons, window signs, stickers, and parades, the Chinese American community called attention to the fact that they were not Japanese.

Charlie Quon was a resident of East Adams and one of the many Chinese Americans who faced anti-Asian discrimination after Pearl Harbor. He and his brother-in-law were arrested in the early 1940s on road trip from San Francisco. In the Central Valley, the pair stopped for coffee and to take photos of the scenery. Charlie Quon recalls: "We finished our coffee and about fifteen or twenty minutes down the road, here comes flashing lights and they stopped us. The highway patrol stopped us. We were held in Bakersfield overnight to find out whether we were Chinese or Japanese. And when they found out that I was Chinese, then they let me go."[47]

After Pearl Harbor, many Chinese Americans felt forced to perform their ethnic identity everywhere they went. According to Charlie Quon, "before the war I used to carry a badge with me, 'I'm Chinese.' . . . We had to identify ourselves all the time."[48] Beginning in December of 1941, the local Chinese Consolidated Benevolent Association created buttons with an image of the Chinese and US flags that Chinese Americans like Charlie Quon wore to protect themselves from anti-Asian violence.[49]

Franklin Roosevelt's Executive Order 9066 initiated the forced incarceration of Japanese immigrants and Americans of Japanese descent on the West Coast, transforming the landscape of Los Angeles neighborhoods like East Adams. Japanese American businesses were boarded up. Japanese American families quickly vacated their homes, selling belongings at a loss. Dorothy Hom remembers with sadness the family who owned a local flower shop being sent off to camp.[50] Charlie Quon remembers that some Chinese Americans sought to profit off the wartime incarceration, buying cars or belongings from Japanese Americans for cheap.[51] On East 20th Street, twenty-five people were forced to leave.[52] Their absence created a gaping hole on the 700 block, where the Loo family lived.

While Chinese Americans like Charlie Quon chose to wear their Chinese identities using buttons, others chose to perform their American patriotism instead. This was Richard Loo's off-screen strategy. By April of 1942, Loo had joined the California State Military Reserve as part the "Chinatown Militia."[53] The group chose its leadership based on a written test.[54] Richard became second in command under New Chinatown founder Peter SooHoo. "Naturally we want to do our part," he told the *Los Angeles Times* in 1942. "After all, our people have been fighting the [Japanese] for five years." The Chinatown Militia was composed of Chinese Americans too old to serve or waiting for induction. The group trained in their free time in a public park under the direction of Stanley Mu, then a nineteen-year-old City College student whose only formal training was ROTC in high school. It is doubtful that the militia would have been effective against an actual Japanese invasion.[55] Even so, while almost certainly not a well-trained fighting unit, it did offer an opportunity for Chinese American men like Richard to be part of a US government–sponsored military reserve unit, which was documented by local photographers like Harry Quillen as it marched before crowds at parades and celebrations around the city.

In a period of heightened anti-Asian violence, when many white Americans were ignorant of the differences between Chinese Americans and Japanese Americans, the militia became one way for Chinese Americans to perform their American patriotism. According to Norine Dresser, "Parades

FIGURE 5.2.   Richard Loo (far right) with the California State Military Reserve in Old Chinatown in 1942. Photo by Harry Quillen. Harry Quillen Collection, Los Angeles Public Library.

and visible training sessions at the California State Armory in Exposition Park called attention to the men's patriotism creating a marker of their non-Japanese status."[56] Dresser argues that joining this group and marching in parades was one way that these men could also publicly reassert their loyalty as Americans. Unsurprisingly, Richard Loo was not the only Chinese American actor to serve in the group. Beal Wong and Roland Got, both of whom played Japanese characters in wartime propaganda films, served alongside Loo. In the same way that the militia allowed Chinese Americans to perform their patriotism, many Chinese American performers, including Richard Loo, saw their roles in propaganda films as performing their patriotism. In contrast to their militia performances where they marched under US flags—constantly reinforcing their American citizenship—in films their portrayals reinforced longtime stereotypes of Japanese people.

The outbreak of World War II saw an increase in demand for Chinese American performers in Hollywood. At Central Casting, Bessie Loo became the primary agent responsible for filling background roles as Japanese in propaganda films. In 1961, she recounted: "Before Pearl Harbor, hardly a Japanese character was used in a Hollywood movie, occasionally a gardener or a bartender. Writers knew nothing about Japan and cared less."[57] With the US entry into the war in 1941, the industry changed overnight. "After Pearl Harbor, the interest in everything Japanese boomed," Loo said. "Hollywood began turning out one war film after another. The only trouble was that during World War II there were no Japanese in Los Angeles. . . . So I sent Chinese and Filipinos to play Japanese soldiers, and no one knew the difference." She recalled that during the war years "they needed hundreds of Japanese soldiers. I can't say how many. When they needed two hundred of this, two hundred of that, then I called down to Chinatown."[58] Extra work playing Japanese was plentiful.

Not just background roles but bit parts became more prevalent as well. Benson Fong recalled the ease of securing work during World War II. His Hollywood break occurred while eating with friends at a Sacramento restaurant, when he had a modest job as a grocer.[59] A talent scout approached him and asked if he wanted to appear in a movie. Fong recalled: "I had no acting experience, but Paramount gave me $250 a week on a ten-week contract. It looked like a tremendous fortune and I accepted quickly, afraid they might think twice about it and back out."[60] He took a part in the 1943 Paramount film *China* staring Loretta Young and Alan Ladd. Once he was in Hollywood, it was easy to find other work: "I couldn't read lines too well, but World War II was under way, and all the studios were looking for actors. I bicycled around from one set to another playing a Japanese here, a Filipino there, a Chinese on still other days."[61] He landed nearly 20 roles between 1943 and 1945 alone and continued to act sporadically in Hollywood through the 1980s.

While Benson Fong took a variety of parts during the war years, there were a few performers who specialized in Japanese roles. Jew Yut Gim, who went by the stage name Joseph Kim, was one of them. Kim was born in Los Angeles, fought against the Japanese in China in the late 1930s, and then returned to the US to serve in the U.S. Army Coast Artillery during the war. After injuring his leg, he was discharged, returned to Los Angeles, and worked as bit player in films such as *Blood on the Sun* and *China's Little Devils*.[62] In 1945 the Associated Press reported: "[Kim] works nights in a Chinese café and portrays his country's enemies in the daytime."[63]

The outbreak of the war not only increased the number of roles as Japanese characters; it also heralded a change in the representations of Japanese people, which had long been shaped by global and national forces and institutions. Prior to the war, Hollywood films were subject to censorship by the Production Code Administration (PCA), the body that oversaw the Production Code of 1930.[64] After the outbreak of the Second Sino-Japanese war in 1937, the Chinese and Japanese governments as well as the US State Department all sought to influence the representations of Chinese and Japanese people in films. As a result, before the US entry into World War II, depictions of Japanese military aggression were effectively kept out of Hollywood films.

Following Pearl Harbor, Hollywood became explicitly anti-Japanese and pro-Chinese. In June of 1942, the US government created the Bureau of Motion Pictures in the Office of War Information (OWI). The OWI took on oversight of domestic film production,[65] urging Hollywood studios not to produce films that "inspire hatred for the whole German, Japanese, and Italian people."[66] Yet as Hye Seung Chung has shown, the OWI bureaucrats were much more concerned with ensuring that depictions of China and the Chinese people were nuanced than they were in encouraging that depictions of Japan and the Japanese people were nuanced.[67] As a result, Chinese American actors often found themselves in roles as Japanese villains that were little more than one-sided caricatures.

Wartime representations of Japanese people drew on a long history of Orientalist depictions in Hollywood that sought to define the imagined sanctity of the nuclear white family against an imagined yellow peril. Hollywood propaganda built on posters, comic books, and other forms of mass culture that painted all people of Japanese descent as the enemy.[68] Films made little effort to distinguish between the Japanese military and Japanese Americans. Actors who chose to take these roles did so knowing they were reinforcing the worst of Yellow Peril stereotypes.

Richard Loo seems to have seen his acceptance of these roles as villains as part of his duty as an American citizen. In 1942, he expressed his thoughts on playing Japanese military officer Saburo Kusuru in the film *Wake Island*: "I don't mind playing a villain . . . least of all a Japanese villain. And I'll play it as heavy as I can. It will, if you catch the drift of my meaning, be a patriotic opportunity."[69] Two years after this interview with the *Los Angeles Times*, Loo would be given the role of General Mitsubi in the film *The*

Purple Heart, changing his career forever. Turned down originally because the producers believed that at more than six feet he was too tall to play a Japanese general, Loo eventually landed the role after a change of heart by director Lewis Milestone. As Loo would recall of his experiences in that film: "There were no more problems after that. . . . I became an arch villain and had to turn down parts."[70] More so than almost any other Chinese American actor, Loo would be forever linked to his wartime roles as Japanese and Japanese American characters because of that part.[71]

While not exceptional in theme, *The Purple Heart* demonstrates the ways in which Chinese American actors in Hollywood films helped craft dominant narratives about Japanese and Japanese Americans. True propaganda, the movie was screened for members of the armed forces during the war. Unlike earlier propaganda films like *Little Tokyo U.S.A,* which featured white actors in yellowface as Japanese villains, *The Purple Heart* featured Chinese Americans, Filipino Americans, and Korean Americans in all bit and background roles as Japanese soldiers. In addition to Richard Loo, the film featured Philip Ahn, Benson Fong, Peter Chong, Luke Chan, Spencer Chan, Joseph Kim, James B. Leong, Beal Wong, and Moy Ming.

The film follows an American bomber crew shot down in Japanese-controlled China. The Japanese threaten and torture the eight Americans hoping to discover the location where their bombing mission was launched. After refusing to provide the information, the Americans are tried and convicted by the Japanese wartime government and sentenced to death for their alleged involvement in bombing civilian targets in Japan. The story was loosely based on a real-life American bombing flight downed by the Japanese government in April of 1942 while participating in the Doolittle Raids.[72] In October of 1942, the Japanese government reported that it had captured and executed eight American crewmen. At the time the film was produced, little information was known about the fate of the captured men.[73] The film imagines what their fate might have been.

Despite the dearth of information, press coverage pushed audiences to see *The Purple Heart* as representing a type of realism. A week before its release Hedda Hopper lauded its "horrible realism" in her column "Looking at Hollywood" in the *Los Angeles Times.*[74] She wrote that the film "gets you so fighting mad that you'll want to go out and kill [Japanese] personally." Bosely Crowther of the *New York Times* wrote that the film was? "so clearly in keeping with the nature of the enemy in its grim detail that we are safe in accepting this picture—along with the atrocity reports—as general truth." In an editorial in the *Los Angeles Examiner*, Benjamin DeCasseres wrote: "No motion picture, no stage play, so far as I can recall, has ever laid bare more completely and convincingly the psychology of a people than the *Purple Heart*."[75]

Collectively, such articles implied that *The Purple Heart* offered insights into the nature of the Japanese people that the news did not. Film critics asserted that there were two truths—factual from the news and psychological from the film. Indeed, Crowther told his readers that they should view *The Purple Heart* "alongside the atrocity reports," suggesting that the film and the reportage played complementary roles in helping Americans understand the war. In making this argument, reviewers like Crowther directed viewers to see the film's performances by Chinese Americans as integral to its alleged psychological truth.

With *The Good Earth*, the press claimed that Chinese Americans alone added to the film's authenticity. With *The Purple Heart*, the press highlighted the performances—rather than the alleged authenticity of Chinese Americans in the film. For perhaps the first time in Hollywood history, the press urged viewers to see the Chinese American performances as integral to their experience of the film. News coverage continually noted that Richard Loo and most of the other actors were of Chinese, not Japanese, descent.[76] In reminding viewers of this, it encouraged them not to mistake the performers for Japanese.[77] Instead, the press pushed viewers to see the Chinese Americans' performances as integral to revealing alleged truths of the Japanese people.

Taking roles as Japanese villains put Chinese American performers in a quandary. Despite the news coverage, none of them wanted to be mistaken for being of Japanese descent. In short, Richard Loo and his compatriots wanted to act in speaking roles but when these roles were Japanese characters, they did not want to be associated with anti-Japanese stereotypes in these propaganda films. As a result, Chinese American performers needed to signal to movie audiences that they were Chinese American themselves and not Japanese American. Off screen, some, like Richard Loo and Roland Got performed their American patriotism by marching in the Chinatown Militia. Many wore buttons in their daily lives declaring their Chinese heritage. Of course, these options were not available to them while on screen.

Richard Loo approached this contradiction by overacting. He exaggerated his movements on screen; he expressed drastic emotional changes over the course of a single scene; and he performed heightened affective responses to lines and situations. In choosing to overact, to play it "heavy" as he described it to the *Los Angeles Times*, Loo reminded viewers that he was a performer playing a role. In short, his style of acting called attention to itself as a form of performance. Chinese American actors like Loo did not want viewers to forget that they were performers. His overt theatricality reminded viewers that he was a Chinese American playing a role and not the Japanese character her portrayed. Ironically, this same theatricality also ensured that he could never be seen by critics as a serious actor.[78]

Overt theatricality hadn't always been Loo's style. Earlier in his career, when he played a loyal Japanese American who supported White authorities, he affected a naturalistic acting style. In *Little Tokyo USA,* he played Oshima, a Japanese American friend and ally to the protagonist, detective Michael Steele. His acting did not call attention to itself. There was no need to distance himself from his role. It did not matter if viewers mistook Loo for the character he played as this was the role of a loyal Asian sidekick.

In contrast, Richard Loo did have a reason to remind viewers of *The Purple Heart* that he was an actor who did not possess the attributes of his character, General Mitsubi. His style as the lead Japanese villain can only be described as excessive. He laughs maniacally one moment only to sit stoically in the next. With bold facial expressions and an over-the-top laugh, his style constantly calls attention to itself. As a result, most viewers would remember Loo much more than any of his White co-stars. His acting was so memorable that in the 1950s, more than a decade after the film was originally released, the comedian Dick Cavett would devote an entire portion of his act to impersonating Loo's wartime performances and in particular his performance in *The Purple Heart.*[79]

For Chinese American performers, the ability to be seen as an actor performing a role must have felt liberating. Up to this point, Richard Loo had been cast as nondescript Chinese characters. He had played Tong members and Chinese peasants. None of these roles required much acting. Rather all they required was a Chinese-looking performer. Even when he spoke lines, Loo was positioned as atmosphere; his presence alone was meant to add authenticity. In *The Purple Heart,* for first time in his life Loo was given a starring role as the lead antagonist in a major Hollywood motion picture.

Richard Loo and the other Chinese American cast members in *The Purple Heart* knew they were producing a propaganda film, and as American citizens they embraced the opportunity to do so. Loo's co-star, Benson Fong, expressed as much when he told an interviewer of his own work in the film: "It's a propaganda picture. . . . At the time, *Purple Heart* was being shown in all the armed forces, so as far as we were concerned we were doing our patriotic duty for our country."[80] Fong's stance seemed to echo Richard Loo's view of playing roles as Japanese villains as a "patriotic opportunity."

Patriotism aside, there is no doubt that Richard Loo's turn as the Japanese General Mitsubi in *The Purple Heart* not only demonized the enemy nation of Japan but also racialized Japanese Americans as the enemy of US film audiences. We can see this in a pivotal scene in the film, when Mitsubi brings Captain Harvey Ross, played by Dana Andrews, to his office to get information on the location from which the American bomber launched its attack on Japanese targets. Captain Ross appears in the scene wearing his brown leather bomber jacket and holding his hat in his hands, providing a marked contrast to the general's shaved head and formal military uniform.

At the start of the scene, the two men are filmed in one continuous shot, which lasts more than a minute and a half. Rather than cutting back and forth in a shot-reverse-shot sequence, the camera frames both men in focus in the same shot, visually presenting them in contrast to one another. In this opening shot and then in successive shots, Richard Loo switches between emotional extremes, often in the middle of the same sentence. While drinking and smoking, he smiles and laughs, becomes serious and then laughs again, all while Andrews stands stoically by. With these emotional extremes over the course of moments while Andrews shows little emotion at all, Loo's acting draws continuous attention to itself.

Switching between friendly and serious multiple times, he embodies the "sneaky" persona stereotypically assigned to Japanese by the American press of the period. General Mitsubi reveals to Captain Ross that he once lived in Santa Barbara and worked on a fishing boat between San Diego and Seattle. He then smiles at Andrews and tips his glass toward him before saying that the charts of the West Coast "will be useful someday." In this way, the scene collapses differences between Japanese American fisherman and Japanese enemy combatants. It suggests not so subtly that simply because a Japanese American fisherman like Mitsubi may appear friendly, his demeanor may not reflect his actions or loyalties. At the same time, Richard's

FIGURE 5.3. Richard Loo's expression just moments before his expression in Figure 5.4 in the same scene in *The Purple Heart*. They demonstrate the exaggerated emotional shifts of Loo's performance from laughing one moment to stoic the next. Overacting characterized his wartime performances as Japanese villains. *The Purple Heart*, Twentieth Century Fox, 1944 (screen shot by author).

FIGURE 5.4. *The Purple Heart*, Twentieth Century Fox, 1944 (screen shot by author).

performance promotes a popular wartime stereotype of Japanese Americans as duplicitous.

By overacting in this and other wartime roles, Richard Loo reminds audiences that he is not the characters he played but an actor performing a role. At the same time, the press urged viewers to see his performances and those of his Chinese American compatriots as revealing hidden truths about the "psychology" of the Japanese people. In this way, these roles had a powerful propaganda effect that shaped the lives of Japanese Americans during and directly after the war. As a result, Richard Loo and his excessive performances came to represent the Japanese people in the minds of a generation of American moviegoers.

Taking anti–Japanese American roles did not necessarily signal that Richard Loo or any Chinese Americans harbored explicitly anti-Japanese American sentiments—though some of them may have. Regardless of their personal feelings about Japanese Americans, the choices these Chinese Americans made in in the film industry during the war years undoubtedly facilitated anti-Japanese racism and contributed to the anti-Asian violence faced by Japanese Americans as they returned to the West Coast. That Richard became a well-known character actor with a decades-long career in Hollywood was due in part to his choice to play Japanese villains in 1944 and 1945. In this way, his personal success was forever tied to roles that helped shape anti–Japanese American sentiments and actions during World War II. His wartime roles brought him fame and a career in Hollywood during a period when few Chinese Americans managed to survive for long in the industry, and yet these roles defined his career for the rest of his life. On November 22, 1983, his obituary in the *Los Angeles Times* summed up the way most of America remembered his career: "Richard Loo, War Film Villain, Dies." Loo's career spanned nearly half a century, yet his obituary focused on these four years during World War II. By the time of his death, few viewers remembered any of his performances other than those of Japanese villains.

For Japanese Americans, the toll that Loo's performances took was direct and undeniable. They added to an overall climate of hostility for Japanese Americans during one of the darkest moments of the community's history. Unsurprisingly, after his passing, Japanese Americans also remembered Loo for his wartime roles. Interviewed in 1994 by researchers from the Japanese

American National Museum, Eiichi Miyagishima, who was in elementary school when the war broke out, recalled that wartime "prejudice and discrimination was pervasive."[81] In discussing the influence of movies in this period, he named only one actor: Richard Loo. Miyagishima labeled the characters Richard played "despicable. " Japanese American viewers understood quite clearly the social cost of Richard's wartime performances in their daily lives in the 1940s.

Of course, not all Chinese American performers spent the war years portraying vicious stereotypes of the Japanese. As war ravaged the Pacific, a group of high school and college students found a way to shape popular ideas of Chinese Americans. Performing on the streets of Los Angeles Chinatown, they made a name for themselves in much more empowering ways.

CHAPTER 6

Mei Wah Girls' Drum Corps and the 1938 Moon Festival

On October 8, 1938, as dusk fell over Los Angeles, crowds from around the city converged on what remained of Old Chinatown for a celebration of the Moon Festival. Passing under one of three elaborate gates constructed for the occasion, visitors entered a roped-off section of Los Angeles Street decorated with lanterns and flags and lined with concession stands. In the center of the festival area, adjacent to the Lung Kong Tin Yee Association headquarters, Chinese American youth volunteers had constructed an "Alter of Blessings" to the Moon Goddess, where Dr. Edward Lee told fortunes and sold horned nuts.[1] The Chinese Cinema Players, a group of Chinese Americans who worked in the film industry as bit players, designers, and artists, created most of the festival decorations. At one booth, the Los Angeles–born movie star Anna May Wong signed autographs and took photos with fans. The festivities included street dancing, music, and shadow boxing. At the height of the festival, a Chinese dragon operated by dozens of residents wound its way along Los Angeles Street to the delight of curious onlookers while Chinese lion dancers performed for the crowds.[2]

Alongside the Chinese dragon and the lion dancers, fourteen-year-old Barbara Jean Wong prepared to lead eleven Mei Wah Club members in their first official performance as a drum corps. The Mei Wah Club had begun seven years earlier as a basketball team, and many of its members were teenagers who attended local high schools like Belmont and Polytechnic.[3] American citizens by birth, these young women were part of a generation of Chinese Americans then coming of age, and many shared interests with other American youth. Under the guidance of Barbara's mother Maye Wong and her uncle David SooHoo, the teenagers designed costumes and choreographed a routine.[4] Their performance as an all-female Chinese American youth drum corps stood in sharp contrast to many of the more Orientalist aspects of the festival.

With its panoply of Chinese Americans performing for White audiences, the 1938 Moon Festival bore little resemblance to the centuries-old Mid-Autumn Festival from which it borrowed its name. The event was not a Chinese festival in the traditional sense but rather a fundraising performance that mixed tropes from Chinese culture with those from the Orient of the Western imagination. It was the second such fundraiser held in Los Angeles in 1938 after the success of the China Nite Festival earlier that summer. Both China Nite and the 1938 Moon Festival resembled national "Bowl of Rice" fundraisers more closely than they did traditional Chinese celebrations. Held largely between the outbreak of the Second Sino-Japanese War in 1937 and the entry of the United States into World War II in 1941, they were war relief fundraisers created through partnerships between newly formed China aid societies—controlled primarily by white businessmen and former missionaries to China—and local Chinese American organizations. From New York to San Francisco, Portland to Santa Barbara, Bowl of Rice fundraisers brought large crowds into Chinese American communities, raised millions of dollars for China war relief, and garnered extensive coverage in the nation's press.[5] As historian K. Scott Wong has argued, their popularity increased the visibility of Chinese Americans and in the process played a fundamental role in eroding the negative image many White Americans held about China and Chinese people.[6]

In Los Angeles, the 1938 Moon Festival took on an added importance when the Chinese American merchants who controlled the local Chinese Consolidated Benevolent Association (CCBA) decided to hold the fundraiser in Old Chinatown. This decision not only offered them an opportunity to reshape long-held stereotypes about the neighborhood as an urban slum; the festival also gave them a chance to reassert the neighborhood's continued existence in the face of the ongoing demolition. With the construction of Union Station well under way, only a few blocks of Old Chinatown remained.[7] Like the openings of New Chinatown and China City, which had occurred only a few months earlier, the Moon Festival provided the Chinese American residents of Los Angeles a chance to rehabilitate

Chinatown's popular image at a moment of precarity and change for the entire community.

As a result of being held in Old Chinatown, the Moon Festival engaged with the twin yellow peril stereotypes that defined the neighborhood. The first of these was that Old Chinatown hid underground tunnels and secret passages and had its own relationship to time and modernity. The second stereotype was that the community was a homosocial environment composed of primarily male bachelors who engaged in tong violence, opium smuggling, and trafficking in prostitution. These popular images symbolized the perceived deviant sexuality of the Chinese bachelors and its affront to the heteronormative white family in its suburban home.

Through the festival, Chinese Americans consciously challenged stereotypes of the neighborhood by promoting representations of a romantic and feminine Orient. The 1938 Moon Festival included a dragon boat with Chinese women, a parade of more than two hundred lantern-carrying young Chinese American women and girls, and the presence of Anna May Wong, whose star persona embodied the contradictions in many popular representations of Chinese women of the period. Yet the festival's relationship to the imagined Orient was much more complex than simply replacing one set of Orientalist representations with another. The festival also contained subversive elements that conformed neither to long circulating yellow peril representations nor to representations of a romantic, feminine East. Key among these elements was the performance of the Los Angeles Mei Wah Girls' Drum Corps. The group's costuming and performance produced a contradiction in the festival that allowed the young women of the Mei Wah Club to be seen in ways that challenged the more Orientalist representations in other parts of the festival.

In the decisions Chinese Americans made about how to portray their communities to the public, Chinatown performances at war relief festivals had a lasting influence on the way White Americans understood the place of Chinatowns in US society. At the local level, the 1938 Moon Festivals, along with a similar festival called China Nite, shaped popular understandings of Chinatown's relationship to Los Angeles. On a national level, these two festivals worked alongside China war relief events such as the Bowl of Rice festivals, to reshape the place of China and Chinese people in the US popular imagination. A close examination of the two 1938 festivals allows us to foreground the agency of US-born Chinese Americans—and

US-born Chinese American women in particular—to engage racial formation. Through a focus on two China war relief festivals held in Old Chinatown in 1938, this chapter focuses on the instrumental role these performances played in facilitating the incorporation of Chinese Americans into the imagined community of the United States during a pivotal moment in national and global history.

After the Japanese army invaded China in 1937, the San Francisco CCBA began organizing fundraisers throughout the immigrant community. It was the logical choice to coordinate fundraising. Formed in 1882 in part to provide an organized response to the Chinese Exclusion Act, the organization was composed of representatives from the city's district and family associations that provided immigrant mutual aid based on members' common surnames and regions of origin in Southern China.[8] The CCBAs' functions included granting temporary lodging, providing burial expenses for the indigent, and settling disputes. Larger communities like Los Angeles developed their own CCBAs that operated autonomously, though they generally recognized the CCBA in San Francisco as the head of a confederation that reached throughout the United States and Latin America.[9]

Following the outbreak of the Second Sino-Japanese War, the San Francisco CCBA created the Chinese War Relief Association (CWRA) to coordinate relief efforts across the Americas through its forty-seven branches across the United States and Latin America.[10] The CWRA united various political factions within the Chinese American community in ways that had proved impossible in earlier fundraising efforts. It was one of the most visible Chinese American aid organizations nationally. However, it did not hold jurisdiction over all Chinese American communities in the United States. Those in larger cities formed their own war relief associations, often under the guidance of local CCBAs. Ninety-five war relief organizations were started, some in communities with as few as fifty Chinese American residents.[11]

In Los Angeles, the local Chinese war relief organization was dubbed the Chinese Patriotic Society. Although ostensibly an independent organization, it was housed in CCBA headquarters at 415½ Los Angeles Street in Old Chinatown. Run almost completely by volunteers, it paid only a general secretary and an office administrator.[12] While the society occasionally printed broadsides in English in an attempt to influence White popular opinion, it focused its efforts on Chinese immigrants.[13] Each month, CCBA representatives, most likely on behalf of the society, went house to house in Los Angeles collecting funds from Chinese immigrants in support of war relief.[14] Those who did not contribute faced public humiliation—at least one person was paraded through the streets for failing to give to the cause.[15] Like other fundraisers in the immigrant community, the society made almost no effort to shape public opinion. Following the outbreak of the Second Sino-Japanese War in 1937, Chinese Americans widened their efforts to reach members of the public outside the ethnic enclave. These efforts did have the added goal of shaping public opinion.

In Los Angeles, this was a natural transformation given that the leadership of the Chinese Patriotic Society was several adult American-born Chinese who served as a bridge between Chinese-speaking immigrants and the White English-speaking world. The Society was founded by CCBA officers that included Dick Tom, an American-born Chinese grocery store owner; and Thomas Wong, an American-born produce wholesaler who was married to Maye Wong, the Mei Wah Club sponsor.[16] Wong used his position as a community leader to work with United China Relief in planning the Moon Festival held in 1941.[17] Having leaders who could negotiate the internal politics of the community as well as interact with the larger white society became increasingly important as immigrant organizations began to shift their attention from raising money within the ethnic enclave to working with outside organizations to fundraise while shaping popular opinion.[18] Local Chinese American organizers in Los Angeles mimicked the Bowl of Rice campaign.

The national Bowl of Rice campaign was the first large-scale effort to both influence popular opinion about the war in China and raise war relief funds among the general public. In the summer of 1938, the United Council for Civilian Relief in China, a recently formed umbrella organization that included the American Bureau for Medical Aid in China (ABMAC) among other white-led aid groups, partnered with Chinese American organizations to hold a nationwide day of fundraising on June 17, 1938. The national chairman of the council was Colonel Theodore Roosevelt Jr., the son of the former president.[19] By early June, fundraisers were planned in more than 2,000 cities across the nation. More than seven hundred mayors proclaimed June 17 "Humanity Day,"[20] which brought national attention to Chinese war relief and focused the nation's attention on the Chinese American community.

While the Bowl of Rice fundraisers did raise money, they were more successful at raising awareness. China war relief did not garner the same success as the British and Greek war relief efforts. In 1940, all China war relief efforts together raised slightly more than 1 million dollars, while Greek efforts raised $5 million and British efforts raised $10 million.[21] A report prepared for the ABMAC Executive Committee at the end of 1940 stated that Bowl of Rice parties sponsored by ABMAC member committees had raised only $11,543. But it urged the committee to remember the important value of the publicity they garnered.[22]

In San Francisco, the Bowl of Rice Festival became a pop cultural event. Chinatown was blocked off, and visitors purchased "humanity badges" for fifty cents to gain entry to the event, which lasted until four in the morning. The festivities included a dragon dance and other performances by local Chinese Americans. District, family, and fraternal organizations in Chinatown all opened their doors. The *Chinese Digest* reported that the residents of San Francisco Chinatown "recreated something of the splendor and exotic atmosphere of old Chinatown—the Chinatown that Will Irwin once wrote [about] in ecstatic prose and once Arnold Genthe captured in treasured photographs."[23] Paul Smith, editor of the *San Francisco Chronicle* and chairman of the festival, saw that the event was covered in the city's papers. Ranging from large spectacles like those held in New York to local banquets held in small towns across the country, Bowl of Rice events played an important role in the cultural shift in American representations of China.

As the fourth largest Chinese American community in the United States, one may have expected its Bowl of Rice party in Los Angeles to mirror festivities held in San Francisco and New York. However, it drew only a few thousand people to the Los Angeles Breakfast Club.[24] The local party featured chairwoman Der Ling, a self-proclaimed "princess," and the daughter of a former Chinese diplomat in Paris who claimed to have served as a lady-in-waiting to the Empress Dowager in China. The featured entertainment was a beauty contest to find a woman who could symbolize "the Humanitarian Heart of America."[25] Almost all contestants were White. Local Chinese Americans did not make up a significant portion of the night's entertainment nor did local Chinese American groups like the Los Angeles CCBA lend their support in any noticeable way.

The Chinese American community's comparative lack of support for the Los Angeles Humanity Day was primarily the result of local factors. National Humanity Day was held on June 17, which in Los Angeles fell between the June opening celebrations for both New Chinatown and China City. These events occupied the attention of nearly the entire Chinese American community and attracted tens of thousands of visitors, including celebrities, politicians, and dignitaries. The failure to fully embrace National Humanity Day was only one of many ways that fundraising in the Chinese American community in Los Angeles differed from that in San Francisco and elsewhere. Without the support of either the United Council for Civilian Relief in China or the CWRA in San Francisco, the community soon held its own fundraising events, China Nite and the Moon Festival, which the US-born generation would play a fundamental role in planning and executing.

The relationship of the U.S.-born generation to American society was distinct from that of their immigrant parents. This was especially true in Southern California. Since the Chinese American community in Los Angeles was more geographically dispersed than its counterparts elsewhere, its second- and third-generation youth attended racially mixed schools and often shared interests with White American youth their age: football, basketball, and tennis; dances; popular fiction; and Hollywood films.[26] These youth were citizens by birth, but because they were of Chinese descent, once they entered the work force overt racism and xenophobia often limited their employment opportunities and kept them from fully integrating into the larger, White-dominated society.[27] At the same time, however, as US-born citizens they did not always identify closely with China. For this reason, many in the younger generation did not feel connected to the internal war relief efforts organized by their immigrant elders. Barbara Quon expressed this ambivalence in an article she wrote for the *Los Angeles Times* in February 1938:

> I have taken part in the local activities, and what I have done has partly been at the suggestion of my parents. Mother asked me to gather together my old clothes so she could take them to the relief station. I was glad to do it. Of course, there were cash contributions too. It's not that I think the war is none of my business, for that isn't true. It's just that it doesn't affect my personal life as much as it does my mother's. [28]

Quon's views on the fundraisers held by her immigrant parents undoubtedly reflected those of a growing number of her US-born peers.

Following the outbreak of the Sino-Japanese War, increasing numbers of US-born Chinese American youth in Los Angeles began organizing their own fundraisers, which took different forms from those organized by their parents' generation. Between the winter of 1937 and the spring of 1938, Chinese American youth in Los Angeles organized a series of charity football games against Chinese American youth in San Francisco.[29] The Mei Wah Club also sponsored a joint fundraiser that featured dance performances at the Nationalist Hall in Los Angeles.[30] The *Chinese Digest,* an English-language publication written for and by second-generation Chinese Americans, explained why activities such as dances were important for involving the younger generation: "In times of financial need, whether that need is within one's community or in the homeland, the older generation contributes without any thought of any kind of return. But somehow you don't approach any second generation youth and ask for a direct donation. You ask 'Won't you buy a ticket to a benefit dance?' Somehow the psychology is different."[31] Football games, musical performances, dances—the fundraising efforts of these U.S.-born youth reflected their own life experiences.

In April 1938, under the guidance of the Chinese Patriotic Society, seventeen Chinese American youth clubs formed the Los Angeles Federation of Chinese Clubs to raise funds for war relief.[32] They included the Mei Wah Club, the Kwan Ying Club, the Guardsmen, the Lo Wah Club, the Lo Wah Auxiliary, the Chinese Cinema Players, and the Chinese student clubs at Jefferson, Belmont, and Polytechnic high schools.[33] Following the formation of a similar federation in San Francisco, the Los Angeles federation issued a statement: "We the Chinese youth of Southern California, whether citizens of China or citizens of the sympathetic democracy of the USA should . . . assume the responsibilities which are ours."[34] The federation boasted more than four hundred members and included Chinese students studying in the US as well as US-born youth.[35]

Even though many of its members were still of high school age, the federation chose twenty-seven-year-old Marshall Hoo as its president.[36] Originally from Oakland Chinatown, Hoo moved to Los Angeles in 1930 hoping to find employment during the Depression. He was active in social movements around Los Angeles and held an interest in the evolving geopolitical situation in Asia. A charismatic speaker, Hoo exerted much energy raising awareness of events in Asia among his fellow Chinese American youth in Los Angeles.[37] Under his leadership, the Federation of Chinese Clubs put out its own bilingual newsletter as a way to keep both Chinese- and American-born members informed.[38] The bilingual nature of newsletter made it distinct from the San Francisco-based *Chinese Digest* and spoke to the organization's attempts to incorporate both Chinese- and American-born youth into the local war relief effort. Once established, the Federation of Chinese Clubs became the main venue through which members of the younger generation became involved in war relief.

When the CCBA in Los Angeles sponsored China Nite in the summer of 1938, the federation played a fundamental role in making the event a success. China Nite was held at a time when many district and family associations in Los Angeles where reeling from the destruction of much of Old Chinatown.[39] The Kong Chow Association, which helped manage the local temple, was one of the only district associations whose headquarters was not destroyed by the construction of Union Station.[40] While there is no way of knowing the roles of individual family or district associations in the planning of either China Nite or the 1938 Moon Festival, the local turmoil in Old Chinatown certainly hindered their ability to contribute. In contrast, the members of the Federation of Chinese Clubs were based throughout Los Angeles, not just in Old Chinatown.

Working alongside an older generation of US-born leaders like Wong and SooHoo, these youth groups played a significant role in planning China Nite.[41] The federation formed a division to support the event, chaired by the twenty-one-year-old Mei Wah Club president, Eleanor SooHoo.[42] Building on the federation's success in managing concession stands at the New Chinatown opening, the CCBA handed control of the China Nite concession stands to the local youth groups.[43] The influence of the young people on China Nite appeared not just in concessions but also in the festival's entertainment, which included live music by Suen Luen Due, "the Chinese Bing Crosby," along with "street dancing" in a reserved area of the plaza.[44] The success of China Nite provided the template for the Moon Festival held later the same year.

Taking place over a weekend in early October, the Moon Festival attracted 25,000 people to Old Chinatown and garnered media coverage in most of the city's major papers.[45] Even as Chinese American self-representations at

CHINA NITE
SOUVENIR PROGRAM
—and—
DIRECTORY

AUGUST 6th - 7th

LOS ANGELES, CALIFORNIA

ENTIRE PROCEEDS FOR CIVILIAN RELIEF IN CHINA

FIGURE 6.1.   Eleanor SooHoo on the cover of the China Nite program. David and Dora SooHoo Collection. Courtesy of the Chinese American Museum.

the festival largely rejected older Yellow Peril stereotypes that had defined Old Chinatown by its Chinese bachelors, the festival remained deeply engaged with representations of the Orient of Western imagination. Rather than completely reject the Orientalism at heart of so many mainstream representations, Chinese American organizers and performers used the illusionary and theatrical elements inherent in Orientalist conceptions of the neighborhood to draw visitors while simultaneously asserting Old Chinatown's presence in the face of Union Station construction.

Unlike earlier, largely unsuccessful attempts by Chinese American merchants to define the theatrical elements of the tourist economy of Old Chinatown, the organizers and performers of the Moon Festival controlled nearly every aspect of it. The festival was roped off and open only to paying visitors. In the festival area, the Federation of Chinese Clubs ran concession stands with games and food. Side stages along Los Angeles Street featured performances by both the Chinese Bing Crosby and the Chinese Cultural

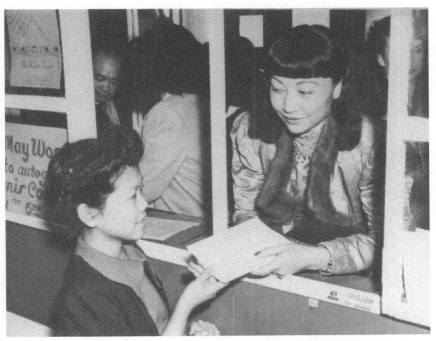

FIGURE 6.2.   Anna May Wong signing an autograph for Lilly Mu at a fundraising festival. Chinese Historical Society of Southern California.

Mission, while Anna May Wong took photos with fans and signed autographs at a booth near the entrance to Ferguson Alley.

In the evenings, Los Angeles Street became a stage for scheduled performances that did not end until eleven. They included the Mei Wah Girls' Drum Corps, a children's parade, a 1,000-foot golden dragon, and a dragon boat proceeded by more than 200 local Chinese American women carrying lanterns and dressed in Chinese gowns. On Saturday night, the Jinnistan Grotto Band also performed.

In order to highlight these performances, festival organizers drew on the experiences of community members in the Hollywood film industry in defining the festival's atmosphere. The Chinese Cinema Players of the Federation of Chinese Clubs decorated sections of Chinatown like a Hollywood set. They placed a giant smiling moon on a roof at the entrance to Ferguson Alley next to Anna Wong's autograph booth. With one eye closed and a large grin, the moon bore more than a passing resemblance to the one made famous in Georges Melies's 1902 silent film, *A Trip to the Moon*. On the roof of an adjacent building, club members crafted a sign announcing "Moon

FIGURE 6.3.   Old Chinatown decorated for the 1938 Moon Festival. Chinatown Remembered Project, Chinese Historical Society of Southern California.

Festival Oct 8–9." By decorating the corner of Ferguson Alley in this way, the Chinese cinema players gave it the quality of a movie set.[46]

Unlike the 1941 Moon Festival, which featured more than a hundred Hollywood stars in a parade of open-air vehicles, the 1938 Moon Festival featured only Anna May Wong, the biggest Chinese American Hollywood movie star of the time. As a Chinese American born in Los Angeles, Wong was an important member of the Chinese American community even if she had not been born in Chinatown. By 1938, she was a rising star who faced constant typecasting in her Hollywood films. Her most famous role of the decade had been opposite Marlene Dietrich in the 1932 film *Shanghai Express* in which she played a Chinese prostitute. Newspapers in China had been heavily critical of Wong's role, which many saw as a disgrace to China and the Chinese people.[47] Nevertheless, White American and Chinese American festival goers overwhelmed her booth, which "was always filled to capacity with her fans."[48]

While organizers used set design techniques from Hollywood to highlight Wong, they also drew on the existing architectural environment to advertise that the Moon Festival would allow visitors to see parts of Old Chinatown usually not open to those outside the community. Like China Nite, which had been held in August, the Moon Festival used the setting of Old Chinatown as a draw.

In doing so, the CCBA linked fundraisers and Old Chinatown at a time when the idea of Chinatown itself was being contested in the popular imagination. Old Chinatown had been the heart of the Chinese American community for more than fifty years, but by the summer of 1938 all that was left was of Old Chinatown was Los Angeles Street and a few connecting alleyways. Despite the destruction wrought on the old community, holding the Moon Festival on Los Angeles Street in Old Chinatown made sense on a pragmatic level. In 1938, Los Angeles Street was still home to the headquarters of the local CCBA, along with the offices of the Chinese Patriotic Society, and several district and family associations. While most of the major businesses and restaurants had relocated to New Chinatown or elsewhere, Old Chinatown continued to be the Chinese immigrant community's civic hub.

In addition to these considerations, Los Angeles Street in Old Chinatown meant that the festival organizers could represent Old Chinatown as unchanging in a bid to draw spectators.[49] Over the years, even as its

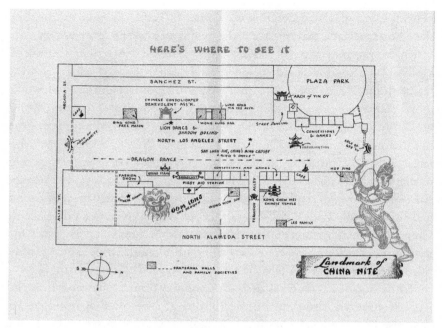

F I G U R E   6 . 4 .   Map of China Nite from the China Nite program. David and Dora SooHoo Collection. Courtesy of the Chinese American Museum.

destruction proceeded, the popular press depicted Old Chinatown as a mystical world untouched by modernity or progress. In December 1933, the *Los Angeles Times* ran an article and photo essay, "Chinatown, Hail and Farewell," in which these sentiments were expressed:

> "There is to be a new Chinatown; the plans for it already have been drawn. Of old Chinatown, fronting on the Plaza's oval oasis all that will be left will be memories of pungent, complicated, Oriental odors, the slup, slup of slippered feet or the throbbing from the joss house of a gong to mark hours that, somehow, march much more slowly there than in the outside Occidental world . . ."[50]

The paper describes the neighborhood as an extension of the mystical and timeless Orient of the Western imagination. The Old Chinatown of the writer's imagination is a place of odors, sounds, and other sensations that cannot be captured by photos or film. The writer positions Old Chinatown as a place soon to be relegated to memory, the technologies of the present unable to capture or retain its essence. In Old Chinatown not only is the passing of time signaled differently—with the beating of a gong—but the nature of time itself passes more slowly than in the rest of the "Occidental world."[51]

Moon Festival organizers drew on such Orientalist conceptions when they used the Kong Chow Temple to attract tourists, since it had been an important draw in publicizing the earlier China Nite. *The Los Angeles Times* announced: "Through the closed shutters of an overhanging balcony near Ferguson Alley, the reverberating boom and clang of a huge prayer drum and gong will sound a call for devout worshipers to the Altar of Blessings in the Kong Chow Temple, which will be open to visitors. Sightseers will learn much of the ancient Chinese worship."[52] In this way, pre-festival news coverage advertised the temple as an attraction where spectators could consume Chinese religious practices. Rather than depict it or other sites in Chinatown as embodying yellow peril, the *Times* presented Chinese culture as an unchanging site of culture and difference.

While the *Times* mentioned "devout visitors," it omitted the full range of activities and services that the temple provided to the Chinese American community in Los Angeles. Rather, representations of Chinatown as existing outside of time made the Kong Chow Temple visible to tourists in ways that belied its place as a functioning house of worship overseen by a priest and visited regularly by local residents.[53] By the mid-1930s, in the midst of the Great Depression, the temple housed at least five indigent, elderly Chinese who had nowhere else to turn. One man in his late seventies had come to America as a fourteen-year-old and worked as a cook for railroad workers. Now too frail to support himself, he told his story to an interviewer from the Federal Writers Project in 1936, "I am such an old man now that I can't work at all. If I try to stand long on my feet I fall down and I have nothing to do. . . . I am so helpless that I wish I die because I can't get along well enough without working. I live in the temple with four other men who old like myself and can't work either."[54]

Yet the temple was not the only way in which organizers used the built environment to attract spectators. Like other major Chinatowns across the country, Old Chinatown had long been represented as a world of underground tunnels and secret rooms. According to a 1930 *Los Angeles Times* article, "Tong wars, murders, dope raids, hop-house scandals, white and yellow slavery, underground tunnels, secret trap doors; all have been here.

Outside in the streets old men bask lazily in the sunshine and life is peaceful to the eye, but behind barred doors one feels that mystery is eternally seething."[55] In popular articles like this, Old Chinatown was depicted as not just *unseen* but *unseeable* by White visitors. Underground tunnels reflected broader fears of many city leaders that Chinatown and the Chinese people were invisible to police and government power and that the neighborhood existed outside the legal boundaries of the rest of the city. The notion that Chinatown was ridden with tunnels and secret passages reflected dominant fears that its residents could not be seen or governed by the state, the police, or the White power structure of the city.

China Nite and the 1938 Moon Festival provided venues for residents of Old Chinatown to actively engage these popular perceptions of inscrutability the festivals actively challenged the notion that Chinatown was unseeable, most explicitly by allowing visitors to access buildings that they otherwise may not have visited. The Bing Kong Tong, the Lung Kung Tin Yee Family Association, and the CCBA all opened their halls to the public, and in the process challenged its visual perceptions of the community.[56] Visitors to the CCBA hall could watch festival performances from its balconies and windows. Visitors thus had a way to see the neighborhood from a vantage point usually reserved for of these organizations, and organizers had an opportunity to respond to popular depictions of Old Chinatown as an underground labyrinth outside of the visual control of White society. It did so by inviting visitors to view the festivities and performances from an inside perspective. In short, the Moon Festival drew visitors in with the promise of seeing parts of the community they may not have had access to otherwise, only to then subvert that promise by positioning them to watch the festival from the point of view of Chinese Americans.

Of course, presenting Chinatown as embodying an unchanging and ancient culture was not the only long-standing racial trope that the 1938 Moon Festival engaged. At the center of the festival schedule were the several Chinese American youth performances, many of which featured women and girls. In several of the festival's performances, Chinese American women in their teens and twenties promoted Orientalist ideas of Asian femininity. As historians Karen Leong and Judy Wu have argued, Bowl of Rice events portrayed Chinese women as either exotic or helpless and suffering.[57] Descriptions of several performances at the 1938 Moon Festival support this observation. According to the newsletter of the Federation of Chinese Clubs, "two hundred girls dressed in colorful Chinese gowns, forming Chinese characters," and carrying lanterns preceded the dragon boat.[58] Similarly, on the Saturday morning following the first night, the *Los Angeles Times* said that "pretty Chinese girls rode in a grotesque dragon boat, seeking to appease the wrath of the dragon on the fifteenth day of the eighth moon in the Chinese Calendar." While such female performances promoted the idea of a mystical fantasy world that was divorced temporally and spatially from the rest of the city, embedded within this narrative were counter-narratives that contradicted the exotic images. More than any other performers at the festivals, the Mei Wah Club challenged these Orientalist depictions.

The Mei Wah Girls' Drum Corps began in July of 1938, shortly after the opening of New Chinatown, when the CCBA invited the Mei Wah Club to perform for China Nite. One of the members of the club recalled the moment the drum corps was formed in the club's minutes:

> One Sunday afternoon in July right after the Chinatown opening, we (Iris, Dora, Eleanor, Loraine, and David) were drinking tea at Mei Lan Foods. Someone brought up that the Chinese Consolidated Benevolent Association were going to give a China Nite in Chinatown. They wanted the Mei Wah girls to perform. The girls didn't know of anything so David and Iris suggested the girls should form a drum corps since there were a few drums at the Chung Wah [CCBA]. [59]

In inviting the Mei Wah Club to perform, the CCBA gave it nearly complete control over the form their performance would take. With little practice, a handful of Mei Wah members put on a short performance with drums borrowed from the CCBA. While not mentioned in the China Nite program or in newspaper coverage, that initial performance was such a success that when the CCBA announced they would host a second fundraiser, the club was invited to perform again. Soon after the invitation, the original performers gathered other young women and began practicing for what would be the official debut of the Los Angeles Mei Wah Girls' Drum Corps at the 1938 Moon Festival.[60]

More so than any other performance, the Mei Wah Girls' Drum Corps served to disrupt notions of Old Chinatown as linked to conceptions of femininity rooted in the Orient of the Western imagination. The corps made their own uniforms and choreographed their routine. Unlike the

F I G U R E   6 . 5 .   Mei Wah Girls' Drum Corps at the 1938 Moon Festival. Chinatown
Remembered Project, Chinese Historical Society of Southern California.

costumes of Chinese American women who performed in the dragon boat
and lantern parades, the uniforms were not culturally marked as Chinese in
any overt way. According to historian Shirley Jennifer Lim, they were mod-
eled on those of military bands. She points out that they paid homage to
China in subtle ways: "In allegiance to their Chinese heritage, their shirts
bore frog fastenings and cheong-sam type collars and sleeves which they
paired with American white pants and shoes."[61] The drum corps dressed in
matching uniforms with the exception of the those worn by drum major
Iris Wong and majorette Barbara Jean Wong. Unlike most of the other band
members whose dark shirts contrasted with their lighter pants, Iris wore a
light-colored top and a flowing sash around her waist. Barbara Jean, who as
majorette led the band with her baton, wore a light-colored shirt, outlined
in sequins, and matching white shoes.[62]

    In later years, when the drum corps competed in regional competitions
and local parades, this costuming allowed their uniforms to resemble those

of other marching bands in California. Yet in their performance at the Moon Festival, it played a different role. Because so much of the festival drew on Orientalist fantasies about Chinatown, the military band–inspired costumes provided a subtle and recognizable contrast to much of the Orientalist atmosphere. Certainly, the high school students who made up the Mei Wah Girls' Drum Corps provided a striking contrast to the Moon Festival Queen, the dragon boat, and the "two hundred girls dressed in colorful Chinese gowns, forming Chinese characters" described by the Federation of Chinese Clubs' newsletter.[63]

In short, the Mei Wah Girls' Drum Corps created a cultural contradiction within the world of the festival, one that could not be easily reconciled with the expectations of many white spectators. The rupture in the fantasy world created by the Mei Wah Club's performance made the corps members visible in a way that other performers at the festival were not. The festival created the theatrical space for the Mei Wah Club to perform; yet at the same time the members created a representation of themselves simultaneously as part of Chinatown and not part of the "Orient"—which so many spectators expected. Through their performance, these Chinese American women demanded to be seen as modern in a way that traditional Orientalist iconography denied was possible.

With her costume and placement at the front of the drum corps, Barbara Jean Wong occupied a prominent place in this performance of Chinese American cultural expression. In many ways her role as majorette was fitting given her experience as a childhood radio actor and Hollywood background performer. Yet her drum corps performances differed in one important way from her radio and film work. In films she always performed in the background; on radio she was made prominent, but listeners heard her without attaching her voice to an Asian American face. In contrast, as the majorette of the Mei Wah Girls' Drum Corps, Wong discovered that the Moon Festival provided a platform on which she could be both Chinese American and a star.

Planned primarily by the CCBA with the support of the Federation of Chinese Clubs, the 1938 Moon Festival allowed local Chinese Americans to engage their place in the national imagination in ways that would have been nearly impossible even one decade earlier. As the war in Asia progressed, China relief fundraising also evolved. In 1940, under the guidance of Henry

FIGURE 6.6. Coverage of the Mei Wah Girls' Drum Corps. *Federation News*, 1938. David and Dora SooHoo Collection. Courtesy of the Chinese American Museum.

Luce, the publisher of *Time* and *Life* magazines, eight major aid groups in America joined to form United China Relief.[64] This new organization continued to partner with local communities to host wartime festivals, and the support of Luce ensured that the festivals received national media coverage. In the Los Angeles area, United China Relief created a separate Hollywood committee to fundraise in the film industry. The committee was headed by David O. Selznick, the powerful movie producer behind *Gone with the Wind*, and Alfred Hitchcock's *Rebecca*.[65] When United China Relief partnered with the CCBA to plan the second Moon Festival in 1941, the event was under the direction of Selznick and the Hollywood United China Relief committee.[66]

No longer held in the autumn as the Moon Festival traditionally had been in China, the 1941 event was held between August 4 and 10 as part of Mayor Fletcher Bowron's city-wide China Relief Week.[67] Lasting three nights, the 1941 Moon Festival was divided between China City, New Chinatown, and Old Chinatown. Spectators who wished to enter the three "pay areas" had to purchase a fifty-cent ticket, the proceeds of which went toward United China Relief.[68] The Chinese dragon returned, as did the fashion show. Anna May Wong also appeared. A local teenager, Margaret Kwong, was chosen as the Moon Festival Queen and mentioned in the *Los Angeles Times*. The Mei Wah Club performed once again, and this time Barbara Jean Wong's photo appeared in *Life* magazine.

Despite the continued involvement of the Chinese American community, the added involvement of Hollywood meant less control in the community's hands. The CCBA appears to have ceded much of the planning to United China Relief. A parade between the pay areas featured fifty bands, two Chinese dragons—one of which was more than two hundred feet long—two camels, two hundred women carrying Chinese lanterns and at least six rickshaws. More than a hundred Hollywood stars, including Bob Hope and Marlene Dietrich, participated in the parade over the three nights. Meanwhile, Old Chinatown was transformed into an amusement zone including a Ferris wheel and a merry-go-round. New Chinatown featured a one-ring circus.[69]

Amid all this, the local community found its roles different from those in the 1938 fundraising festivals. The Mei Wah Girls' Drum Corps did not wear the military-inspired uniforms they designed but instead uniforms that appear to have been made from silk with elaborate embroidered borders surely meant to evoke the Orient of the Western imagination.[70] The photo of Wong and the drum corps that appeared in *Life* did not identify Wong by name or even mention the corps' name. While the 1941 festival remained a platform for everyday Chinese Americans to engage dominant notions of race, gender, and nationality, that platform now had to be shared with others, many of whom had more experience and ability in shaping public opinion. Aspects of the group's Chinese American vision still came through, but the festival did not provide the same opportunities as in 1938.

By the start of the war, the Mei Wah Girls' Drum Corps would be displaced altogether. In Mei-Ling Soong, popularly known as Madame Chiang Kai-shek, the US government found an Asian celebrity around whom they could build a performance unlike any the nation had ever seen. Henry Luce placed her on the front cover of *Time*. Touring the US in 1943, she became the first Chinese national to address both houses of Congress. In Los Angeles, she arrived by train at Union Station, visited Old Chinatown, and was featured at a gala dinner held at the Ambassador Hotel. The highlight of her visit was an appearance on April 4, 1943, at the Hollywood Bowl. David O. Selznick oversaw a stage production worthy of a Hollywood blockbuster featuring hundreds of Chinese American extras from Los Angeles alongside Mary Pickford, Spencer Tracy, Ingrid Bergman, and Marlene Dietrich. A stage show covered the history of China, and then Mei-ling Soong took the microphone and gave an impassioned speech in English that lasted nearly an hour. The event was the finale to her speaking tour of the United States. By the end of the year, Congress had passed the Magnuson Act officially overturning Chinese exclusion.

The US government may have found its Chinese star, but the celebration of Madame Chiang Kai-shek's tour and finale at the Hollywood Bowl masked discontent among Chinese Americans. Among many who had helped raise funds for China Relief over the past few years, grumblings of discontent began to arise. Reflecting on the fundraising that she and others had taken part in, Jennie Lee Taylor recalled of Mei-ling Soong's visit: "I just saw her. I didn't meet her. She was at the [Hollywood Bowl]. She came with about twenty fur coats and all that. That was really a surprise to me that she came over with all that luxury, and all these people were dying in China. And here I was collecting money [to] help these poor refugees."[71]

Perhaps even more telling than the feelings of volunteers like Jennie Lee Taylor were the reactions of Sou Jen Chu, who was one of the official representatives of the Chinese American community who met Mei-ling Soong on her visit to Old Chinatown. An immigrant from China who had received his business degree from the University of Southern California, he worked as a teller for Security First National Bank.[72] He had always been deeply involved in the community, as the head of the Gee How Oak Ten Family Association and a leader in the Los Angeles CCBA. When New Chinatown launched in 1938, the Los Angeles Chinatown Corporation approached him to write the Chinese calligraphy on its gates. Despite his close ties, Sou Jen Chu broke with the Chinatown leadership and left the community shortly after Madame Chiang Kai-shek's visit because of what he perceived as the mishandling of China relief funds by the Chinese Nationalist government.[73]

The visit by Madame Chiang Kai-shek meant the official end of Chinese exclusion. But even the Magnuson Act of 1943 was partially for show. With its passage, Chinese Americans for first the time were allowed into the US under the quota system of the 1924 Johnson Reed Immigration Act. However, the US government only allowed a token quota of 105 Chinese per year to legally immigrate. The community would have to wait until the passage of the 1965 Immigration Act for more substantial immigration reforms.

With tens of thousands of spectators and expansive coverage by the local press, the 1938 Moon Festival can be seen as the film that so many local Chinese Americans had dreamed Hollywood would produce. Organized primarily by the community, it provided a platform on which Chinese Americans in Los Angeles could present their own vision of Chinatown to a broader public audience. Long regarded as perpetual foreigners, a generation of American citizens found in the 1938 Moon Festival a moment when their heritage was recognized, rather than denigrated, and when their relatives across the Pacific were supported. In short, the Moon Festival provided hundreds of Chinese Americans, for the first time in many of their lives, an opportunity to perform on a stage of their own creation.

Conclusion

In November of 1943, Peter SooHoo spoke to the press from the offices of Consul T. K. Chang. Consul Chang and Mr. SooHoo addressed reports of anti-Black discrimination by Chinese restaurant owners in Los Angeles.[1] SooHoo was emphatic that Chinese Americans were opposed to discrimination of any kind. He asserted that Chinese restaurants and other Chinese American–owned establishments served all customers, regardless of race or ethnic background. In the five years since New Chinatown had opened, Black residents of Los Angeles, like their White counterparts, had come to enjoy visiting and dining in the district. In the years before Pearl Harbor, the Black press contained several reports of the Black families in the city frequenting Chinatown businesses.[2] But despite SooHoo's opposition, discrimination against Black patrons by certain Chinese restaurant owners during the war years appears to have been widespread, particularly for those that catered primarily to White patrons.

In her 1944 master's thesis on Chinese American life in Los Angeles, University of Southern California graduate student Kim Fong Tom contrasted the way Chinese restaurants in different areas of the city treated Black patrons. According to Tom, Chinese restaurant owners welcomed Black customers to the many chop suey joints that dotted the neighborhood near Ninth and San Pedro. With counter service rather than booths or tables, these working-class establishments served patrons of all backgrounds who did manual labor in the nearby City Market. Tom wrote: "The workers in this market, be they colored or white, frequently hang around these small restaurants where they can chat, laugh, and yell freely as if there were no

FIGURE C.1. New Chinatown restaurant in the 1940s. *Los Angeles Daily News*, UCLA Library Special Collections, copyright © 1940, Creative Commons, Attribution 4.0 International License.

barrier between them."[3] In the multi-ethnic corridors of Ninth Street, working-class Blacks found Chinese American restaurants to be a safe place to dine, converse, and relax among a diverse crowd.

Tom found a completely different situation in the more upscale Chinese restaurants around New Chinatown, which sought a primarily White middle-class clientele. She described these restaurants as "most aristocratic,"[4] writing that they did not take reservations on weekends or during peak hours in part because "there are so many [White] American customers waiting to be served."

And yet, Tom noted, "race discrimination is not uncommon." She wrote of the experiences of one group of Black customers who visited one of these Chinese restaurants. When the group arrived, no one waited on them to "discourage them so that they would walk out."[5] When they remained, the restaurant felt forced to serve them, but cooks added an extra amount of salt to all of the food so that it tasted disagreeable.

Tom asked the owner of the restaurant why he discriminated against Black customers in this way. He told her:

> I have no prejudice against the Negroes, but I want to keep my [White] American customers. If there are too many Negroes in my restaurant, the white customers will go away. I am a businessman and the competition here is so keen. What can I do![6]

Following Pearl Harbor, the Black population of the city surged as Blacks and their families arrived to work in the shipyards and other wartime industries. Amidst these demographic changes, some Chinese restaurants decided they were not going to serve Black patrons. In discriminating against them, this particular restaurant owner believed he was catering to the prejudices and desires of his White patrons.

By the middle of World War II, the ways in which the city's White residents perceived of race and space in Los Angeles had been completely transformed. At the beginning of the twentieth century, Black visitors and residents of Los Angeles understood the city to be marginally more hospitable than many other urban areas throughout the US. In 1902, Jefferson Edmonds, editor of the *Liberator*, a Black-owned newspaper, declared: "California is the greatest state for the Negro."[7] In 1913 W.E.B DuBois visited Los Angeles for a Black church–hosted reception attended by "2,300 people from the White, yellow and black races."[8] Of his visit to Los Angeles, DuBois said, "Los Angeles was wonderful. Nowhere in the United States is the Negro so well and beautifully housed, nor the average of efficiency and intelligence in the colored population so high."[9] While Black visitors like DuBois were impressed with the relative prospects for African American residents of the city, DuBois also noted the Black Angelenos still faced ample discrimination.[10]

Even as Black residents were able to buy homes and open businesses in Los Angeles, White residents and city leaders segregated them in certain neighborhoods in the central part of the city. Historian Josh Sides notes that, even as policies in cities like Detroit, Chicago, and New York produced Black-segregated neighborhoods, in Los Angeles "covenants used to protect and maintain White neighborhoods had the effect of creating some of the most racially and ethnically diverse neighborhoods in the country."[11] If ever there were a place where interethnic racial solidarity might develop in the early twentieth century, Los Angeles was it. While proximity between

Black and Chinese people did create some genuine cross-racial friendships and even interracial families in communities like East Adams and the City Market neighborhood, these districts never played as prominent a role in the White imagination of the city as Chinatown did.[12]

The war brought rapid changes to areas in the central parts of the city. As tens of thousands of Black workers and families arrived from the South seeking jobs in wartime industries, they found themselves crowded into this small area in the center of the city by racist housing restrictions. Almost overnight, the former Little Tokyo, emptied of its Japanese American residents, was transformed into a thriving Black community.[13] Vacant housing quickly became overcrowded with newly arrived Black workers. It did not take long for White reporters and leaders to call this new Black neighborhood a "slum."[14] Even as White reporters denigrated the changes happening in this central Los Angeles district, their reportage of Chinatown began to improve.

In her work on the construction of the model minority myth, historian Ellen Wu describes how the predominant view of Chinese and Japanese Americans in the United States shifted between World War II and the 1960s. Wu asserts that, before the war, White Americans saw Asian Americans as unassimilable aliens who were "*definitively not-white*" [italics in the original]. By the 1960s, White Americans saw Asian Americans as model minorities who were "well assimilated, upwardly mobile, politically non-threatening, and *definitively not-black*."[15] [italics in the original]. Efforts by Chinese American merchants to make Chinatown more palatable to White visitors were informed by their belief that the racism of White patrons would keep them from wanting to shop or eat near Black visitors. As a result, some Chinese American business owners discriminated against Black people, attempting to limit the Black presence in Chinatown. The goal was to disassociate Chinatown in the minds of White tourists from associations with Blackness.

For more than half a century, anti-Black and anti-Chinese sentiments overlapped in the minds of White Los Angeles residents. Between the late nineteenth century and the start of the 1930s, Chinatown was one of the few segregated districts in the city to which White cultural producers assigned a distinguishable set of racial characteristics. City boosters and media elite cast Los Angeles Chinatown as a racialized Other against which the White suburban image of the city was constructed. Beginning in the nineteenth century, anti-Black racism and yellow peril fears co-constructed an image of Chinatown as a site of intertwined racial Otherness. One need look no further than the name White residents gave to the street that housed Chinatown in the final decades of the nineteenth century—[N-word] Alley—for an example of this. Up until the early 1930s, White Americans saw Chinatown as "definitively not White."

Against the backdrop of the war in the Pacific, upwardly mobile Chinese American merchants engineered their own acceptance by White residents and city leaders through the launch of New Chinatown. Sadly, some of them, like the restaurant owner interviewed by Kim Fong Tom in 1944, sought this acceptance by engaging in anti-Black racism themselves. By discriminating against their Black patrons, business owners hoped to garner favor from White visitors. Though he would not have used these terms, the restaurant owner interviewed by Tom understood that the Chinatown pastiche aesthetic that defined New Chinatown had rendered its Chinese restaurants as safe, consumable products in the minds of White patrons. With an understanding that White prejudice and racism informed where White patrons decided to spend their money during the war years, this restaurant owner sought to define his establishment as "definitively not Black" in the minds of his White guests by excluding Black guests.

Even as Chinese American leaders like Peter SooHoo sought to reassure the broader public that New Chinatown businesses opposed all forms of racial discrimination, interviews with New Chinatown restaurant owners conducted in the 1940s suggest otherwise. SooHoo himself may have spoken out against anti-Black racism, but his views were not shared by all in the Chinese American community at the time. Just as several Chinese American performers launched their careers during World War II by playing roles that perpetuated anti-Japanese American sentiments among White audiences, so too did several Chinese restaurant owners seek acceptance from their White patrons through their anti-Black discrimination.

This was the contradiction at the heart of Chinatown's wartime acceptance by White Americans. For more than half a century, Chinese American merchants led by the Chinese Consolidated Benevolent Association in San Francisco protested and sought justice in the courts against immigration and racial exclusion. Simultaneously, these same merchants sought Chinatown's inclusion in the popular culture by advancing a Chinatown pastiche aesthetic that rendered its perceived difference exotic yet nonthreatening and consumable by Whites. During a moment when Chinese people were barred from immigrating to the US, denied the right to naturalize, and kept from buying property in many western states, Chinatown's merchants transformed the imagined yellow peril into a form of ethnic difference palatable to their White visitors. From the Chinese Village at the World's Columbian Exposition of 1893 to San Francisco Chinatown rebuilt after the 1906 earthquake and fire, to the opening of New Chinatown in Los Angeles in 1938, Chinese American merchants found success selling the Chinatown Pastiche aesthetic to White tourists. In doing so, they lay the cultural groundwork to challenge Chinese exclusion long before the geopolitical shifts in the Pacific of the 1930s made this a legal possibility. Certainly, the Magnuson Act of 1943, which officially repealed Chinese exclusion, could not have passed without the cultural shift brought about by Chinese American merchants' widespread adoption of the Chinatown Pastiche over the previous half-century.

The problem with Chinatown pastiche as a cultural strategy of inclusion was that it asked Chinese American merchants to work within the existing structures of social stratification that had maintained US racism for centuries. Rather than challenging them, the merchants sold a palatable form of Chinese Otherness to tourists while leaving underlying structures of Orientalism and anti-Blackness in place. To advance their own interests and seek inclusion in the global city of Los Angeles, some Chinese American business owners sought to exclude Black patrons while welcoming White ones in the hope of advancing their position in American society. After having been discriminated against for so long, some Chinese Americans chose their own advancement even as they recognized that doing so excluded Black residents of the city. In short, many Chinese American merchants advanced a new image of a cosmopolitan Los Angeles that included Chinatown but excluded Black residents and visitors.

In the decades following World War II, the city's predominantly Black communities, and its Mexican American communities, were increasingly used by city leaders and media elites as the imagined spaces against which the White family in the suburban home was defined. This is not to say that these communities had not been used by city leaders in similar ways before, but previously anti-Black or anti-Mexican American stereotypes often intersected and overlapped with yellow peril images in depictions of the city's central core. By the early 1960s, Chinatown had ceased to be the imagined urban space against which the region defined its White suburbs. Nowhere was this change more recognizable than on the silver screen.

In the winter of 1961, Universal Studios released *Flower Drum Song* across the nation to much fanfare. On Stage 12 on Universal's back lot, the studio recreated Grant Avenue in San Francisco Chinatown. The set comprised 54 buildings, some three stories high, spread over more than 50,000 square feet.[16] While *Flower Drum Song* was not publicized or covered in the press nearly as widely as *The Good Earth* had been two decades earlier, it still elicited a significant amount of national news coverage. In "Hollywood's New Lotus Blossom Look," published five months before the film's release, the *Los Angeles Times* asked, "What's behind Hollywood's big Oriental Kick?" The article profiled Asian American actresses who had appeared in recent Hollywood films, including Nancy Kwan and Miyoshi Umeki from *Flower Drum Song*.[17] This film heralded a change in Hollywood's usual casting protocols and the press took note.

In 1961, with the civil rights movement in the South splashed across the nation's papers and racial equity on the minds of many of the White media elite in Los Angeles and beyond, Hollywood finally replaced the underground Chinatown film with the first studio film to truly celebrate the inclusion of Chinese Americans in the nation. Originally written as a novel by Chinese American author C. Y. Lee and adapted for Broadway by none other than Rogers and Hammerstein, *Flower Drum Song* was the first major Hollywood film set in the present day to feature an almost completely Asian American cast.[18]

In a story set in contemporary America, director Henry Koster cast Asian Americans in nearly every starring role. Unlike *The Good Earth*, *Flower Drum Song* cast no White actors in yellowface makeup. The movie featured newcomer Nancy Kwan in her second starring role after *The World of Suzie Wong* (1960). In her starring role as Linda Low, Kwan appeared alongside James Shigeta, a Japanese American performer from Hawai'i, who was already a bestselling recording artist in Japan.[19] Longtime character actor Benson Fong played Wang Chi-Yang, the family patriarch. Miyoshi Umeki, Jack Soo, and Patrick Adiarte reprised their stage roles as Mei Li, Sammy Fong, and Wang San. The sole non-Asian American lead was the Black actress Juanita Hall, who reprised her stage role as Madame Liang.

The release of *Flower Drum Song* signaled a cultural shift. The major urban Chinatowns of the United States had almost all transformed into sites of tourism and consumption, benefiting their Chinese American merchants, but before this film, the Chinatown pastiche aesthetic had not reached the silver screen. *Flower Drum Song* represented a key step in the incorporation of Chinese Americans into the imagined community of the nation. In his review of the film for the *New York Times,* Bosley Crowther wrote: "Don't get the idea, however, that the characters and comedy put forth in this fable of Chinese-Americans residing in San Francisco Chinatown are in any way basically different from the characters and comedy that used to bloom in any number of plays about German or Swedish or Jewish immigrants coming from the old to the new country (via the comedy route) in years gone by."[20] White critics had finally accepted Chinese Americans symbolically in the melting pot of the nation. Four short years after the film was released, Congress passed the 1965 Immigration Act, welcoming Asian immigrants to the United States on equal footing with immigrants from Europe.

In *Flower Drum Song,* my grandfather's sister Margie Chee, wife of my Uncle Richard, finally got her chance to appear in a Hollywood film along with her son, my Uncle Rick. As casting for extras commenced in 1961, Auntie Margie and Uncle Richard lived in the Crenshaw District of Los Angeles with their three children: nine-year-old Rick, seven-year-old Lisa, and two-year-old Lori. While the Chee family visited Chinatown occasionally for dinners, they remained outside the circle of Chinatown elite ever since the family patriarch, Sou Jen Chu, broke with Chinatown leadership over the alleged mishandling of funds related to Mei-ling Soong's Los Angeles visit.

When Rick was born, rather than growing up in Chinatown, he and his family lived in a nearly all-Black apartment complex. By the time he was nine, the family had moved into a single-family home in a multi-ethnic neighborhood. He recalled that there were many Chinese and Japanese Americans in their neighborhood and that his elementary school was largely Asian American. Despite this, the family almost never saw stories about Chinese Americans on the silver screen. According to Rick, "I did not see or think about Asians being in the movies. There weren't that many."[21] Instead, the family enjoyed movies at the local drive-in, where they saw *101 Dalmatians* (1961) and The *Absent-Minded Professor* (1961).

While Rick and his sisters rarely saw Asian Americans performers on screen, they knew that they existed. Their family was close with the family

FIGURE C.2.   Margie Chee, Rick Chee, Lisa Chee, and Lori Chee. Chee Family Collection. Courtesy of Rick Chee.

of Cherylene and Virginia Lee, Chinese American childhood actors who went on to travel the country and perform in Las Vegas.[22] By 1961, Cherylene had already danced with Gene Kelly. Virginia had already appeared in uncredited roles in the movie *The King and I* (1956) and *Soldier of Fortune* (1955). In *Flower Drum Song*, the two sisters gave a scene-stealing performance with the song, "The Other Generation."

Cherylene and Virginia Lee encouraged Rick and his sisters to try out as extras. "They knew that *Flower Drum Song* was going to be filmed," Rick said, "and because it was a predominately Asian film, they needed a lot of Asian actors and started calling for everybody. Auntie Holly [mother of

Virginia and Cherleyne] said, "Hey, why don't you try out to be an extra?" [...] So, Auntie Ann and [Cousin] Cindy, my mom, myself, Lisa, all went to try out. They only picked my mother and me." Rick and his mom spent three days on set, where young Rick earned a total of $76. He and my Auntie Margie appeared in the crowd at the Chinese New Year cheering on Linda Lowe's float. Rick sat on the curb, with other Chinese American youth while his mom stood in back in the crowd.

When the film was released later that year, Rick, his family, his classmates, and his friends crowded into a local theater to watch it. In the theater, no matter how hard he looked, Rick could not find himself in the crowd scene. Decades later he tried again. The whole family gathered around hoping to find a glimpse of nine-year-old Rick somewhere on the Chinatown curb as Nancy Kwan's New Year's float passed by. Even with the DVD, Rick was unsure he ever did identify himself. Despite never actually seeing himself on screen, he has fond memories of being in the movie: "I liked it a lot. I liked the songs. I thought it was fun." Laughing, he said, "I always say my claim to fame was as a *Flower Drum Song* extra."

Flower Drum Song symbolized the end of one era and the start of another. Before the passage of the 1965 Immigration Act, the city's Chinese American population remained relatively small. Studios wishing to cast large numbers of background extras for a Chinese American–themed film did not have a large pool from which they could draw. As such, *Flower Drum Song* would also be the last film that gave a significant proportion of the Chinese Americans who lived in Los Angeles the opportunity to appear as extras in a major Hollywood production. With the passage of the 1965 Immigration Act, the Chinese American population of Los Angeles grew rapidly, expanding the pool of would-be performers.

Up until 1965, Los Angeles Chinese Americans had a special relationship with the movies. As extras and occasional bit players, they saw themselves on screen. Chinese American representations were far fewer, but for much of the first half of the twentieth century, if you were Chinese American living in Los Angeles and saw another Chinese American on screen, there was a good chance you personally knew that person. Perhaps they were your brother, or cousin, or neighbor. You might have gone to church with them or seen them at the gas station, but with a community of only a few thousand it was difficult to see Chinese faces in the background that you did not recognize.

Today, when people talk about "seeing themselves on screen," they are usually speaking metaphorically. Seeing yourself on screen is a metaphor for watching media representations that reflect your life experiences—usually as they relate to race, class, gender, and sexuality. But if you had been a Chinese American living in Los Angeles in the 1930s or 1940s, wanting to see yourself on screen meant exactly that. It did not mean seeing a story that reflected your life experience. Rather, it meant actually seeing yourself in the background of a crowd scene. Chinese Americans might not have been able to star in films, but those who lived in Los Angeles could, and often did, see themselves on screen.

Epilogue

In late February 2023, the actor James Hong took the stage at the Fairmont Century Plaza Hotel with his castmates from the film *Everything Everywhere All at Once*.[1] The group was there to accept the award for Outstanding Performance by a Cast in a Motion Picture from the Screen Actors Guild (SAG). *Everything Everywhere All at Once* was in the midst of an historic sweep of awards. In addition to SAG, it had already swept the Writers Guild of America, the Producers Guild of America, and the Directors Guild of America. The film would go on to win two Golden Globes, five Critics Choice Awards, and seven Independent Spirit Awards. In March, the film took home seven of the eleven Oscars it was nominated for, including Best Picture. The accolades that the film accumulated were impressive. Even among *Everything Everywhere*'s many awards, SAG's was a special one. After all, it was for outstanding performance by a cast and had been chosen by fellow performers in Hollywood.

Fittingly, when the cast of the film accepted their SAG award, the 94-year-old Hong spoke for the group. Few Asian American performers in Hollywood history have experienced the longevity of James Hong. By 2023, he had appeared in more than 600 television and movie roles dating back to the mid-1950s. He had had bit roles in *Flower Drum Song* (1961), *Chinatown* (1974), and *Blade Runner* (1982). He had made reoccurring appearances on *Bonanza* and *Kung Fu*. In the 1960s, when starring roles were a rarity for Chinese Americans, Hong and a group of fellow Asian American performers founded the East West Players. This Asian American theater group allowed them to produce and star in their own plays. The year prior to the SAG win, thanks in part to a campaign by his fellow actor Daniel Dae Kim, Hong became the oldest actor ever to receive a star on the Hollywood Walk of Fame.[2]

With a career spanning half a century, Hong embodied the struggles of Chinese American performers in an industry that had long marginalized them. After fifty years in Hollywood, this consummate bit and supporting player was finally getting the recognition he deserved. Hong took his moment on stage to reflect on how far Chinese Americans had come: "In *The Good Earth,* the leading roles were played by guys with their eyes taped up *like this* and they talked *like this* because the producers said that Asians were not good enough, and they [were] not box office. Look at us now!" Standing on the stage at the Fairmont, Hong did not need to look past Paul Muni and Louise Rainer's yellowface performances to see the extras and bit players in the background. Instead, eighty-five years after *The Good Earth*'s release, he could call out the racist casting that had kept Asian Americans like him from gaining starring roles in movies like *The Good Earth.*

The press was rapturous in lauding *Everything Everywhere All at Once* and in celebrating the arrival of Asian Americans in Hollywood. *The Guardian* described it as an "Asian American wave crashing on Hollywood's highest honor."[3] NBC news declared: "Asian Americans are over just being included. They're defining mainstream culture."[4] Of course, this was not the first time the mainstream press had heralded the entry of Asian Americans into Hollywood's exclusive club. They framed the release of *Crazy Rich Asians* (2018), *Better Luck Tomorrow* (2002), *The Joy Luck Club* (1993), *Flower Drum Song* (1961), and even *The Good Earth* (1937) with similar narratives. As James Hong could attest, the problem with the recurring theme of Asian American cinematic arrival is that Asian Americans in general, and Chinese Americans in particular, have performed in films since the beginning of Hollywood.

As *Performing Chinatown* has shown, Los Angeles Chinatown was so interconnected with Hollywood in the first half of the twentieth century that it is impossible to tell the history of Chinese Americans in Los Angeles without discussing the movie industry or performance more broadly. Asian Americans in general and Chinese Americans specifically have been in the movie industry the entire time: sometimes in the background, other times in bit roles, and occasionally as supporting players. In the wake of the success of *Everything Everywhere*, the question we must ask ourselves is not whether Asian Americans have finally arrived in Hollywood. Rather, the question to ask is why the rest of America has not noticed our presence before.

Notes

Introduction

1. Richard Chee, interview by William Gow, July 7, 2008, Chinatown Remembered Project, Chinese Historical Society of Southern California (CHSSC).

2. Esther Lee Johnson, interview by William Gow, March 9, 2008, Chinatown Remembered; Tyrus Wong, interview by Genie Moon, November 1, 2007, Chinatown Remembered; Charlie Quon, interview by Nancy Thai, April 22, 2007, Chinatown Remembered.

3. Scholarship on Chinese Americans in Los Angeles has tended to focus either on the 1871 Los Angeles Chinatown Massacre or on the development of Chinese American ethnoburbs like Monterey Park beginning in the 1980s. Exclusion-era Los Angeles remains vastly understudied. See Scott Zesch, *The Chinatown War: Chinese Los Angeles and the Massacre of 1871* (New York: Oxford University Press, 2012); Leland T. Saito, *Race and Politics: Asian Americans, Latinos, and Whites in a Los Angeles Suburb* (Champaign: University of Illinois Press, 1998); Timothy Fong, *The First Suburban Chinatown: The Remaking of Monterey Park, California* (Philadelphia: Temple University Press, 1994); Wei Li, *Ethnoburb: The New Ethnic Community in Urban America* (Honolulu: University of Hawai'i Press, 2009); Wendy Cheng, *The Changs Next to the Diazes: Remapping Race in Suburban California* (Minneapolis: University of Minnesota Press, 2013); James Zarsadiaz, *Resisting Change in Suburbia: Asian Immigrants and Frontier Nostalgia in L.A.* (Berkeley: University of California Press, 2022). Scholarship on Chinese Americans in Los Angeles during the exclusion era includes memoirs, a public history produced by the CHSSC, and a limited number of theses and dissertations. See, for example, Lisa See, *On Gold Mountain: The One Hundred Year Odyssey of My Chinese American Family* (New York: Vintage

Books, 1995); Louise Leung Larson, *Sweet Bamboo: A Memoir of a Chinese American Family* (Berkeley: University of California Press, 1989); CHSSC, ed., *Linking Our Lives: Chinese American Women of Los Angeles* (Los Angeles: CHSSC, 1984); Susie Ling, ed., *Bridging the Centuries: History of Chinese Americans in Southern California* (Los Angeles: CHSSC, 2001); Jenny Cho and the Chinese Historical Society of Los Angeles, *Chinatown in Los Angeles* (Mount Pleasant, SC: Arcadia Press, 2009); Mabel Sam Lee, "The Recreational Interests and Participation of a Selected Group of Chinese Boys and Girls in Los Angeles, California" (master's thesis, University of Southern California, 1939); Wen-hui Chen, "A Study of Chinese Family Life in Los Angeles as Compared to the Traditional Family Life in China." (master's thesis, University of Southern California, 1940); Kim Fong Tom, "The Participation of the Chinese in the Community Life of Los Angeles," (master's thesis, University of Southern California, 1944); Wen-hui Chen, "Changing Socio-Cultural Patterns of the Chinese Community in Los Angeles" (PhD diss., University of Southern California, 1952).

4. Key works on Asian American public performances include Lon Kurashige, *Japanese American Celebration and Conflict: A History of Ethnic Identity and Festival in Los Angeles, 1934–1990* (Berkeley: University of California Press, 2002); Karen Shimakawa, *National Abjection: The Asian Body on Stage* (Durham, NC: Duke University Press, 2002); Chouh-Ling Yeh, *Making an American Festival: Chinese New Year in San Francisco's Chinatown* (Berkeley: University of California Press, 2008); Josephine Lee, *Performing Asian America: Race and Ethnicity on the Contemporary Stage* (Philadelphia: Temple University Press, 1997); James Moy, *Marginal Sights: Staging the Chinese in America* (Iowa City: University of Iowa, 1993); Takeo Rivera, *Model Minority Masochism: Performing the Cultural Politics of Asian American Masculinity* (Oxford, UK: Oxford University Press, 2022).

5. In creating this definition, I draw on the work of performance studies scholar Richard Schechner, who describes one of the key building blocks of performance as "restored behavior." He defines restored behavior as "physical, verbal, or virtual actions that are not-for-the-first time; that are prepared or rehearsed." *Performance Studies: An Introduction* (London: Routledge, 2013), 29.

6. Ju Yon Kim, *Racial Mundane: Asian American Performance and the Embodied Everyday* (New York: New York University Press: 2015), 10–16.

7. I am reminded of performance studies scholar Diana Taylor's observation that performance "is a wide ranging and difficult practice to define and holds many, at times conflicting meanings and possibilities." In this context, I am aware that analyzing a filmed performance is not the same as analyzing a live one. As Taylor states, "documentation gives us a sense of what happened but cannot capture the 'live' performance itself." While I acknowledge these differences, recorded and live Chinatown performances shared similarities in the way they shaped conceptions

of race and engaged systems of power in the 1930s and 1940s. The juxtaposition of these two types of performance produces a more complex understanding of Chinese American racial formation in the mid-twentieth century. *Performance* (Durham, NC: Duke University Press, 2016), 6, 186.

8. I believe that the intersectionality of race, gender, sexuality, and class should be taken as a given. The literature on intersectionality, which developed out of Black feminist thought, is extensive and crosses disciplines. Key works include Kimberlé Crenshaw, "Demarginalizing the Intersection of Race and Sex: A Black Feminist Critique of Antidiscrimination Doctrine, Feminist Theory and Antiracist Politics," *University of Chicago Legal Forum* 1989, no.1 (1989): 139–167, "Mapping the Margins: Intersectionality, Identity Politics and Violence against Women," *Stanford Law Review* 433, no. 6 (July 1991): 1241–1299; Patricia Hill Collins, *Black Feminist Thought: Knowledge, Consciousness, and the Politics of Empowerment* (New York: Routledge, 2000); and Evelyn Nakano Glenn, *Unequal Freedom: How Race and Gender Shaped American Citizenship and Labor* (Cambridge, MA: Harvard University Press, 2002).

9. Ella Shoat and Robert Stam point out that there is nothing inherently wrong with debating the realism of racial representation on film: "Spectators (and critics) are invested in realism because they are invested in the idea of truth and reserve the right to confront a film with their own personal or cultural knowledge." This is not the project of this book. *Unthinking Eurocentrism: Multiculturalism and the Media* (New York: Routledge, 1994), 178.

10. Decades of scholarship on race in film reject the positive-image approach to analyzing racial representations. See, for example, bell hooks, *Black Looks: Race and Representation* (Boston: South End Press, 1992), 4; Valerie Smith, *Representing Blackness: Issues in Film and Video* (New Brunswick, NJ: Rutgers University Press, 1997), 4; Jun Xing, *Asian America Through the Lens: History, Representation, and Identity* (London: AltaMira, 1998), 20–28.

11. Ah Wong, "The Joy Luck Experience," *Los Angeles Times*, October 2, 1993.

12. Alex Wong, "The Oral History of Better Luck Tomorrow," *GQ*, August 16, 2008.

13. Alice Truong, "The Trailer for *Crazy Rich Asians* Has Some Asking: Where Are the Brown Faces?" *Quartz*, April 24, 2018.

14. There is a broad body of literature on the ways that film has represented race, including Donald Bogle, *Toms, Coons, Mulattoes, Mammies and Bucks: An Interpretive History of Blacks in American Films* (New York: Bantam Books, 1974); Eugene Franklin Wong, *On Visual Media Racism, Asian Americans in Motion Pictures* (New York: Arno Press, 1978); Chon Noriega, *Chicanos and Film: Representation and Resistance* (Minneapolis: University of Minnesota Press, 1992); Ed Guerrero, *Framing Blackness: The African Image on Film* (Philadelphia: Temple University Press, 1993); Daniel Bernardi, ed., *The Birth of Whiteness: Race and the Emergence of U.S. Cinema*

(New Brunswick, NJ: Rutgers University Press, 1996), and *Classic Hollywood, Classic Whiteness* (Minneapolis: University of Minnesota Press, 2001); Peter X. Feng, ed., *Screening Asian Americans* (New Brunswick, NJ: Rutgers University Press, 2002); Michelle H Raheja, *Reservation Reelism: Redfacing, Visual Sovereignty and Representations of Native Americans in Film* (Lincoln: University of Nebraska Press, 2010); Manthia Diawara, ed., *Black American Cinema* (New York: Routledge, 2012); Lisa Black, *Picturing Indians: Native Americans in Film, 1941–1960* (Lincoln: University of Nebraska Press, 2020).

15. Michael Omi and Howard Winant, *Racial Formation in the United States* (New York: Routledge, 2014).

16. There is an extensive literature on the Chinese Exclusion Act, including Alexander Saxton, *The Indispensable Enemy: Labor and the Anti-Chinese Movement in California* (Berkeley: University of California Press, 1975); Andrew Gyory, *Closing the Gate: Race, Politics, and the Chinese Exclusion Act* (Chapel Hill: University of North Carolina Press, 1998); Charles McClain, *In Search of Equality: The Chinese Struggle against Discrimination in Nineteenth-Century America* (Berkeley: University of California Press, 1996); Erika Lee, *At America's Gates: Chinese Immigration During the Exclusion Era* (Chapel Hill: University of North Carolina Press, 2003); Beth Lew-Williams, *The Chinese Must Go: Violence, Exclusion, and the Making of the Alien in America* (Cambridge, MA: Harvard University Press, 2018).

17. Building on Beth Lew-Williams' work, I contend that this was followed by a second restriction period from 1943 to 1965. *Chinese Must Go*, 8–9.

18. Beth Lew-Williams argues that we should call this law the Chinese Restriction Act of 1882, in keeping both with the way contemporaries referred to it and with the immigration goals of the legislation.

19. While "yellow peril" was likely coined by German emperor Wilhelm II in the nineteenth century, the concept stretches back much further to Marco Polo's visit to China in 1275. See Gary Okihiro, *Margins and Mainstream: Asians in American History and Culture* (Seattle: University of Washington Press, 1994), 119. For an overview of yellow peril discourse, see Kent Ono and Vincent Pham, *Asian Americans and the Media* (Malden MA: Polity Press, 2009), 25–62; John Kuo Wei Tchen and Dylan Yeats, *Yellow Peril! An Archive of Anti-Asian Fear* (New York: Verso, 2014).

20. On popular American representations of China and Chinese Americans, see Dorothy B. Jones, *Portrayals of China and India on Screen, 1896–1955* (Cambridge, MA: MIT Press, 1955); Harold Isaacs, *Scratches on the Minds: American Views of China and India* (New York: John Day, 1958); Stuart Creighton Miller, *The Unwelcome Immigrant: The American Image of Chinese, 1785–1882* (Berkeley: University of California Press, 1969); John Kuo Wei Tchen, *New York Before Chinatown: Orientalism and the Shaping of American Culture, 1776–1882* (Baltimore: Johns Hopkins

University Press, 1999); Gordon Chang, *Fateful Ties: A History of America's Preoc-cupation with China* (Cambridge, MA: Harvard University Press, 2015).

21. Lisa Lowe has argued that the American citizen was defined against the figure of the Asian immigrant, legally, economically, and culturally. *Immigrant Acts: On Asian American Cultural Politics* (Durham, NC: Duke University Press 1996), 4.

22. David R. Roediger, *Working Toward Whiteness: How America's Immigrants Became White* (New York: Basic Books, 2005); Ian Haney Lopez, *White by Law: The Legal Construction of Race* (New York: New York University Press, 2006), 56–77.

23. In her discussion of Asian American theatrical performances, Karen Shi-makawa says, "Asian American performers never walk onto an empty stage. . . . That space is always already densely populated with phantasmas of Orientalness through and against which an Asian American performer must struggle to be seen." For Shimakawa, popular "images and representations, as well as legal rulings and gov-ernment policies" all vacillate "between positioning Asian Americans as foreigners/ outsiders/deviants/criminals or domesticated/invisible/exemplary/honorary whites." While Shimakawa's observation that Asian American performers are forced to ne-gotiate between these two poles is certainly correct in contemporary times, this was not the case during the exclusion era, when American popular culture and American law nearly always marked Chinese Americans exclusively as foreigners, outsiders, deviants, or criminals. *National Abjection*, 15, 17.

24. In tracing this history of racial formation, I draw a distinction between Chi-natown performances, which shaped ideas about race and simultaneously profited from White audiences, and performances in American Chinatowns that were not directed at White audiences for profit, such as musical performances for fellow members of the ethnic enclaves. As Krysten Moon has shown, the latter perfor-mances did shape conceptions of race for Whites who happened to witness them, but they were not directed at White audiences; as a result, their effects on popular conceptions of race were a byproduct, not a goal. *Yellowface: Creating the Chinese in American Popular Music and Performance,1850s–1920s* (New Brunswick, NJ: Rutgers University Press, 2005), 66–70, 84–85.

25. Roger Daniels, *Asian America: Chinese and Japanese in the United States since the 1850s* (Seattle: University of Washington Press, 1988), 188.

26. Peter Kwong and Dušanka Miščević, *Chinese America: The Untold Story of America's Oldest New Community* (New York: New Press, 2005), 20.

27. Shelley Sang-Hee Lee, *A New History of Asian America* (New York: Rout-ledge, 2014), 222.

28. To the extent that scholars give Chinese Americans any agency in this his-tory, it is the residents of San Francisco Chinatown who are held up as the main protagonists. See, for example, Yong Chen, *Chinese San Francisco: A Transpacific Community* (Stanford, CA: Stanford University Press, 2000), 239–260; Nayan Shah,

Contagious Divides: Epidemics and Race in San Francisco's Chinatown (Berkeley: University of California Press, 2001), 204–258.

29. Mae Ngai, *Impossible Subjects: Illegal Aliens and the Making of Modern America* (Princeton, NJ: Princeton University Press, 2004), 96–126.

30. David Palumbo-Liu calls this process of incorporation "introjection" *Asian/American: Historical Crossings of a Racial Frontier* (Stanford, CA: Stanford University Press, 1999), 18.

31. On class division in North American Chinatowns, see Renqui Yu, *To Save China, To Save Ourselves: The Chinese Hand Laundry Alliance in New York* (Philadelphia: Temple University Press, 1992); Jan Lin, *Reconstructing Chinatown: Ethnic Enclave, Global Change* (Minneapolis: University of Minnesota Press, 1998), 57–79; Peter Kwong, *Chinatown, N.Y. Labor and Politics, 1930–1950* (New York: New Press, 2001). On gender in Chinatowns, see CHSSC, ed., *Linking Our Lives*; Judy Yung, *Unbound Feet: A Social History of Chinese Women in San Francisco* (Berkeley: University of California Press, 1995); Isabella Seong-Leong Quintana, "National Borders, Neighborhood Boundaries: Gender, Space, and Border Formation in Chinese and Mexican Los Angeles" (PhD diss., University of Michigan, 2010); Xiaojian Zhao, *Remaking Chinese America Immigration, Family, and Community, 1940–1965* (New Brunswick, NJ: Rutgers University Press, 2002).

32. Elaine Kim, *Asian American Literature: An Introduction to the Writings and Their Social Context* (Philadelphia: Temple University Press, 1982), 4.

Chapter 1

1. Suellen Cheng and Munson Kwok, "The Golden Years of Los Angeles Chinatown: The Beginning," *Los Angeles Chinatown 50th Year Guidebook* (Los Angeles: Chinese Historical Society of Southern California, 1988).

2. Cheng and Kwok, "The Golden Years," 40.

3. Robert Lee draws a distinction between *alien* and *foreign*, with *foreign* meaning "outside or distant" and *alien* meaning "things that are immediate and present yet have foreign nature or allegiance." *Orientals: Asian Americans in Popular Culture* (Philadelphia: Temple University Press, 1999), 3.

4. Nayan Shah, *Contagious Divides: Epidemics and Race in San Francisco Chinatown* (Berkeley: University of California Press, 2001), 13–14.

5. A large proportion of these men were not bachelors at all but married men separated from their wives and children in China. Madeline Hsu, *Dreaming of Gold, Dreaming of Home: Transnationalism and Migration Between United States and South China, 1882–1943* (Stanford, CA: Stanford University Press, 2000), 99.

6. Mae Ngai is one of the few scholars to connect the rebuilding of San Francisco Chinatown after the 1906 earthquake with the various Chinese Village attractions at

world's fairs. *The Lucky Ones: One Family and the Extraordinary Invention of Chinese America* (Princeton, NJ: Princeton University Press, 2012), 95–116.

7. I build on the history of Asian American cultural production by scholars including: Shirley Jennifer Lim, *A Feeling of Belonging: Asian American Women's Public Culture, 1930–1960* (New York: New York University Press, 2006); and Gloria Heyung Chun, *Of Orphans and Warriors: Inventing Chinese American Culture and Identity* (New Brunswick, NJ: Rutgers University Press, 2000).

8. On the "surface aesthetics" of Chinatown, see Sabine Haenni, *The Immigrant Scene: Ethnic Amusements in New York, 1880–1920* (Minneapolis: University of Minnesota Press), 149–154.

9. Anne Anlin Cheng, *Ornamentalism* (New York: Oxford University Press, 2019). The conception of the United States as a melting pot entered the national imagination with the production of Israel Zangwill's play *The Melting Pot* in 1909.

10. Ben Singer, *Melodrama and Modernity: Early Sensational Cinema and its Contexts* (New York: Columbia University Press, 2001), 101–130.

11. There is a growing literature on visuality that asserts that vision itself has a history. For example, see Hal Foster, ed. *Vision and Visuality* (Seattle: Bay Press, 1988); and Nicholas Mirzoeff, *The Right to Look: A Counter History of Visuality* (Durham, NC: Duke University Press, 2011).

12. On the Orient of the Western imagination and the domination of actual lands and people, see Edward Said, *Orientalism* (New York: Vintage Books, 1979).

13. On shifting ideas of the yellow peril, see Erika Lee, *The Making of Asian America: A History* (New York: Simon and Schuster, 2015), 123–128.

14. Kay Anderson has suggested that the "imagined geography" of Chinatown is largely the product of the White imagination. "The Idea of Chinatown: The Power of Place and Institutional Practice in the Making of a Racial Category," *Annals of The Association of American Geography* 77, no. 4 (December 1987): 581, and *Vancouver's Chinatown: Racial Discourse in Canada, 1875–1980* (Montreal: McGill-Queen's University Press, 1992), 28–33, 80–82.

15. By 1960, nearly half of Chinese Americans in the US traced their origins to the county of Toisan (*Taishan*) in the Pearl River Delta. Hsu, *Dreaming of Gold*, 3. Toisan was one of the four counties that made up the Sze Yup (*Siyi*) region surrounding the city of Canton (*Guangzhou*).

16. Frank Soule, John Gihon, and Jim Nisbet, *The Annals of San Francisco* (New York: D. Appleton and Company, 1855), 381.

17. Yong Chen, *Chinese San Francisco: A Trans-Pacific Community* (Berkeley: University of California Press, 2000), 55, 57.

18. *Appletons' Hand-Book of American Travel. Western Tour* (New York: D. Appleton and Company, 1873), 131. William Robertson and W. F. Robertson, *Our*

American Tour: Being a Run of Ten Thousand Miles from the Atlantic to the Golden Gate, in the Autumn of 1869 (Edinburgh: W. Burness Printer, 1871), 85.

19. Ronald Takaki, *Strangers from a Different Shore: A History of Asian Americans* (New York: Little, Brown, 1998), 80; Sucheng Chan, *Asian American: An Interpretive History* (NewYork: Twayne Publishers, 1991), 28–35.

20. Jean Pfalezer, *Driven Out: The Forgotten War Against Chinese Americans* (Berkeley: University of California Press, 2009).

21. Pfaelzer, *Driven Out* 256–290.

22. Takaki, *Strangers from a Different Shore*, 80.

23. Singer, *Melodrama and Modernity*, 17–35.

24. On the connection between spectacularization of nineteenth-century urban life and the emergence of mass culture, see Vanessa Schwartz, *Spectacular Realities: Early Mass Culture in Fin-de-Siècle Paris* (Berkeley: University of California Press, 1998), 2.

25. Barbara Berglund, "Chinatown's Tourist Terrain: Representation and Racialization in Nineteenth-Century San Francisco," *American Studies* 46, no. 2 (Summer 2005): 7–17.

26. Gordon Chang and Shelley Fisher Fishkin, *Chinese and the Iron Rail* (Stanford, CA: Stanford University Press, 2019), 16–18.

27. Catherine Cocks, *Doing the Town: The Rise in Urban Tourism in the United States, 1850–1905* (Berkeley: University of California Press, 2001), 52–60.

28. Cocks, 72; J. Philip Gruen, *Manifest Destinations: Cities and Tourists in the Nineteenth Century American West* (Norman: University of Oklahoma Press, 2014), 147–150.

29. Cocks, *Doing the Town*, 6–8

30. Walter Benjamin, "On Some Motif's in Baudelaire," in *Illuminations*, ed. Hannah Arendt (New York: Schocken Books, 1968), 155–200.

31. Tom Gunning, "From the Kaleidoscope to the X-Ray: Urban Spectatorship, Poe, Benjamin, and Traffic in Souls (1913)," *Wide Angle* 19 (1997): 29–61.

32. Lauren Rabinovitz, *For the Love of Pleasure: Women, Movies, and Culture in Turn-of-the-Century Chicago* (New Brunswick, NJ: Rutgers University Press, 1998), 8–9.

33. Haenni, *The Immigrant Scene*, 44; Rabinovitz, *For the Love of Pleasure*, 6–7; Judith R. Walkowitz, *City of Dreadful Delight: Narratives of Sexual Danger in Late Victorian London* (Chicago: University of Chicago Press, 1992), 15–40.

34. Walkowitz, *City of Dreadful Delight*, 20–21.

35. Soule, Gihon, and Nisbet. *Annals of San Francisco*, 386.

36. "How Our Chinamen Are Employed," *Overland Monthly*, March 1869, 236.

37. Victor G. Nee and Brett de Bary Nee, *Longtime Californ': A Documentary Study of An American Chinatown* (Stanford, CA: Stanford University Press, 1972), 15.

38. Takaki, *Strangers from a Different Shore*, 115.

39. On Chinese returning on Sundays, see *Report and Proceedings of the Investigation of the New York City Police*, Vol. II (1895), 2242. Mary Lui demonstrates that by the 1880s the majority of the city's Chinese Americans were laundry workers scattered across the city who lived behind their stores. *The Chinatown Trunk Mystery: Murder, Miscegenation, and Other Dangerous Encounters in Turn of the Century New York City* (Princeton, NJ: Princeton University Press, 2005), 51–55.

40. See, for example, Beth Lew-Williams, "'Chinamen' and 'Delinquent Girls': Intimacy, Exclusion, and a Search for California's Color Line," *Journal of American History* 104, no. 3 (2017): 632–655.

41. Anthony Lee, *Picturing Chinatown: Art and Orientalism in San Francisco* (Berkeley: University of California Press, 2001), 9–58.

42. *San Francisco Chronicle*, March 28, 1886.

43. *Outlook*, "Seen by the Spectator: Being a Selection of Rambling Papers First Printed in *The Outlook*, under the title *The Spectator* (New York: Outlook Company, 1902), 193.

44. George H. Fitch, "A Night in Chinatown," *Cosmopolitan*, February 1887.

45. Charles Dilke describes seeking out two "detectives" to lead him around Little China in San Francisco. *Greater Britain: A Record of Travel in English-Speaking Countries, During 1866–7* (New York: Harper and Brothers, 1869), 187–194; See also *Bancroft's Tourist Guide* (San Francisco: Bancroft and Company, 1871), 197–199.

46. Josephine Clifford, "Chinatown," *Porter's American Monthly*, May 1880; Fitch, "Night in Chinatown," 351.

47. Berglund, "Chinatown's Tourist Terrain," 10.

48. "Police Commissioners," *San Francisco Call*, March 15, 1894, and "Nine Fallen Stars," February 28, 1895.

49. "Supervisors to Hold Special Meeting," *San Francisco Chronicle*, September 14, 1897.

50. Chuck Connors, *Bowery Life* (New York: Richard Fox Publishing, 1904).

51. Berglund, "Chinatown's Tourist Terrain," 6.

52. "The Orient in America: A Stroll Through Chinatown in Day and Night," *San Francisco Chronicle*, June 13, 1875.

53. I build on Sabine Haenni's observation that Chinatown was often depicted as a site that engaged all the senses. *Immigrant Scene*, 155–162.

54. Outlook, *Seen by the Spectator*, 209.

55. Outlook, 210.

56. Outlook, 214–215.

57. Martin Rubin, "Berkeleyesque Traditions," in *Theater and Film: A Comparative Anthology*, ed. Robert Knopf (New Haven, CT: Yale University Press, 2005), 51.

58. Rubin, 53.

59. Raymond Rast, "The Cultural Politics of Tourism in San Francisco's China-town, 1882–1917," *Pacific Historical Review* 76, no. 1 (February 2007): 39.

60. Barbara Berglund also overlooks the theatricality of Chinatown, arguing instead that Chinatown tourist literature represented what Whites believed were "social truths of this new immigrant group." "Chinatown's Tourist Terrain," 6.

61. C. A. Kelley, *Glimpses of the Far West*, (n.p., 1902), https://catalog.hathitrust.org/Record/102288704

62. Haenni, *Immigrant Scene*, 150–155.

63. *San Francisco Chronicle*, "A Municipal Opium Joint," July 25, 1905.

64. Josette Feral, "Theatricality: The Specificity of Theatrical Language," *Sub-Stance* 31, no. 2/3 (2002): 97.

65. Raymond Rast, in "Tourism in San Francisco Chinatown," explains that Chinese entrepreneurs "contested white representations of vice-ridden Chinatown but substituted their own claims that Chinatown authenticity lay in the exoticism of its architecture, theatrical performances, curios, and cuisine" (p. 33).

66. "The Midway Plaisance Map," in *The Dream City: A Portfolio of Photographic Views of the World Columbian Exposition with an Introduction by Halsey C. Ives* (St. Louis: N. D. Thompson, 1894), http://columbus.iit.edu/dreamcity/Midway.html.

67. Gary Okihiro has argued that Asians were often seen by White visitors to the fair as an intermediate group on this scale of civilization. *Common Ground: Reimaging American History* (Princeton, NJ: Princeton University Press, 2001), 36.

68. Mae Ngai mentions these men as the three primary financial backers of the fair. Newspaper accounts of the day mention another Chinese investor, spelling his name Chan Pak Kwai or Chin Pock Quay. "Transnationalism and the Transformation of the 'Other': Responses to the Presidential Address," *American Quarterly* 57, no. 1 (March 2005): 62. Also see "China at the Fair," *San Francisco Chronicle*, December 4, 1892; "Chinese Nipped in Midway Deal," *Chicago Tribune*, March 16, 1894; and "Chinese Actors Reach the City," *Chicago Tribune*, April 23, 1893.

69. Ngai, *The Lucky Ones*, 97.

70. Ngai, "Transnationalism," 52.

71. Hubert Howe Bancroft, *The Book of the Fair: An Historical and Descriptive Presentation of the World's Science, Art, and Industry as Viewed Through the Columbian Exposition at Chicago in 1893* (Chicago: The Bancroft Company, 1893), 873.

72. Bancroft, 873.

73. Anna Pegler Gordon, "Chinese Exclusion, Photography, and the Development of US Immigration Policy," *American Quarterly* 58, no. 1 (March 2006): 51–77.

74. Barbara Venman, "Dragons, Dummies and Royals: China at American World's Fairs, 1876–1904," *Gateway Heritage: The Magazine of the Missouri Historical Society* 17, no. 2 (Fall 1996): 22; "China at the Fair.".

75. Ngai makes a similar observation in "Transnationalism,"61.

76. Historian Robert Rydell has suggested that American world's fairs between 1876 and 1916 created "symbolic universes" that confirmed the authority of the country's corporate, political and scientific leadership." Similarly, James Moy has argued that the purpose of the Chinese Village was to contain the Chinese "in a constructed foreign place." Such readings oversimplify how popular culture is used to maintain social hierarchy. Rather than looking at the Chinese Village as a site of containment, it is better to see it as site of containment *and* resistance. Any given cultural text will have elements of both containment and resistance to social stratification, though the balance between the two will vary, with some doing more to contain and other doing more to resist. Robert Rydell, *All the World's a Fair: Visions of Empire at the American International Expositions, 1876–1916* (Chicago: University of Chicago Press), 2; James Moy, *Marginal Sights: Staging the Chinese in America* (Iowa City: University of Iowa Press, 1993), 62–63. On containment and resistance, see Stuart Hall, "Notes on Deconstructing the Popular," in *People's History and Socialist Theory*, ed. Raphael Samuel (London: Routledge, 1981), 227–239.

77. This was the second incarnation of this newspaper. On Wong Chin Foo, see Scott Deligman, *The First Chinese American: The Remarkable life of Wong Chin Foo* (Hong Kong: Hong Kong University Press, 2013).

78. *Chinese American*, June 24, 1893.

79. Zhang, "Origins of the Chinese Americanization Movement," 52–55.

80. Chinese Equal Rights League, *Appeal of the Chinese Equal Rights League to the People of the United States for Equality of Manhood* (New York: Chinese Equal Rights League, 1892), 3, https://id.lib.harvard.edu/curiosity/immigration-to-the-united-states-1789-1930/39-990098173160203941

81. *Chinese American*, June 24, 1893.

82. "Gee Wo's Great Scheme," *Omaha Daily Bee*, October 22, 1892.

83. Qingsong Zhang, "The Origins of the Chinese Americanization Movement: Wong Chin Foo and the Equal Rights League," in *Claiming America: Constructing Chinese American Identities During the Exclusion Era*, ed. K. Scott Wong and Sucheng Chan (Philadelphia: Temple University Press, 1998), 55.

84. "Freaks of Chinese Fancy at the Fair," *Chicago Tribune*, September 24, 1893.

85. Bancroft, *Book of the Fair*, 873.

86. "Freaks of Chinese Fancy at the Fair," *Chicago Tribune*, February 2, 1893.

87. Bancroft, *Book of the Fair*, 873.

88. "Freaks of Chinese Fancy," February 2.

89. Freaks of Chinese Fancy," February 2.

90. Ivan Light, "From Vice District to Tourist Attraction: The Moral Career of American Chinatowns 1880–1940," *Pacific Historical Review*, 43 no. 3 (1974): 378.

91. Light, 378.

92. "Freaks of Chinese Fancy, " February 2.

93. Rand, McNally, *A Week at the Fair* (Chicago: Rand, McNally, 1893), 232.

94. Freaks of Chinese Fancy," September 24.

95. "Freaks of Chinese Fancy," September 24.

96. "Freaks of Chinese Fancy at the Fair," *Chicago Tribune*, September 23, 1893.

97. "Freaks of Chinese Fancy," September 23.

98. "The Midgets That Make the Midway Merry," *Chicago Tribune*, October 15, 1893.

99. "Freaks of Chinese Fancy, " September 24.

100. An article published after the attraction closed identified a seventeen-year-old named Chan Gee Wah, who was employed in the joss house. It is likely that she was the woman with children described in the *Chicago Tribune* articles. See "Many Cannot Be Sent Back," *Chicago Daily Tribune*, November 12, 1893.

101. Cheng, *Ornamentalism*, 18.

102. Cheng, 23.

103. Halsey C. Ives, "Chinese Beauty," *Dream City*, https://archive.org/details/dreamcityportfolooworl/page/n209/mode/2up

104. Fatimah Rony, *The Third Eye: Race, Cinema, and Ethnographic Spectacle* (Durham, NC: Duke University Press, 1996), 41–43.

105. See Halsey C. Ives"The Chinese Joss-House," in *Dream City*, http://columbus.iit.edu/dreamcity/00024045.html

106. "Chinese Nipped in Midway Deal," *Chicago Tribune*, March 16, 1894.

107. "Chinese Nipped."

108. Chinese Nipped."

109. On the Orientalist architecture that Chinese American merchants built in Chinatown after the earthquake, see Philip Choy, *San Francisco Chinatown: Guide to its History and Architecture* (San Francisco: City Lights Books, 2012), 43–46.

110. Christopher Yip, "San Francisco Chinatown," (Ph.D. diss., University of California, Berkeley, 1995), 198.

111. Emma Teng, "Artifacts of a Lost City: Arnold Genthe's Pictures of Old Chinatown and its Intertexts," in *Recollecting Early Asian America: Essays in Cultural History*, ed. Josephine Lee, Imogene Lim, and Yuko Matukawa (Philadelphia: Temple University, 2002), 73–74.

112. As Christopher Yip points out, the two buildings could not act as a gate to Chinatown as they framed California Street rather than the main thoroughfare of Grant Avenue. "San Francisco Chinatown," 200.

113. Yip, "San Francisco Chinatown," 200.

114. "The Sing Chong Bazaar," *Architect and Engineer* 13, no. 1 (May 1908): 96.

115. Bjorn A. Schmidt discusses the difficulty merchants in San Francisco Chinatown had in their attempts to change popular ideas about Chinatown. Even after Chinatown was rebuilt, postcards of opium dens from the 1890s were still popular.

Moreover, Schmidt shows that, as late as 1909, guidebooks still felt the need to mention that the Chinese did not eat rats. According to Schmidt, Old Chinatown remained a reference for San Francisco Chinatown well into the 1920s. *Visualising Orientalness: Chinese Immigration and Race in U.S. Motion Pictures* (Cologne, Germany: Böhlau Verlag, 2017), 140–150.

116. "Panama Pacific International Exposition," booklet 1, 2nd ed., 1915.

117. Frank Morton Todd, *The Story of the Exposition*, Vol. II (New York: G.P. Putnam's Knickerbocker Press, 1921), 358.

118. On White actors in yellowface, see Kim K. Fahlstedt, *Chinatown Film Culture: The Appearance of Cinema in San Francisco's Chinese Neighborhood* (New Brunswick, NJ: Rutgers University Press, 2020), 131.

119. Abagail Markwyn, "Economic Partner and Exotic Other: China and Japan at San Francisco's Panama-Pacific International Exposition," *Western Historical Quarterly* 39 (Winter 2008): 460–461.

120. Shehong Chen, *Being Chinese, Becoming Chinese Americans* (Champaign: University of Illinois Press, 2002), 100–104; Markwyn, "Economic Partner and Exotic Other," 462; Rast, "Tourism in San Francisco's Chinatown," 55–57.

121. Markwyn, "Economic Partner and Exotic Other," 463.

122. On the carnival attraction's origin, see "Underground Chinatown," *Billboard*, May 11, 1918, 72.

123. On Beatrice Nebraska, see "Parker's Greatest Show," *Billboard*," July 13, 1918, 38. On Coney Island, see "Coney Island Wants Airship Taxi to New York This Year, *New York Clipper*, May 7, 1919, 6.

124. "Important!!! Showmen!" advertisement in *Billboard*, February 16 1918, 40.

125. "Important!!! Showmen!"

126. See "Underground Chinatown Exhibit: Wax Work Called False Picture of Chinese Life," *New York Times*, October 19, 1919, and "America Is Urged to Cultivate China," *New York Times*, October 17, 1920.

127. Castelar Street is now Hill Street.

128. On the history of chop suey, see Haiming Liu, *From Canton Restaurant to Panda Express: A History of Chinese Food in the United States* (New Brunswick NJ: Rutgers University Press, 2015), 49–70; Yong Chen, *Chop Suey USA: The Story of Chinese Food in the United States* (New York: Columbia University Press, 2014).

129. T. K. Chang, Consul, Republic of China, "Congratulations Upon the Grand Opening of Chinatown," (1938), trans. Suellen Cheng, in *Chinatown Los Angeles: The Golden Years* (Los Angeles: Chinese Chamber of Commerce, 1988), 46.

130. Josi Ward, "Dreams of Oriental Romance," *Buildings and Landscape* 20, no.1 (Spring 2013): 34.

131. Garding Lui, *Inside Los Angeles Chinatown* (self-pub., 1948), 20.

Chapter 2

1. "Along El Camino Real" with Ed Ainsworth, *Los Angeles Times*, June 6, 1938.

2. "Los Angeles China City Given Oriental Film Set," *Los Angeles Times*, March 27, 1938.

3. "New Chinatown Previewed; Opens to Public Tonight," *Los Angeles Times*, June 7, 1938.

4. "New Chinatown Dedicated," *Los Angeles Times*, June 26, 1938.

5. Karen Shimakawa draws on the psychoanalytic theory of abjection to describe the place of Asian Americans in the nation. Abjection is defined by "an attempt to circumscribe and radically differentiate something that although deemed repulsively *other* is paradoxically, at some fundamental level, an undifferentiated part of the whole." In the same way that the abjection of Asian Americans played a role in defining Americanness, the abjection of Old Chinatown played a role in defining the city of Los Angeles throughout much of the exclusion era. See *National Abjection: The Asian American Body on Stage* (Durham, NC: Duke University Press, 2002), 2.

6. On the imagined geography of Chinatown see Kay J. Anderson, "The Idea of Chinatown: The Power of Place and Institutional Practice in the Making of a Racial Category," *Annals of the Association of American Geography* 77, no. 4 (1987): 581.

7. "Our New Chinatown," Peter SooHoo Collection, Series 1, Box 2—Ephemera, New Chinatown Los Angeles Collection, Huntington Library, San Marino, CA.

8. Lawrence Lan, "The Rise and Fall of China City, Race, Space, and Cultural Production in Los Angeles Chinatown, 1938–1948," *Amerasia Journal* 42, no. 2 (2016): 4.

9. I build on literary scholar David Fine's description of Los Angeles as "boosted into existence." *Imagining Los Angeles: A City in Fiction* (Reno: University of Nevada Press, 2004), 1–9.

10. Carey McWilliams, *Southern California: An Island on the Land* (Salt Lake City, UT: Peregrine Smith, 1946), 118.

11. Eric Avila, *Popular Culture in the Age of White Flight* (Berkeley: University of California Press, 2006), 23; Stephanie Lewthwaite, "Race, Place, and Ethnicity in the Progressive Era," in *A Companion to Los Angeles*, ed. William Deverell et al (Malden, MA: Wiley Blackwell, 2010), 40–55.

12. Robert Fogelson, *Fragmented Metropolis: Los Angeles, 1850–1930* (Berkeley: University of California Press, 1993), 248–249.

13. Fogelson, *Fragmented Metropolis*, 142–143.

14. Scott Kurashige, "Between White Spot and World City," in *A Companion to Los Angeles*, ed. William Deverel et al. (Malden, MA: Wiley Blackwell, 2010), 57.

15. "View Park Homes," *Los Angeles Examiner*, April 25, 1926.

16. Anthea Hartig, "Promotion and Popular Culture," in *A Companion to Los Angeles*, ed. William Deverell et al. (Malden, MA: Wiley Blackwell, 2010), 295.

17. Avila, *Popular Culture*, 22.

18. Mark Wild, *Street Meeting: Multiethnic Neighborhoods in Early Twentieth-Century Los Angeles* (Berkeley: University of California Press, 2008) 38–39.

19. Harry Ellington Brook, *Los Angeles, California: The City and County* (Los Angeles Chamber of Commerce, 1921), 26.

20. "Eagle Rock," *Los Angeles Times*, October 15, 1925.

21. As Richard Dyer has shown, representations of whiteness—as an imagined normative racial category—are deeply linked to heterosexuality. *White: Essays on Race and Culture* (New York: Routledge, 1997), 20–21.

22. Natalia Molina, *Fit to Be Citizens? Public Health and Race in Los Angeles, 1879–1939* (Berkeley: University of California Press, 2006), 6.

23. Molina, *Fit to Be Citizens*, 6–8. We might think of Los Angeles as being defined by what Wendy Cheng calls regional racial formation. *The Changs Next Door to the Diazes: Remapping Race in Suburban California* (Minneapolis: University of Minnesota Press, 2013), 10–11.

24. William Deverell, "Privileging the Mission over the Mexican: The Rise of Regional Identity in Southern California," in *Many Wests: Place, Culture and Regional Identity*, ed. David Wrobel and Michael Steiner (Lawrence: University Press of Kansas, 1997), 250.

25. McWilliams, *Southern California*, 43.

26. Stephanie Lethwaite, "Race, Place and Ethnicity in the Progressive Era," in *A Companion to Los Angeles*, ed. William Deverell et al. (Malden, MA: Wiley Blackwell, 2010), 43.

27. Lucie Cheng and Suellen Cheng, "Chinese Women of Los Angeles, A Social History" in *Linking Our Lives: Chinese American Women of Los Angeles*, ed. Chinese Historical Society of Southern California (CHSSC) (Los Angeles: CHSSC, 1984), 1.

28. Susie Ling, "Our Legacy," in *Bridging the Centuries: History of Chinese Americans in Southern California,* ed. Susie Ling (Los Angeles: CHSSC, 2001), 16.

29. Cesar Lopez, "Lost in Translation," *Southern California Quarterly* 94. no. 1 (Spring 2012): 25–90.

30. Scott Zesch, *The Chinatown War: Chinese Los Angeles and the Massacre of 1871* (New York: Oxford University Press, 2012).

31. Ng Poon Chew, "The Chinese in Los Angeles," *Land of Sunshine* 1, no. 5 (1894): 103–105.

32. CHSSC, *Bridging the Centuries: History of Chinese Americans in Southern California* (Los Angeles: East West Discovery Press, 2001).

33. Isabela Seong Leong Quintana, "Making Do: Making Home: Borders and the Worlds of Chinatown and Sonoratown in Early Twentieth Century Los Angeles," *Urban History* 41, no. 1. (2014): 48.

34. Linda Espana-Maram, *Creating Masculinity in Los Angeles's Little Manila: Working Class Filipinos and Popular Culture 1920s–1950s* (New York: Columbia University Press, 2006), 20.

35. In 1930 Lee Shippey mentioned "Filipinotown" once in his columns. He mentioned it again in 1932. See columns published on January 27, 1930, and April 2, 1932. The *Los Angeles Times* published "Cosmopolitan Los Angeles—Filipinos," on December 5, 1937. Such articles were exceptions. For the most part, the city's reporters did not imagine Filipinos living in a distinct Filipino neighborhood. White newspaper reporters often portrayed Filipinos as a threat to the city's White residents, but it was the city's dancehalls, not the Little Manila neighborhood, that White writers portrayed as a threat.

36. On Chinatown's vice industries, see Espana-Maram, *Creating Masculinity*, 51–72.

37. Roberta Greenberg, *Down by the Station*, Institute of Archeology, University of California, Los Angeles, 1996, 17.

38. Wild, *Street Meeting*, 23.

39. Quoted in Kit King Louis, "A Study of American-Born and American-Reared Chinese in Los Angeles" (master's thesis, University of Southern California, 1931).

40. Peter SooHoo Jr., interview by William Gow, April 9, 2007, Chinatown Remembered Project, CHSSC.

41. Gilbert Hom, "Chinese Angelenos Before World War II," in *Duty and Honor: A Tribute to Chinese American World War II Veterans of Southern California* ed. Marjorie Lee, 21–16 (Los Angeles: CHSSC, 1998), 22.

42. Don Dolan "Racial Minorities Survey: All Races," August 6, 1936, Racial Elements in Population, Federal Writers Project, File 96, Box 114, UCLA Library Special Collections, Los Angeles.

43. For descriptions of the land dispute and related issues, see Suellen Cheng and Munson Kwok, "Chinatown, the Golden Years: The Beginning" *Chinatown: The Golden Years* (Los Angeles Chinese Chamber of Commerce, 1988), 38-41; Kroznek and Greenwood, "Historical Background" in Roberta Greenwood, *Down By the Station: Los Angeles Chinatown, 1880–1933* (Los Angeles: University of California, Los Angeles, Institute of Archaeology, 1996), 35–37; Edwin Bingham, "The Saga of the Los Angeles Chinese (master's thesis, Occidental College, 1942), 136–140.

44. Marlyn Musicant, *Los Angeles Union Station* (Los Angeles: Getty Research Institute, 2014).

45. Historian Jeremiah Axelrod discusses the importance of Chinatown as a symbol in the Propositions 8 and 9 campaigns. He contends that the campaign for

Union Station was about promoting a vision of Los Angeles that was modern and progressive and that Chinatown was held up as its antithesis. He also argues that opponents "were mobilizing in order to suggest that previously (properly) hidden ethnic districts were now threatening to become prominent," and that the station project itself represented an "ambitious program of ethnic cleansing." While I agree with Axelrod on the symbolic importance of Chinatown to the campaign, I contend that Chinatown had a history of hypervisibility to both White visitors and residents of Los Angeles. After all, for most of the early twentieth century the city's papers and film industry actively highlighted yellow peril stereotypes of Chinatown in contrast to their suburban image of Los Angeles. Rather than seeing the 1926 vote as part of a program of ethnic cleansing, we should see it as a conflict over who would control Chinatown's popular image. See "Keep the 'L' Out of Los Angeles," *Journal of Urban History* 34, no. 1 (2007): 26.

46. Quoted in Axelrod, "Keep the 'L' Out," 26.

47. "People vs. Railroads, Union Station Issue," *Los Angeles Times*, April 20, 1926.

48. "Fabrication vs. Fact," *Los Angeles Times*, April 28, 1926.

49. Musicant, "In Search of a Site," 35.

50. J. M. Scanland, Quaint Chinese Quarter by Civic Center," *Los Angeles Times*, May 6 1926.

51. "Sledges Sound Old Chinatown's knell in Preparing Place for New Railway Terminal," *Los Angeles Times*, December 23, 1933; "Old Chinatown in Exodus as Wreckers Start Work," *Los Angeles Examiner*, December 23, 1933.

52. "Old Chinatown in Exodus."

53. On the SooHoo family background and Peter SooHoo's life as a young man, see Ella Yee Quan, "Pioneer Families Share Their History," *Chinatown: The Golden Years* (Los Angeles: Chinese Chamber of Commerce, 1988), 29–30; also see Eleanor SooHoo Yee, interview by William Gow, October 7, 2007, Chinatown Remembered Project, CHSSC.

54. In 1930, there were 74,954 Chinese in the US. Of these, 30,808, or 41.2 percent, were born in the United States and of these, 4,325 had US-born parents. Thus, we can say that around 5 percent in 1930 were third- or fourth-generation Americans. See Bureau of the Census, "Color or Race, Nativity, and Parentage," chap. 2 in *Fifteenth Census of the United States: 1930: Population, Volume II* (Washington DC: Government Printing Office, 1933), 34, 59. In Los Angeles in 1940, 2,540 of the city's 4,736 Chinese Americans were US-born, or 53.6%. See Bureau of the Census, *Sixteenth Census of the United States: 1940: Population: Characteristics of the Nonwhite Population by Race* (Washington, DC: United States Government Printing Office, 1943), 86.

55. Kit King Louis, "A Study of American-Born," 87.

56. Charlotte Brooks, *American Exodus: Second Generation Chinese Americans in China, 1901–1949* (Berkeley: University of California Press, 2019).

57. Peter SooHoo, interview by William C. Smith, August 7, 1925, Survey of Race Relations Collection, Box 37, Folder 442, Hoover Institution Archives, https://purl.stanford.edu/dv730sz7464

58. Y. C. Hong, CACA obituary for Peter SooHoo Sr., May 1945, Peter SooHoo Collection, Series 2, personal clippings, Huntington Library, San Marino, CA.

59. Xiaojian Zhao, *Remaking Chinese America* (New Brunswick, NJ: Rutgers University Press, 2002), 18.

60. On the president of the Chinese American Citizens Alliance, see Hong, CACA obituary for Peter SooHoo Sr. On the Chinese Militia, see Norine Dresser, "Chinatown Militia Units, 1942: Los Angeles and San Francisco," *Gum Saan Journal* 15, no. 2 (1992). On the Boy Scout troop leader, see "New Chinatown Scouts Hold First Meet at Their Log Cabin," *Chinese Press*, February 21, 1941. On voter registration, see "GOP Drive Opens Today," *Los Angeles Times*, July 16, 1934.

61. Department of Water and Power obituary, May 1945, Peter SooHoo Collection, Series 1, New Chinatown community clippings, Huntington Library, San Marino, CA.

62. On middlemen who negotiated between Chinese immigrants and Whites, see Lisa Rose Mar, *Brokering Belonging: Chinese in Canada's Exclusion Era, 1885–1945* (New York: Oxford University Press, 2010), 1–14.

63. Lee Shippey, "Lee Side o' LA," *Los Angeles Times*, August 24, 1936.

64. Wu Shan, "Merchandising Chinese Products on the Los Angeles Market," (master's thesis, University of Southern California, August 1934), 32.

65. See the following *Los Angeles Times* articles: "Spectacle Will Mark Passing of Chinatown," September 18, 1934; "Home for Oriental Village Planned," September 21, 1934; "Farewell Fete on Today," September 22, 1934; and "Ceremony Hails New Era in City Construction," September 23, 1934.

66. "Chinatown Will Stay Despite New Union Depot," *Los Angeles Daily News*, December 17, 1934.

67. "Chinatown and the Old Plaza," in *Hotel Greeters Guide and Hotel Directory of California*, 1934, 29–30, Peter SooHoo Collection, Box 10, Album 3, Huntington Library, San Marino, CA.

68. Bingham, "Saga of the Los Angeles Chinese," 144.

69. William Estrada, *The Los Angeles Plaza: Sacred and Contested Space* (Austin: University of Texas Press, 2008), 192–193.

70. Peter SooHoo, speech to the Los Angeles Chamber of Commerce, August 16, 1937, quoted in Bingham, "Saga of the Los Angeles Chinese," 141.

71. Wen-Hui Chung Chen, "Changing Socio-Culutral Patterns of the Chinese Community in Los Angeles," (Ph.D. diss., University of Southern California, 1952), 81–83.

72. Kim Fong Tom, "Participation of the Chinese in the Community Life of Los Angeles" (master's thesis, University of Southern California, 1944), 13.

73. "Chinese Quarter Launched Today," *Los Angeles Daily News*, August 16, 1937.

74. Cheng and Kwok, "Chinatown the Golden Years" of Los Angeles Chinatown: The Beginning," in *Los Angeles Chinatown: The Golden Years 1938–1988* (Los Angeles: Chinese Chamber of Commerce, 1988), 41.

75. Personal notes, Peter SooHoo Collection, Box 9, Folder 3, Huntington Library, San Marino, CA.

76. "Harry Carr Memorial Gate Featured in Community Project," *Los Angeles Times*, October 3, 1937.

77. "Chinese Quarter Launched Today," *Daily News*, August 16, 1937.

78. "Chinese Quarter Launched Today."

79. An undated draft of the association's statement exists in the SooHoo archive. Its wording is slightly different from that of the final version excerpted in the Los Angeles *Daily News*. See Walter Yip, Quon S. Doon, and Lee Wah Shew, "Los Angeles Chinatown Project Association Statement," August 16, 1937, Peter Soohoo Series 1, Huntington Library.

80. Speech to the Los Angeles Chamber of Commerce, August 16, 1937, Peter SooHoo Collection Box 3, Folder 5, Huntington Library, San Marino, CA.

81. Westwood Village is a Mediterranean-style shopping district planned by the Janss Investment Company. It opened in 1929 next to the UCLA campus. The district featured the Fox Westwood Theatre, Bullock's Westwood department store, and Ralph's grocery store. Like most of West Los Angeles during this period, Westwood Village used restrictive covenants to exclude Black owners and keep the area's business owners exclusively White. See Richard Rothstein, *The Color of Law: A Forgotten History of How Our Government Segregated America* (New York: Liveright Publishing, 2017), 81.

82. "Conflict of Views in New Plans," *Daily News*, August 16, 1937, Peter SooHoo Collection, Box 10, Album 3, Huntington Library, San Marino, CA.

83. Listing of firms and rents for new Chinatown circa 1938, Peter SooHoo Collection, Box 9, Folder 3, Tab 7, Huntington Library, San Marino, CA.

84. William Gow, "Building a Chinese Village in Los Angeles: Christine Sterling and the Residents of China City 1938–1948," *Gum Saan Journal* 32, no. 1 (2010): 39–53.

85. Camille Chan Wing, interview by William Gow, September 27, 2019.

86. Judy Tzu-Chun Wu, *Doctor Mom Chung of the Fair-Haired Bastards* (Berkeley: University of California Press, 2005), 34.

87. Dorothy Siu, interview by Jean Wong, November 21, 1979, Southern California Chinese American Oral History Project, CHSSC; Dr. Ruby Ling Louie,

interview by William Gow, March 28, 2008, Chinatown Remembered Project, CHSSC.

88. Jean Baudrillard, *Simulacra and Simulation* (Ann Arbor, MI: University of Michigan Press, 1981).

89. See Lan, "The Rise and Fall of China City," 2–21; Dr. Ruby Ling Louie, "Reliving China City," in *Bridging the Centuries: History of Chinese Americans in Southern California*, ed. Susie Ling (Los Angeles: Chinese Historical Society of Southern California, 2001), 39–43; Josi Ward, "Dreams of Oriental Romance: Reinventing Chinatown in 1930s Los Angeles," *Buildings & Landscapes: Journal of the Vernacular Architecture Forum* 20, no. 1 (Spring 2013): 19–42.

90. "Gala Fete to Open New L.A. Chinatown," *Los Angeles Herald and Express*, June 23, 1938.

91. Quoted in Charles K. Ferguson, "Political Problems and Activities of Oriental Residents in Los Angeles and Vicinity" (master's thesis, UCLA, 1942), 77.

92. Ferguson, "Oriental Residents in Los Angeles," 78.

93. "New Chinatown Has Tribute to Pioneers," *Los Angeles Daily News*, June 27, 1938.

94. New Chinatown opening speech, Peter SooHoo Collection, Box 3 Folder 5, Huntington Library, San Marino, CA.

95. Allen Mock, interview by Jean Wong, January 13, 1980, Southern California Chinese American Oral History Project, UCLA Library Special Collections, Los Angeles.

Chapter 3

1. Lee Shippey, "The Lee Side," *Los Angeles Times*, August 24, 1936.

2. MGM was not the first Hollywood studio to build a fake Chinese village in Chatsworth. A few years earlier, Paramount had constructed a smaller village in the same area for *Shanghai Express*. Hye Seung Chung, *Hollywood Diplomacy: Film Regulation, Foreign Relations & East Asian Representations* (New Brunswick, NJ: Rutgers, 2020), 36.

3. John R. Woolfenden, "Location Sets So Realistic Swallows Build Nests There," *Los Angeles Times*, June 7, 1936, and "Pearl Buck's 'Good Earth' in Celluloid Soil," *Christian Science Monitor*, March, 4 1937.

4. News reports gave different accounts of the number of extras employed on the film. One thousand is seen in numerous reports but is difficult to verify. "'Good Earth' Casting Stirs Feud Among Chinese Actors," *Los Angeles Times*, December 1, 1935.

5. "English Speaking Chinese Sought for 'The Good Earth,'" *China Press*, December 20, 1935. This is a Reuters wire service article that would have run in different forms in a variety of newspapers.

6. While Asian American Studies scholars have completed substantial research on Chinese American labor history, as well as biographical work on Asian American movie stars like Anna May Wong, Sessue Hayakaya, and Philip Ahn, they have largely overlooked the importance of extra work to Chinese Americans in Southern California. For Asian American movie stars, see Daisuke Miyao, *Sessue Hayakawa: Silent Cinema and Stardom* (Durham, NC: Duke University Press, 2007); Hye Seung Chung, *Hollywood Asian: Philip Ahn and the Politics of Cross Ethnic Performance* (Philadelphia: Temple University Press, 2006); Anthony Chan, *Perpetually Cool: The Many Lives of Anna May Wong, 1905–1961* (Lanham, MD: Rowman and Littlefield, 2003); Karen J. Leong, *China Mystique: Pearl S. Buck, Anna May Wong, Mayling Soong, and the Transformation of American Orientalism* (Berkeley: University of California Press, 2005), 57–105; Shirley Jennifer Lim, *Anna May Wong: Performing the Modern* (Philadelphia: Temple University Press, 2019).

7. Garding Liu, *Inside Los Angeles Chinatown* (self.-pub., 1948), 29.

8. Esther Lee Kim, *Made-Up Asian Americans: Yellowface during the Exclusion Era* (Ann Arbor: University of Michigan Press, 2022), 176.

9. Beginning in the 1990s, film scholars shifted the study of Hollywood stars away from textual readings of films and toward a more materially grounded methodology that examined acting as a form of labor. Building on the earlier work of Los Angeles labor historians, film studies helped facilitate this shift, which has produced several important studies of the historical and material conditions under which extras and bit players in classical Hollywood performed. See Danae Clark, "Acting in Hollywood's Best Interest: Representations of Actors' labor During the National Recovery Administration," *Journal of Film and Video* 42, no. 4 (Winter 1990): 3–19; *Negotiating Hollywood: The Cultural Politics of Actors Labor* (Minneapolis: University of Minnesota Press, 1995); Barry King, "Stardom as an Occupation, in *The Hollywood Film Industry: A Reader*, ed. Paul Kerr (London: Routledge, 1986), and "The Star and the Commodity: Notes towards a Performance Theory of Stardom," *Cultural Studies* 1, no. 2 (1987): 145–161. On labor historians' contributions to this literature, see Louis Perry and Richard Perry, *A History of the Los Angeles Labor Movement, 1911–1941* (Berkeley: University of California Press, 1963); Murray Ross, "Hollywood's Extras," in *The Movie in Our Midst: Documents in the Cultural History of Film in America*, ed. Gerald Mast (Chicago: University of Chicago Press, 1983); Sean Holmes, "The Hollywood Star System and the regulation of Actors' Labor, 1916–1934," *Film History* 12, no. 1 (2000): 97–114; Anthony Slide, *Hollywood Unknowns: A History of Bit Players, and Stand-Ins* (Jackson: University of Mississippi Press, 2012). Slide devotes one chapter to what he calls "ethnic extras," which has three pages on Chinese Americans (p. 192–195). Research has been done on extras from other racial and ethnic communities. See Charlene Regester, "African American Extras in Hollywood during the 1920s and 1930s," *Film History* 9, no. 1

(1997): 95–115; Nicolas G. Rosenthal, *Reimagining Indian Country: Native Migration & Identity in Twentieth Century Los Angeles* (Chapel Hill: University of North Carolina Press, 2012), 31–49.

10. On postwar engagement in Hollywood, see Jenny Cho, *Chinese in Hollywood* (Charleston, SC, Arcadia Press 2013), 55–75.

11. "How Famous Film Stars Have Been Discovered," *Los Angeles Times*, October 18, 1914.

12. Slide, *Hollywood Unknowns*, 21–23.

13. "Society Rules Among Extras," *Los Angeles Times*, January 1, 1922.

14. "How Famous Film Stars Have Been Discovered,"

15. Kevin Brownlow, *Behind the Mask of Innocence* (New York: Knopf, 1990), 332; Slide, *Hollywood Unknowns*, 193.

16. Graham Russel Hodges, *Anna May Wong: From Laundryman's Daughter to Hollywood Legend* (Hong Kong: Hong Kong University Press, 2012), 56.

17. "I am Growing More Chinese with Each Passing Year," *Los Angeles Times*, September 9, 1934.

18. One of the few exceptions to this coverage during the silent film era was the experience of Anna May Wong. Like so many White female stars, she was "discovered" in a crowd. In her own retelling, her discovery was not by a film director but by James Wang, the Chinese American labor recruiter.

19. As one example, see "How Film Stars Have Been Discovered."

20. Denise McKenna, "The Photoplay or the Pickaxe: Extras, Gender, and Labor in Early Hollywood," *Film History* 23, no. 1 (2011): 5–19.

21. McKenna cites figures from 1926 to 1941 showing that there were nearly twice as many men as women extras during this period. "Photoplay or Pickaxe," 5.

22. For a story of one male extra during the silent era, see Charlie Keil, "Leo Rosencrans, Movie-Struck Boy," *Film History Journal* 26, no. 2 (2014): 31–51.

23. Heidi Kenaga, "Making the 'Studio Girl': The Hollywood Studio Club and Industry Regulation of Female Labor," *Film History* 18, no. 2 (2006): 129–139.

24. McKenna, "Photo Play or Pickaxe," 6.

25. Kerry Seagrave, *Film Actors Organize: Union Formation Efforts in America, 1912–1937* (Jefferson, NC: McFarland & Company, 2009), 25.

26. Ross, "Hollywood's Extras," 223–228.

27. California Bureau of Labor Statistics, *Twenty Second Biennial Report of the Bureau of Labor Statistics of the State of California* (Sacramento: California State Printing Office, 1926), 149.

28. Seagrave, *Film Actors Organize*, 29.

29. California Bureau of Labor Statistics, *Twenty Second Biennial Report*, 149.

30. In 1927, Central Casting hired Charles Butler to recruit Black performers into a segregated division. Regester, "African American Extras in Hollywood," 95–115.

31. "Racial Caster Corner Types," *Variety*, March 8, 1932.

32. Surveying a group of 135 Americans in 1958 about their views on Asia, Harold Isaacs found that respondents identified the Japanese invasion of Manchuria as the event that most brought Asia to their attention. *Scratches on Our Minds*, 51.

33. "Warfare in Orient Brings Film Gold to Chinatown," *Los Angeles Times*, June 26, 1932.

34. "Los Angeles Wins Terminal Battle," *New York Times*, September 17, 1933.

35. "Station May Start Soon," *Los Angeles Times*, November 11, 1933.

36. "Wrecking Crews Begin Clearing Depot's Site," *Los Angeles Times*, December 23, 1933.

37. Walter Chung, interview by George Yee, January 20, 1980, Southern California Chinese American Oral History Project, Chinese Historical Society of Southern California (CHSSC.)

38. "Chinese Ask No Aid; They're Used to Depressions," *China Press*, April 22, 1933.

39. Heather R. Lee, "A Life Cooking for Others: The Work and Migration Experiences of a Chinese Restaurant Worker in New York City, 1920–1946," in *Eating Asian America: A Food Studies Reader*, ed. Robert Ji-Song Ku (New York: New York University Press, 2013), 62–63.

40. "Wages and Incomes of Farm Workers," *Monthly Labor Review* 49, no. 1 (1939): 60.

41. George Shaffer, "Movie Change Threatens Rule in Chinatown," *Chicago Tribune*, August 4, 1934.

42. "Wage Provisions for Extras Clarified," *Variety*, March 13, 1934; "Film Code Revamped," *Los Angeles Times*, October 1, 1933.

43. Major studios agreed to continue abiding by the NRA labor codes even after the NRA was found unconstitutional by the Supreme Court in 1935. See "Major Studios Continuing to Op. NRA Pro Tem Regardless," *Variety*, May 29, 1933.

44. Esther Lee Johnson, interview by William Gow, March 9, 2008, Chinatown Remembered Project, CHSSC.

45. Federal Writers Project of the Works Project Administration, *Los Angeles in the 1930s: The WPA Guide to the City of Angels* (Berkeley: University of California Press, 2011), 84.

46. Lilly Mu Lee, interview by Suellen Cheng, July 24, 1982, Southern California Chinese American Oral History Project, CHSSC.

47. "In Hollywood with Jimmy Fiddler," *Washington Post*, August 9, 1937.

48. "Hollywood's 'Fast Set' on the Tennis Courts," *Film Weekly*, December 5, 1931.

49. "The man who put ease in Chin-ese pictures for you. . . ." *Standard* 6, no.3 (July 1925), 137.

50. Swan Yee, interview by Suellen Cheng, June 23, 1983, Southern California Chinese American Oral History Project, UCLA Library Special Collections.

51. Jennie Lee Taylor, interview by Scott Chan, May 9, 2007, Chinatown Remembered Project, CHSSC.

52. Tyrus Wong, interview by Genie Moon, November 1, 2007, Chinatown Remembered Project, CHSSC.

53. While Gubbins, in the English-language press, claimed to be a White man, many of the Chinese Americans who worked for him were certain he was mixed-race and simply passing for White. See, for example, Eddie E. Lee, interview by Jean Wong, January 20, 1979, Southern California Chinese American Oral History Project, CHSSC; Tyrus Wong interview.

54. Sidney Skolsky, "Hollywood: Watching Them Make Pictures," *Washington Post*, December 18, 1935, 20.

55. "Mob Meets Chinese Film Star," *North China Herald and Supreme Court & Consular Gazette*, February 19, 1936; Lim, *Anna May Wong*, 153–180.

56. "English Speaking Chinese Sought for 'The Good Earth'" *China Press*, December 20, 1935. The story is dated November 30, even though it ran in December.

57. "Chinese Throngs in Rush to Get Film Work," *Los Angeles Times*, November 3, 1935.

58. "Casual Casting," *Variety*, December 11, 1935; "Chatter, Hollywood," *Variety*, April 22, 1936.

59. Chung, *Hollywood Asian*, 96.

60. Quoted in Chung, *Hollywood Diplomacy*, 46.

61. Eleanor Barnes, "China Peeved at Hollywood," *Los Angeles Daily News*, undated clipping, Peter SooHoo Collection, Box 3, Scrapbook 1, Huntington Library, San Marino, CA.

62. Barnes, "China Peeved at Hollywood."

63. Shaffer, "Movie Change Threatens Rule."

64. Shaffer, 11.

65. "Purely Chinese," *Variety*, April 3, 1934. Ironically, despite Kiang's support of Chee, *The Cat's Paw* still ran into issues with Chinese censors, in part because the censors were still incensed over *Welcome Danger*. Cheung, *Hollywood Diplomacy*, 33.

66. Edwin Bates, "Actions War on Who Is Who in Chinese Movies," *Illustrated Daily News*, undated clipping, Peter SooHoo Collection, Box 3 Scrapbook 1, Huntington Library, San Marino, CA.

67. Spencer Chan, interview by Suellen Chan, April 7, 1983, Southern California Chinese American Oral History Project, CHSSC.

68. "Dr. George Lew Chee," *Los Angeles Times*, March 8, 1935.

69. John Scott, "'Good Earth' Casting Stirs Feud among Chinese Actors," *Los Angeles Times*, December 1, 1935.

70. Scott, "'Good Earth' Casting."

71. "L.A. Chinatown 'Mayor' Probed on Film Extras," *Variety*, December 18, 1935.

72. Bessie Loo, interview by Emma Louie, May 6, 1981, Southern California Chinese American Oral History Project, CHSSC.

73. "Cueing the Chinese," *Variety*, December 25, 1935.

74. For a description of extra work on the set of the *Good Earth*, See Charles Leong, "Mandarins in Hollywood," in *Moving the Image: Independent Asian Pacific American Media Arts*, ed. Russell Leong (Los Angeles: UCLA Asian American Studies Center and Visual Communications, 1991).

75. Janette Roan, *Envisioning Asia: On Location, Travel and the Cinematic Geography of U.S. Orientalism* (Ann Arbor: University of Michigan Press, 2010), 113–156.

76. Edwin Shallert, "Eurasian Girl Attending U.S.C. Awarded Lotus Role in 'The Good Earth,'" *Los Angeles Times*, April 18, 1936; Douglas Churchill, "The snubbed scribes of Hollywood," *New York Times*, April 26, 1936.

77. Edwin Shallert, "Don Ameche, Newcomer from Radio, Will Play Alessandro Role in 'Ramona'" *Los Angeles Times*, April 16, 1936.

78. Edwin Schallert, "James Dunn Going to Sea in Classic Story," *Los Angeles Times*, June 3, 1936.

79. Schallert, "Important Picture Roles Await Return of Henry Wilcoxon from England," *Los Angeles Times*, December 11, 1935.

80. Churchill, "Snubbed Scribes of Hollywood."

81. "College Student Awarded Role in 'The Good Earth,'" *Los Angeles Times*, May 1, 1936.

Chapter 4

1. "Unique Display Planned for Film Opening," *Los Angeles Times*, January 20, 1937.

2. Edwin Schallert, "Display Will Be Held at the Carthay," *Los Angeles Times*, February 5, 1937; "'Good Earth' Premiere Dazzles Onlookers," *Los Angeles Times*, January 31, 1937.

3. "'Good Earth' Premiere."

4. "AFI Catalogue," available at http://www.afi.com/members/catalog/

5. "AFI catalogue," https://catalog.afi.com/Film/8507-THE-GOODEARTH.

6. Colleen Lye, *America's Asia: Racial Form and American Literature, 1893–1945* (Princeton, NJ: Princeton University Press, 2005), 204.

7. Harold Isaacs, *Scratches on the Mind: American Images of China and India* (New York: John Day Company, 1958), 156.

8. Schallert, "Display Will Be Held at the Carthay."

9. Kendall Read, "Students Will Visit Exhibit at Carthay," *Los Angeles Times*, March 12, 1937.

10. Isaacs, *Scratches on the Mind*, 156.

11. For an academic example, see David C. Oh, *Whitewashing and the Movies: Asian Erasure and Subjectivity in U.S. Film Culture* (New Brunswick, NJ: Rutgers University Press, 2022), 2–3. For a popular example, see Jenn Fang, "Yellowface, Whitewashing, and the History of White People Playing Asian characters," *Teen Vogue*, August 8, 2018.

12. Esther Lee Kim, *Made Up Asians: Yellowface During the Exclusion Era* (Ann Arbor: University of Michigan Press, 2022), 176.

13. Ella Shoat and Robert Stam, *Unthinking Eurocentrism: Multiculturalism and the Media* (London: Routledge, 1994), 190.

14. Kim argues that protests by Asian American actors over yellowface performance in Hollywood did not begin until the 1960s. *Made-Up Asians*, 184.

15. Cultural theorist Stuart Hall has described the field of popular culture as "a sort of constant battlefield." For Hall, popular culture is a site of "containment and resistance," where differing sections of society struggle to shape the social structures that define so much of our shared existence. According to Hall, a film or related piece of popular culture never has a single meaning to all people for all time. Instead, its cultural meaning is historically grounded and socially contested by differing groups in society over time. Building on Hall's understanding of popular culture, we cannot understand *The Good Earth* as having one fixed social meaning for all times and social groups. See "Notes on Deconstructing the Popular," in *People's History and Socialist Theory*, ed. Raphael Samuel (London: Routledge, 1981), 227–240.

16. John C. Oh considers *The Good Earth* an example of whitewashing, which he defines as "a symbolic intervention of Whiteness that erases Asian/American subjectivity by replacing and displacing it with White subjectivity, thus rendering Asian/Americans as objects in their own stories." See *Whitewashing and the Movies*, 3.

17. On oppositional spectatorship, see bell hooks, "The Oppositional Gaze: Black Female Spectators," in *Black Looks: Race and Representations* (Boston: South End Press, 1992).

18. As scholars like Kim K. Fahlstedt have shown, Chinese Americans have had a long history of movie viewing stretching back to the early silent era of cinema. Fahlstedt coins the phrase "post-quake Chinatown film culture" to encompass the film exhibition and audience experiences of people in San Francisco Chinatown directly after the 1906 earthquake and fire. *Chinatown Film Culture: The Appearance of Cinema in San Francisco's Chinese Neighborhood* (New Brunswick, NJ: Rutgers University Press, 2020), 3–4.

19. For a theoretical discussion of the line between adoration and revulsion that surrounds Asian Americans in US popular culture, see Leslie Bow, *Racist Love: Asian Abstraction and the Pleasure of Fantasy* (Durham, NC: Duke University Press, 2022), 5–7.

20. Erika Lee, *At America's Gates: Chinese Immigration during the Exclusion Era, 1882–1943* (Chapel Hill, NC: University of North Carolina Press, 2003), 1–19.

21. Daisuke Miyao, *Sessue Hayakawa: Silent Cinema and Transnational Stardom* (Durham, NC: Duke University Press, 2007), 21–49.

22. Denise Khor, *Transpacific Convergences: Race Migration, and Japanese American Film Culture before World War II* (Chapel Hill, NC: University of North Carolina Press, 2022), 25.

23. On yellow peril films during this period, see Jun Xing, *Asian Americans Through the Lens: History, Representations, and Identities* (Walnut Creek, CA: Alta Mira, 1998), 55–58.

24. Ruth Myer, *Serial Fu Manchu: The Chinese Supervillain and the Spread of Yellow Peril Ideology* (Philadelphia: Temple University Press, 2014), 9.

25. Robert Lee, *Orientals: Asian Americans in Popular Culture* (Philadelphia: Temple University Press, 1999), 114; Franklin Wong, "On Visual Media Racism," (Ph.D. diss., University of Denver Press, 1977), 96–102.

26. Eugene Franklin Wong, "The Early Years: Asians in the American Films Prior to World War II," in *Screening Asian Americans*, ed. Peter X Feng (New Brunswick, NJ: Rutgers University Press, 2002), 56.

27. Wu Fang appears to have been named after a Chinese diplomat to Washington during this period, whose name was Wu Ting Fang. Raymond William Stedman, *The Serials; Suspense and Drama by Installment* (Norman: University of Oklahoma Press, 1971), 39.

28. Wong, "The Early Years," 56.

29. Philippa Gates, *Criminalization/Assimilation: Chinese/Americans and Chinatowns in Classical Hollywood Film* (New Brunswick, NJ: Rutgers University Press, 2019), 53–102.

30. "The Highbinders," *Reel Life*, April 03, 1915.

31. "The Flower of Doom," *Moving Picture Weekly*, April 4, 1916.

32. Gina Marchetti, *Romance and the Yellow Peril: Race, Sex, and Discursive Strategies in Hollywood Fiction* (Berkeley: University of California Press, 1993), 4.

33. Marchetti, 28.

34. Mary Ting Li Lui, *The Chinatown Trunk Mystery: Murder, Miscegenation and Other Dangerous Encounters in Turn-of-the-Century New York City* (Princeton, NJ: Princeton University Press, 2007), 1–16.

35. "Chinese Protest," *The Moving Picture World*, April 4, 1911, 705.

36. "Our Chinese Movie Actors," *Picture Play*, September 1926, 83–85.

37. "Our Chinese Movie Actors."

38. Kevin Brownlowe, *Behind the Mask of Innocence* (New York: Knopf, 1990), 330.

39. "Film Folk Bombarded by Chinese," *Los Angeles Times*, December 16, 1923.

40. "Film Folk Bombarded."

41. Brownlowe, *Behind the Mask of Innocence*, 330.

42. "Chinese Complications," *Motion Picture News*, September 9, 1926, 1236.

43. "It was Lloyd's First Talkie and Last Silent," *Los Angeles Times*, August 13, 2008.

44. Chung, *Hollywood Diplomacy*, 31.

45. "'Welcome Danger,' Motion Film Case Adjourned Again," *China Press*, March 22, 1930.

46. Yiman Wang, "'The Crisscrossed Stare,' Protest and Propaganda in China's Not-So-Silent Era," in *Silent Cinema and the Politics of Space*, ed. Jennifer M. Bean, Laura Horak, and Anupama Kapse (Bloomington: Indiana University Press, 2014), 192.

47. Wang, "The Crisscrossed Stare," 192.

48. "Harold Lloyd Apologizes for 'Welcome Danger,'" *China Press*, August 1, 1930.

49. Wang, "Crisscossed Stare," 192.

50. Xhiwei Xiao, "Nationalism, Orientalism, and an Unequal Treatise of Ethnography: The Making of *The Good Earth*," in *The Chinese in America: A History from Gold Mountain to the New Millennium*, ed. Susie Lan Cassel (New York: AltaMira: 2002), 278–279.

51. Cheung, *Hollywood Diplomacy*, 25–26.

52. Eric Smoodin, *Regarding Frank Capra: Audience, Celebrity, and American Film, 1930–1960* (Durham, NC: Duke University Press, 2004), 57.

53. Smoodin, 57.

54. Smoodin, 58.

55. Chung, *Hollywood Diplomacy*, 29.

56. Chung, 39.

57. Xiao, "Nationalism, Orientalism, and an Unequal Treatise," 276

58. Xiao, 278–279.

59. "Chinese language May Be Used in 'Good Earth,'" *Los Angeles Times*, November 23, 1933.

60. The 1933 film was entitled *Eskimo*. On Shallert's reportage, see "Chinese language May Be Used," 11. On the film, see Angela Aleiss, *Making the White Man's Indian: Native Americans and Hollywood Movies* (Westport, CT: Greenwood Publishing, 2005), 42–45.

61. The film co-starred an Asian American actress identified at the time of the film's release as Lotus. The actress would later go by the screen name Lotus Long. According to at least one Alaska Native who saw the film, Lotus Long's attempts to speak Inupiaq were unintelligible. Alan Gevison, *Within Our Gates: Ethnicity in American Feature Films, 1911–1960* (Berkeley: University of California Press, 1997), 317. On Lotus Long's inability to speak Inupiaq see Margaret Blackman, *Sadie Brower Neakok: An Inupiaq Woman* (Seattle: University of Washington Press, 1989), 92.

62. "'Olan,' 'Wang Lung' Sought Here for 'Good Earth' Film," *China Press*, December 28, 1934.

63. "Work on the Film of the 'Good Earth' at a Standstill," *China Press*, August 3, 1935.

64. On General Tu's arrival, see "Parsian Locale for Tuneful Production," *Los Angeles Times*, December 20, 1934; "Chinese General a Film Censor," *New York Times*, June 3, 1935. On White actors, see "Asther Back at M-G for 'Good Earth Test,'" *Variety*, January 15, 1934.

65. "'The Life of John Paul Jones' Will Be Produced by Darryl F. Zanuck," *Los Angeles Times*, October 22, 1935.

66. "'East is West' Cast Is All Complete," *Sacramento Union*, September 24, 1922.

67. In her discussion of *The Good Earth*, Janette Roan demonstrates the ways in which the producers of the film were concerned first and foremost with selling the film's authenticity. *Envisioning Asia: On Location, Travel and the Cinematic Geography of U.S. Orientalism* (Ann Arbor: University of Michigan Press, 2010).

68. "Star Acquires Heavy Tan for 'Good Earth' Role," *Los Angeles Times* March 6, 1936.

69. "Muni on Treadmill," *Los Angeles Times*, June 22, 1936 (1923–current file).

70. Philip Sheuer, "A Town Called Hollywood," *Los Angeles Times*, July 5, 1936.

71. John Woolfenden, "Location Sets So Realistic Swallows Build Nests There: Crops Grow, Grain Ripens in Transplanted Chinese Villages as Cameras Continue to Roll on '*The Good Earth*.'" *Los Angeles Times*, June 7, 1936.

72. Janette Roan, *Envisioning Asia*, 113–156.

73. *Quoted in "Amusements in Heron," Evening Huronite* [South Dakota], October 1, 1937.

74. Quoted in "Amusements in Heron."

75. Philip K. Scheuer, "'The Good Earth' Truly Great Film Drama," *Los Angeles Times*, July 29, 1937, 8.

76. "Frank Nugent, "The 1937 Cinema Achieves a Flying Start with 'The Good Earth' Leading," *New York Times*, February 7, 1937, 165.

77. Scheuer, "'The Good Earth,'" July 29, 1937, 8.

78. Marchetti, *Romance and the Yellow Peril, 10–45*; Nayan Shah, *Contagious Divides: Epidemics and Race in San Francisco Chinatown* (Berkeley: University of California Press, 2001).

79. Tom McDannold, "The Development of Los Angeles Chinatown: 1850–1970" (master's thesis: California State University, Northridge, 1973), 109.

80. While it is easy to conceive of citizenship as only applying to legal rights, scholars have demonstrated the extent to which the rights and privileges of citizenship are also connected to culture. Anthropologist Renato Resaldo, in *Cultural Citizenship in Island Southeast Asia: Nation and Belonging in the Hinterlands* (Berkeley: University of California Press, 2003), asserts the importance of what he calls "cultural citizenship," which demonstrates the extent to which promoting cultural diversity and allowing diverse cultural expressions is an important aspect of maintaining a multiracial democracy. As Lori Kido Lopez, in *Asian American Media Activism Fighting for Cultural Citizenship* (New York: New York University Press, 2016), reminds us, "people can be excluded from first class citizenship for having non-normative cultural practices" (p. 12–13). Lopez's work shows how cultural citizenship is often tied to media practices. Lopez writes: "In order for individuals to feel like their cultural practices are accepted and that people like them are included within the nation, they must see themselves and their specific communities represented within the media." Chinese American youth reframed *The Good Earth* in ways that allowed them to see the film as a representation of their community, thus claiming US cultural citizenship.

81. K. Scott Wong, *Americans First: Chinese Americans and the Second World War* (Cambridge, MA: Harvard University Press 2005), 24–26.

82. "Ching Wah Lee," *Los Angeles Times*, April 18, 1937.

83. Wong, *Americans First*, 25.

84. Judy Yung, *Unbound Feet: A Social History of Chinese Women in San Francisco,* (Berkeley: University of California Press, 1995), 303.

85. Wong, *Americans First*, 221, n.36.

86. "'Good Earth' Started," *Chinese Digest*, March 27, 1936.

87. All quotes are from "Hollywood Review: "Who's Who of the Chinese in The Good Earth," *Chinese Digest*, March 1937.

88. Lim P. Lee, "Sociological Data: An Inside View of a Motion Picture studio," *Chinese Digest*, March 1937.

89. Lee, "Sociological Data."

90. Ida Lee, interview by Beverly Chan, July 29, 1980, Southern California Chinese American Oral History Project, Chinese Historical Society of Southern California (CHSSC).

91. Margaret K. Lee, interview by Beverly Chan, April 29, 1980, Chinese American Oral History.

92. Alice Hum, interview by Beverley Chan, July 28, 1980. Chinese American Oral History.

93. Frank York Lee, interview by Bernice Sam, July 7, 1980, Chinese American Oral History.

94. Bessie Loo, interview by Jean Wong, Beverly Chan, and Emma Louie, February 21, 1979, and January 10, 1980, Chinese American Oral History.

95. Keye Luke, interview by Jean Wong, February 23, 1979, Chinese American Oral History.

96. Celine Parrenas Shimizu, *The Hypersexuality of Race: Performing Asian/American Women on Screen and Scene* (Durham, NC: Duke University Press, 2007), 59.

97. General Tu, who advised on *The Good Earth*, claimed that the perception of Wong in China was "very bad." See Leong, *China Mystique*, 75.

98. Judy Chu, "Anna May Wong," in *Counterpoint: Perspectives on Asian America*, ed. Emma Gee et al. (Los Angeles: Asian American Studies Center, 1976); Rene Tajima, "Lotus Blossoms Don't Bleed: Images of Asian Women," in *Making Waves: An Anthology of Writings by and about Asian American Women*, ed. Asian Women United (Boston: Beacon Press, 1989), 308–317; Cynthia W. Liu, "When Dragon Ladies Die Do They Come Back as Butterflies? Re-imagining Anna May Wong," in *CounterVisions: Asian American Film Criticism*, ed. Darrell Y. Hamamoto and Sandra Liu (Philadelphia: Temple University Press, 2000); Anthony Chan, *Perpetually Cool: The Many Lives of Anna May Wong, 1905–1961* (Lanham, MD: Rowman and Littlefield, 2003); Leong, *China Mystique*, 57–105; and Shirley Jennifer Lim, *Anna May Wong: Performing the Modern* (Philadelphia: Temple University Press, 2019).

99. Herbert Leong, interview by Jean Wong, December 22, 1980, Chinese American Oral History.

100. Ching Wah Lee, interview by Frank China and Philip Choy, July 30, 1970, Asian American Resources Project, Bancroft Library, University of California, Los Angeles.

101. Jennie Lee Taylor, interview by Scott Chan, May 9, 2007, Chinatown Remembered.

Chapter 5

1. On the history of Chinese farmworkers, see Sucheng Chan, *This Bittersweet Soil: The Chinese in California Agriculture, 1860–1910* (Berkeley: University of California Press, 1986).

2. Bessie Loo, interview by Jean Wong, March 21, 1979, Southern California Chinese American Oral History Project, Chinese Historical Society of Southern California (CHSSC).

3. Bessie Loo, interview.

4. Bessie Loo, interview.

5. Bessie Loo, interview by Frank Chin, May 4, 1970, Combined Asian American Resources Project (CAARP), Department of Special Collection, University of California, Santa Barbara.

6. Patrick McNulty, "Actress' Odd Career: Locating Orientals," *Los Angeles Times*, August 31, 1958.

7. The other two members of this triumvirate were Keye Luke and Philip Ahn. See Hye Seung Chung, *Hollywood Asian: Philip Ahn and the Politics of Cro-Ethnic Performance* (Philadelphia: Temple University Press, 2006), 45.

8. This is my count from the American Film Institute Catalog entry on *The Purple Heart*. Loo landed the role of General Mitsubi in the film, and in the process went from unknown background player to recognizable character actor. In addition to Loo, Beal Wong appeared as Toma Nogato, Lee Tung-Foo and Moy Ming as Japanese judges, and James Leong, Victor Wong, and Eddie Lee as Japanese army aides. See American Film Institute, "The Purple Heart," *AFI Catalog*, http://www.afi.com/members/catalog

9. In analyzing Hollywood's representation of Japanese characters on screen, it is important to remember Karla Rae Fuller's assertion: "The structure of this Oriental advisory was neither simplistic nor fixed, as the figure of the Japanese enemy shifted and adjusted overt the course of the war years (1941–1945)." *Hollywood Goes Oriental: CaucAsian Performance in American Film* (Detroit, MI: Wayne State University Press, 2010), 124.

10. Benson Fong, interview by Frank Chin, May 9, 1970, CAARP, Department of Special Research Collections, University of California, Santa Barbara.

11. Bessie Loo, Interview, American Oral History. Note that there is a discrepancy in the historical record as to when the Loos moved from San Francisco to LA. One article in the Richard Loo biography file at the Margaret Herrick Library says that the couple moved in 1929. This is refuted by the 1930 census manuscript, which show the Loo's living in San Francisco, and by information from this interview. See 1930 Federal Census.

12. "Los Angeles Chinese Twins Proficient in Use of Slang," *Los Angeles Times*, February 27, 1937.

13. Bessie Loo, interview, Chinese Oral History.

14. Burt A. Folkart, "Richard Loo, War Film Villain Dies," *Los Angeles Times*, November 22, 1983.

15. Shirley Lim, *Anna May Wong: Performing the Modern* (Philadelphia: Temple University Press, 2019), 20–26.

16. "Films in Review," April 1962, Richard Loo biography file, Margaret Herrick Library, Beverly Hills, CA.

17. "Biography of Richard Loo," November 22, 1943, Richard Loo Biography File, Margaret Herrick Library.

18. "Richard Loo, Film Villain, Dies."

19. "Richard Loo, Actor 5 Decades," *New York Times*, November 22, 1983; "Biography of Richard Loo"; *Los Angeles Examiner*, May 7–13, 1967, Richard Loo biography file, Margaret Herrick Library.

20. Mabel Sam Lee, "The Recreational Interests and Participation of a Selected Group of Chinese Boys and Girls in Los Angeles, California" (master's thesis, University of Southern California, 1936), 44–46.

21. Bessie Loo, interview, Chinese American Oral History.

22. Tyrus Wong, interview by Genie Moon, November 1, 2007, Chinatown Remembered Project, CHSSC.

23. Jack Ong, "From Hanford to Hollywood: Remembering Bessie Loo," *Gum Saan Journal* 30, no 1. (2007): 49.

24. Victor Sen Yung, interview by Frank Chin, April 18, 1971, CAARP, Department of Special Research Collections, University of California, Santa Barbara.

25. Victor Sen Yung, interview.

26. Bessie Loo, interview, Chinese American Oral History.

27. Bessie Loo speaking at the general meeting of CHSSC, May 6, 1981.

28. Quoted in Ong, "From Hanford to Hollywood," 50.

29. On Richard Loo's films see American Film Institute, *AFI Catalog.*

30. Bernice Louie, "Yellow Jacket Well played," *Chinese Digest*, 1938, 18.

31. "'Yellow Jacket' Staged at SC," Los Angeles *Daily News*, November 14, 1938.

32. Bessie Loo, interview.

33. On the Loo family home, see Bessie Loo, interview ; see also 1940 Census manuscript.

34. WPA Household Census Cards and Employee Records, 1939, WPA-C-LACity-1591–004, University of Southern California.

35. Tabulation from 1920 US Census manuscripts.

36. *Revisiting East Adams*, dir. Jenny Cho (2004); Gilbert Hom, "Chinese Angelenos Before World War II," in *Duty and Honor*,21–16.

37. See Garding Lui, *Los Angeles Chinese Telephone Guide* (Los Angeles: self-pub., 1948), 28–34.

38. Richard Chee, interview by William Gow, October 5, 2008, Chinatown Remembered.

39. All information about the block is from the 1940 US Census, California, Los Angeles, District 60–813.

40. Hom, "Chinese Angelinos," 22.

41. George and Elsie Yee, "The Chinese and the Los Angeles Produce Market, *Gum Saan Journal* 9, no. 1 (1986), 4–17.

42. Garding Lui, *Inside Los Angeles Chinatown* (Los Angeles: 1948), 114–115.

43. Valerie Matsumoto, *City Girls: The Nisei Social World in Los Angeles, 1920–1950* (New York: Oxford University Press, 2014), 42.

44. Dorothy Hom, interview by William Gow, September 15, 2007, Chinatown Remembered.

45. Charlie Quon, interview by Nancy Thai, April 22, 2007, Chinatown Remembered.

46. Ben Fong, interview by Annie Luong, May 25 2008, Chinatown Remembered.

47. Charlie Quon, interview by Nancy Thai, May 19, 2007, Chinatown Remembered.

48. Charlie Quon, interview.

49. William Gow, "I am Chinese: The Politics of Chinese American Lapel Buttons in Los Angeles During World War II," *Western Historical Quarterly* 53, no. 1 (Spring 2022): 47–75.

50. Dorothy Hom, interview, Chinatown Remembered.

51. Charlie Quon, interview, Chinatown Remembered.

52. 1940 US Census manuscript.

53. Marjorie Lee, "On the Home Front: Curtis-Wright Technical Institute and an Introduction to the Chinatown Militia Unit," in *Duty and Honor*,37–38. Norrine Dresser, "Chinatown Militia Units—1942 Los Angeles and San Francisco," *Gum Saan Journal* 15, no. 2 (December 1992): 17.

54. Lee, "On the Home Front," 37–38.

55. "California Chinese Reserves Put in Day of Training," *Los Angeles Times*, April 20, 1942. Stanley Mu, interview with Mabel Kong, November 3, 2007, Chinatown Remembered.

56. Dresser, "Chinatown Militia Units," 20.

57. Lloyd Shearer, "Hollywood Comes to Bessie Loo for Orientals, *Independent Press-Telegram*, January 15, 1961, 78.

58. Bessie Loo, interview.

59. Arthur Dong, *Hollywood Chinese: The Chinese in American Feature Films* (Los Angeles: Angel City Press, 2019), 134.

60. Marshall Berges, "Gloria and Benson Fong, Home Q&A" *Los Angeles Times*, May 7, 1978.

61. Berges, "Gloria and Benson Fong.

62. "Joseph Kim" in *The Motion Picture Encyclopedia 1950 Edition* (Hollywood: Hollywood Reporter Press, 1950), 98.

63. Rosalind Shaffer, "Japanese Roles Go Hard with Hollywood Villains," *Rushville [Indiana] Republican*, August 3, 1945.

64. Chung, *Hollywood Asian*, 87–88.

65. Chung, 101.

66. Quoted in Chung, *Hollywood Diplomacy*, 87.

67. Chung, 86–88.

68. John Dower, *War Without Mercy: Race and Power in the Pacific War* (New York: Norton, 1986).

69. "'Wake Island' Colorado," *Los Angeles Times*, August 2, 1942.

70. "Biography of Richard Loo."

71. These roles would be mentioned in the lead of his obituary. See "Richard Loo, Actor 5 Decades.

72. Paolo E. Coletta, "Launching the Doolittle Raid on Japan," April 18, 1942, *Pacific Historical Review* 62, no. 1 (February 1993): 73–86.

73. Chung, *Hollywood Diplomacy*, 71–72.

74. Hedda Hopper, "Looking at Hollywood," *Los Angeles Times*, February 25, 1944.

75. The March 7, 1944, editorial was reprinted as a full-page advertisement in *Hollywood Reporter*, March 7, 1944.

76. Richard Loo is identified as "the Chinese actor" in an article about his role as Saburo Kurusu. See "Wake Island Colorado": "Chinese cast as Japanese in the film, leave no evil, no infamy, unexposed, but their portrayal is subtle and memorable." See "Purple Heart Praised for Relentless Aspects," *Los Angeles Times* March 7, 1944; in one of her weekly columns, Hedda Hopper explains that all "Chinese acting talent" are wanted to "play [Japanese] since no [Japanese] are around." *Los Angeles Times*, January 3, 1943.

77. In her study of the performance of Philip Ahn, film scholar Hye Seung Chung presents a theory of ethnic masquerade to explain the way in which audiences viewed Ahn in his non-Korean roles in the period between the 1930s and 1950s. Chung asserts that in many roles during this period Ahn passed as a non-Korean, which called for Ahn, the actor passing as a non-Korean, the duped the mainstream viewers who do not recognize that Ahn is passing, and the bilingual bicultural viewers who see that Ahn is in fact Korean and not the ethnicity he claims to be passing for. By explicitly identifying Richard Loo and other Chinese American performers as Chinese, the press kept them from engaging in any sort of ethnic masquerade.

78. Here it might be useful to think about the comparison that Michael Fried draws between "absorption" and "theatricality." In his discussion of eighteenth-century French painting, Fried discusses those paintings that "absorb" the observer by drawing them into the work of art and allowing them to forget time and place. In contrast, he discusses works that foreground their theatricality. In paintings such as portraiture from the period, "the basic action depicted . . . is the sitter's presentation of himself or herself to behold." In these paintings, the observer is not drawn into the art. Instead, the observer remains constantly aware of the presence of the artistic

subject, thus highlighting the "inherent theatricality of the genre." Fried argues that this theatricality—calling attention to the subject of the painting—contributed to critiques of these works. See *Absorption and Theatricality, Painting and Beholder in the Age of Diderot* (Chicago: University of Chicago Press, 1980), 108–109.

79. Cavett discusses his Richard Loo impersonation and performs an excerpt on *Gilbert Gottfried's Amazing Colossal Podcast*, episode 299, February 17, 2020.

80. Benson Fong, interview.

81. Eiichi Miyagishima, interview, May 1994, Terminal Island Life History Project, Online Archive of California, Japanese American National Museum.

Chapter 6

1. *Federation News* 1, no. 8 (November 1938), David and Dora SooHoo Collection, Chinese American Museum, University of California, Los Angeles; "Chinese Plan Celebration of Eighth Moon Festival," *Los Angeles Times*, October 5, 1938.

2. "Chinese Hold Moon Festival," *Los Angeles Times,* October 9, 1938; see also *Federation News.*

3. Marjorie Lee dates the founding of the Mei Wah Club to January 5, 1931, without attribution, in "Building Community," in *Linking Our Lives: Chinese American Women of Los Angeles* (Chinese Historical Society of Southern California, 1984), 107. In contrast, club sponsor Maye Wong recalls the founding as some time in 1932. See Wong, interview by Jean Wong and Emma Louie, May 8, 1979, Southern California Chinese American Oral History Project, Chinese Historical Society of Southern California (CHSSC).

4. Lee, "Building Community," 97.

5. Him Mark Lai, "Roles Played by Chinese in America during China's Resistance to Japanese Aggression and during World War II," *Chinese America: History and Perspective* (1997): 75–128.

6. K. Scott Wong, *Americans First: Chinese Americans and the Second World War* (Cambridge, MA: Harvard University Press, 2005), 42.

7. "Sledges Sound Old Chinatown's knell in Preparing Place for New Railway Terminal," *Los Angeles Times*, December 23, 1933.

8. Him Mark Lai, "The Historical Development of the Chinese Consolidated Benevolent Association/Higuan System," *Chinese America: History and Perspective* (1987): 24–25. Throughout the nineteenth century, the CCBA hired white lawyers and provided financial backing for legal challenges to anti-Chinese legislation like the exclusion act. See Peter Kwong and Dušanka Miščević, *Chinese America: The Untold Story of America's Oldest New Community* (New York: New Press, 2007), 111, 125.

9. Lai, "Chinese Consolidated Benevolent Association," 27, 39.

10. Judy Yung, *Unbound Feet: A Social History of Chinese Women in Los Angeles* (Berkeley: University of California Press, 1995), 225-227; Lai, "Roles Played by Chinese," 78, 89–90.

11. Lai, 89.

12. Kim Fong Tom, "Participation of the Chinese in the Community Life of Los Angeles" (master's thesis: University of Southern California, 1944), 70; *Federation News*.

13. Chinese Patriotic Society, "Chinese Appeal to Americans," Special Collections, Oviatt Library, California State University, Northridge.

14. Wen Hui Chen, "Changing Socio-Cultural Patterns of the Chinese Community in Los Angeles and the Vicinity" (Ph.D. diss., University of Southern California, 1952), 243–44; Tom, "Participation of the Chinese," 71.

15. Lai, "Roles Played by Chinese," 93.

16. Dick Tom recalled founding a group to raise funds for China within the Los Angeles CCBA with the help of Thomas Wong and other CCBA officers. It is likely that this group was the Chinese Patriotic Society. Dick Tom, interview by Beverly Chan, February 13, 1980, Chinese American Oral History.

17. Billy Lew, interview with Beverly Chan and Suellen Cheng, October 19, 1979, Chinese American Oral History, CHSSC.

18. Lim Suey Chong was president of the CCBA in 1938 but not necessarily the organization's most powerful member. The presidency was a role that many leaders avoided, and Chinese brokers like Thomas Wong, Dick Tom, and Peter SooHoo probably had more influence over China war relief fundraisers. *Federation News*; Tom, "Participation of the Chinese," 52.

19. "Chinatown Throng Aids War Refugees," *New York Times*, June 18, 1938.

20. "1,000,000 to Attend Chinese Aid Fetes," *New York Times*, June 14, 1938.

21. Karen Leong and Judy Wu, "Filling the Rice Bowls of China: Staging Humanitarian Relief during the Sino-Japanese War," in *Chinese Americans and the Politics of Race and Culture*, ed. Sucheng Chan and Madeline Hsu (Philadelphia: Temple University Press, 2008), 136.

22. Executive Committee meeting minutes, December 17, 1940, p. 3, box 95, American Bureau for Medical Aid in China collection, Columbia University Rare Book Library.

23. *Chinese Digest*, July 1938.

24. "Nation to Rally Tomorrow to Aid Civilians In China," *Los Angeles Times*, June 16, 1938; "Miss Model Los Angeles Sought for China Aid Fete," *Los Angeles Times*, June 12, 1938; "Rice Bowl Beauty Qualifications Given," *Los Angeles Times*, June 7, 1938.

25. "Miss Model Los Angeles Sought."

26. Mabel Sam Lee, "The Recreational Interests and Participation of a Select Group of Chinese Boys and Girls in Los Angeles, California," (master's thesis, University of Southern California, 1939), 39–48. On Chinese American youth participation in sports during this period, see Kathleen Yep, *Outside the Pain: When Basketball Ruled the Chinese Playground* (Philadelphia: Temple University Press, 2009).

27. Kit King Louis, "A study of American-born and American-reared Chinese in Los Angeles" (master's thesis, University of California, 1931), 73–94.

28. Barbara Quon, "By Barbara Quon," *Los Angeles Times*, February 13, 1938.

29. *Chinese Digest*, December 1937.

30. Lee, *Linking Our Lives*, 96.

31. "The Chinatown Crier," *Chinese Digest*, March 1938. Ethnic Studies Library, University of California, Berkeley.

32. On the relationship to the Chinese Patriotic Society, see Marshall Hoo, "In Which Federation Is Believed," *Federation News* 1 no. 1 (April 1938), folder 14, box EO50, Y. C. Hong Collection, Huntington Library; on the number of clubs in the federation see *Chinese Digest*, April 1938.

33. *Federation News* 1, no.4 (August 1938)., Billy Lew interview, SCCAOHP, Chinese American Museum.

34. Quoted in *Chinese Digest* 4, no. 4 (August 1938), 2.

35. *Federation News* (April 1938), n,p.

36. Marshall Hoo, interview by Beverly Chan, May 24, 1980, Chinese American Oral History.

37. Marshall Hoo, interview.

38. *Federation News* (April 1938): n.p.

39. Tom, "The Participation of the Chinese," 56. Chen, "Chinese Community in Los Angeles," 235.

40. Chen, "Chinese Community in Los Angeles," 235–236.

41. Gilbert Leung mentions that a younger group was responsible for the 1938 Moon Festival; interview, Emma Louie, March 27, 1979, Southern California Chinese American Oral History Project, CHSSC; the *Federation News* also mentions many of the duties that various youth groups performed at the festival. *Federation News* 1, no. 8 (November 1938), Chinese American Museum.

42. *China Nite Souvenir Program and Directory*, Chinese American Museum.

43. "New Chinatown Opening a Grand Success," and "China Nite," *Federation News* 4, no. 4 (July 1938): n.p, David and Dora SooHoo Collection, Chinese American Museum.

44. *China Nite Souvenir Program*.

45. "Chinese Festival of Moon," *Los Angeles Daily News*, October 7, 1938; "Moon Festival to Begin Tonight," *Los Angeles Daily News*, October 8, 1938; "Chinese Plan

Celebration of the Eighth Moon Festival, *Los Angeles Times*, October 5, 1938; "Gigantic Dragon to Feature Chinese Moon Fete Tonight," *Los Angeles Times*, October 8, 1938; "Chinese Hold Moon Festival," *Los Angeles Times*, October 9, 1938.

46. Missing from the archival record are sources documenting the way the 1938 Moon Festival was perceived by visitors. In fact, except for one article in the *Federation News*, articles in the English-language press only publicized the festival schedule, and did not describe what had already occurred. Thus, the archival record limits the way perceptions of the event can be understood by contemporary scholars.

47. Karen Leong, The *China Mystique: Pearl S. Buck, Anna May Wong, Maling Soong, and the Transformation of American Orientalism* (Berkeley: University of California Press, 2005), 73–74.

48. "Colorful Moon Festival," *Federation News* (November 1938): n.p.

49. As geographer Kay Anderson has pointed out, the notion of Chinatown is itself a social construction "with a cultural history and tradition of imaginary and institutional practice that has given it a cognitive and material reality in and for the West." "The Idea of Chinatown: The Power of Place and Institutional Practice in the Making of a Racial Category," *Annals of the Association of American Geographers* 77, no 4. (December 1987): 581.

50. "Chinatown Hail and Farewell," *Los Angeles Times*, December 3, 1933.

51. Kay Anderson has argued that Chinatown, much like the Orient, is a creation of the white imagination." Idea of Chinatown," 581.

52. "Chinese Plan Celebration of Eighth Moon Festival," October 5, 1938.

53. "God of War Rules Heaven," *Los Angeles Times*, December 8, 1935.

54. "History of C. H. Hung Yung, Pauper," Federal Writer Project of California Records, 1930–1942, Box 95, Folder 10, Racial Minorities Survey, 1936–1937, UCLA Library Special Collections.

55. Gordon L'Allemand, "Old Chinatown," *Los Angeles Times*, October 5, 1930.

56. "Chinese Hold Moon Festival," *Los Angeles Times*, October 9, 1938, "Moon Festival Program," box e50 folder 14, Y. C. Hong Collection, Huntington Library.

57. Leong and Wu, "Filling Bowls of Rice," 144–147.

58. *Federation News* (November 1938): n.p.

59. "Mei Wah Club Minutes," David and Dora SooHoo Collection, Chinese American Museum.

60. "Mei Wah Club Minutes."

61. Shirley Jennifer Lim, *Feeling of Belonging: Asian American Women's Popular Culture, 1930s–1960* (New York: New York University Press: 2005), 93.

62. *Federation News* 1, no. 8 (November 1938): n.p.

63. "Mei Wah Club Minutes.".

64. Leong and Wu, "Filling the Rice Bowls of China," 136–137.

65. David O. Selznick to B. A. Garside, June 16, 1941, box 18, folder 1, Public Policy Papers, United Service to China Records, Department of Rare Books and Manuscripts, Princeton University Library.

66. David O Selznick, "United China Relief Office Memorandum," August 30, 1941, box 18, folder 1, Public Policy Papers, United Service to China Records Department of Rare Books and Manuscripts, Princeton University Library.

67. *Chinese Press*, August 8, 1941.

68. "Moon Festival Will Be World's Biggest Four-Bit Show," *Los Angeles Daily News*, August 7, 1941, unpaginated clipping, Chinese American Museum.

69. "Moon Festival Will Be World's Biggest."

70. The photo of the Mei Wah Girls' Drum Corps is captioned "Chinese Drum Majorette Leads Chinatown Band with a Flourish of Symbols," in "Hollywood Stars Help Los Angeles Celebrate China Relief Festival," *Life*, September 1, 1941.

71. Jennie Lee Taylor, interview by William Gow, April 22, 2007, Chinatown Remembered.

72. Richard Chee, interview by William Gow, October 5, 2007, Chinatown Remembered.

73. Chee, interview.

Conclusion

1. Herman Hill, "Chinese Anti-Negro Discrimination," *Pittsburgh Courier*, Pacific Coast Bureau, December 11, 1943.

2. Lilian Johnson, "The Social Whirl," *California Eagle* [Los Angeles], February 29, 1940.

3. Kim Fong Tom, "The Participation of the Chinese in the Community Life of Los Angeles" (master's thesis, University of Southern California, 1944), 33. There appear to be at least two versions of this thesis with different pagination.

4. Tom, 33.

5. Tom, 34.

6. Tom, 34.

7. Quoted in Josh Sides, *L.A. City Limits: African American Los Angeles from the Great Depression to the Present* (Berkeley: University of California Press, 2003), 11.

8. W.E.B DuBois, "Colored California," *The Crisis* 37, no. 5 (May 1913): 193

9. W.E.B DuBois, "Southern California, *The Crisis* 6. no. 3 (July 1913): 131.

10. DuBois, "Colored California."

11. Sides, *L.A. City Limits*, 18.

12. For example, the mixed-race Chin brothers, who were Chinese and Black, owned the CFO Gas Station on Ninth and San Pedro. *Revisiting East Adams*, dir. Jenny Cho (CHSSC, 2004).

13. Scott Kurashige, *Shifting Grounds of Race: Black and Japanese Americans in the Making of Multiethnic Los Angeles* (Princeton, NJ: Princeton University Press, 2007).

14. "Postwar Plans to Absorb Negro Workers Urged," *Los Angeles Times*, September 8, 1944.

15. Ellen Wu, *Color of Success: Asian Americans and the Origins of the Model Minority Myth* (Princeton, NJ: Princeton University Press, 2015), 2.

16. "Flower Drum Song Blooms on Lavish Set," *Los Angeles Times*, April 23, 1961.

17. Joe Hyams, "Hollywood's New Lotus Blossom Look: What's the Secret of Oriental Charm," *Los Angeles Times*, June 17, 1962.

18. Andrew Shin, "'Forty Percent is Luck': An Interview with C. Y. (Chin Yang) Lee," *Melus* 29. no. 2 (2004): 77–104.

19. "Howard Thompson, Hawaiian Actor Star of Two Films," *New York Times*, October 14, 1961.

20. Bosley Crowther, "Screen: 'Flower Drum Song' Opens," *New York Times*, November 10, 1961.

21. Rick Chee, interview by William Gow, August 12, 2022.

22. Cherylene Lee, *Just Like Really: An Uncommon Chinese American Memoir* (San Francisco: Longevity Press, 2015).

Epilogue

1. "*Everything Everywhere All at Once* Wins Big at SAG Awards," *CBS News*, February 27, 2023, https://www.cbsnews.com/news/sag-awards-winners-highlights/

2. Nardine Saad, "Daniel Dae Kim Just Raised $55,000 for James Hong's Hollywood Star, Now It Gets Harder," *Los Angeles Times*, August 10, 2020.

3. Lisa Wong Macabasco, "What Everything All at Once's Oscar Win Means for Asian American Representation," *Guardian*, March 13, 2023.

4. Brahmjot Kaur and Angela Yang, "Asian Americans are Over Just Being Included," *NBC News*, May 12, 2023, https://www.nbcnews.com/news/asian-america/asian-americans-are-just-included-re-defining-mainstream-culture-rcna77455.

Selected Bibliography

Books and Articles

Aleiss, Angela. *Making the White Man's Indian: Native Americans and Hollywood Movies.* Westport, CT: Greenwood Publishing, 2005.

Anderson, Benedict. *Imagined Communities: Reflections of the Origin and Spread of Nationalism.* New York: Verso, 1991.

Anderson, Kay. *Vancouver's Chinatown, Racial Discourse in Canada, 1875–1980.* Montreal: McGill-Queens University Press, 1995.

Anderson, Kay J. "The Idea of Chinatown: The Power of Place and Institutional Practice in the making of a Racial Category." *Annals of the Association of American Geography* 77. no. 4 (December 1987).

Appleton's Hand-Book of American Travel. Western Tour. D. Appleton and Company, New York, 1873.

Avila, Erica. *Popular Culture in the Age of White Flight: Fear and Fantasy in Suburban Los Angeles.* Berkeley: University of California Press, 2006.

Axelrod, Jeremiah. "Keep the 'L' Out of Los Angeles: Race, Discourse and Urban Modernity in 1920s Southern California." *Journal of Urban History.* 34, no. 1. (2007): 3–33.

Bancroft's Tourist Guide: Yosemite, San Francisco, and Around the Bay Area. San Francisco: Bancroft and Company, 1871.

Bancroft's Tourist Guide: Yosemite, San Francisco, and Around the Bay Area. San Francisco: Bancroft and Company, 1871.

Bancroft, Hubert. *The Book of the Fair: An Historical and Descriptive Presentation of the World's Science, Art, and Industry as Viewed Through the Columbian Exposition at Chicago in 1893.* Chicago: Bancroft Company, 1893.

Benjamin, Walter. "On Some Motif's in Baudelaire." In *Illuminations*. Edited by Hannah Arendt. New York: Schocken Books, 1968.

Berglund, Barbara. "Chinatown's Tourist Terrain: Representation and Racialization in Nineteenth Century San Francisco." *American Studies* 46, no. 2 (2005): 5–36.

Bernardi, Daniel, ed. *The Birth of Whiteness: Race and the Emergence of U.S. Cinema*. New Brunswick, NJ: Rutgers University Press, 1996.

———. *Classic Hollywood, Classic Whiteness*. Minneapolis: University of Minnesota Press, 2001.

Blackman, Margaret. *Sadie Brower Neakok: An Inupiaq Woman*. Seattle: University of Washington Press, 1989.

Bogle, Donald. *Toms, Coons, Mulattoes, Mammies and Bucks: An Interpretive History of Blacks in American Films*. New York: Bantam Books, 1974.

Bow, Leslie. *Racist Love: Asian Abstraction and the Pleasure of Fantasy*. Durham, NC: Duke University Press, 2022.

Brook, Harry Ellington. *The County and City of Los Angeles in Southern California*. Los Angeles: Los Angeles Chamber of Commerce, 1921.

Brownlow, Kevin. *Behind the Mask of Innocence*. New York: Knopf, 1990.

Brooks, Charlotte. *American Exodus: Second Generation Chinese Americans in China, 1901–1949*. Berkeley: University of California Press, 2019.

California Bureau of Labor Statistics. *Twenty Second Biennial Report of the Bureau of Labor Statistics of the State of California*. California State Printing Office, 1926.

Cannon, Raymond. *China City*. Los Angeles: China City Publishing, 1938.

Chan, Anthony. *Perpetually Cool: The Many Lives of Anna May Wong*. Lanham, MD: Scarecrow Press, 2007.

Chan, Sucheng. *Asian American: An Interpretive History*. NewYork: Twayne Publishers, 1991.

———. *This Bittersweet Soil: The Chinese in California Agriculture, 1860–1910*. Berkeley: University of California Press, 1986.

Chang, Gordon. *Fateful Ties: A History of America's Preoccupation with China*. Cambridge: Harvard University Press, 2015.

Chen, Shehong. *Being Chinese, Becoming Chinese Americans*. Champaign: University of Illinois Press, 2002.

Chen, Yong. *Chinese San Francisco: A Transpacific Community, 1850–1943*. Stanford, CA: Stanford University Press, 2000.

———. *Chop Suey USA: The Story of Chinese Food in the United States*. New York: Columbia University Press, 2014.

Cheng, Anne Anline. *Ornamentalism*. New York: Oxford University Press, 2019.

Cheng, Suellen, and Munson Kwok. "The Golden Years of Los Angeles Chinatown: The Beginning." In *Los Angeles Chinatown 50th Year Guidebook*, 39–45. Los Angeles: Chinese Historical Society of Southern California, 1988.

Cheng, Wendy. *The Changs Next Door to the Díazes: Remapping Race in Suburban California*. Minneapolis: University of Minnesota Press, 2013.

Chinese Historical Society of Southern California. *Linking Our Lives: Chinese American Women of Los Angeles*. Los Angeles: East West Press, 1984.

Cho, Jenny, and the Chinese Historical Society of Southern California. Chinatown and China City in Los Angeles. Charleston, SC: Arcadia Press, 2011.

———. *Chinese in Hollywood*. Charleston, SC: Arcadia Press, 2013.

Choy, Philip. *San Francisco Chinatown: Guide to Its History and Architecture*. San Francisco: City Lights Books, 2012.

Chu, Judy. "Anna May Wong." In *Counterpoint: Perspectives on Asian America*. Edited by Emma Gee et al. Los Angeles: Asian American Studies Center, 1976.

Chun, Gloria Heyung. *Of Orphans and Warriors: Inventing Chinese American Culture and Identity*. New Brunswick, NJ: Rutgers University Press, 2000.

Chung, Hye Seung. *Hollywood Diplomacy: Film Regulation, Foreign Relations & East Asian Representations*. New Brunswick, NJ: Rutgers University Press, 2020.

———. *Hollywood Asian: Philip Ahn and the Politics of Cross Ethnic Performance*. Philadelphia: Temple University Press, 2006.

Clark, Danae. "Acting in Hollywood's Best Interest: Representations of Actors' Labor During the National Recovery Administration." *Journal of Film and Video* 42 no. 4 (1990), 3–19.

———. *Negotiating Hollywood: The Cultural Politics of Actors' Labor*. Minneapolis: University of Minnesota Press, 1995.

Cocks, Catherine. *Doing the Town: The Rise of Urban Tourism in the United States, 1850–1915*. Berkeley: University of California Press, 2001.

Collins, Patricia Hill. *Black Feminist Thought: Knowledge, Consciousness, and the Politics of Empowerment*. London: Routledge, 2008.

Connors, Chuck. *Bowery Life*. New York: Richard Fox Publishing, 1904.

Crenshaw, Kimberlé. "Demarginalizing the Intersection of Race and Sex: A Black Feminist Critique of Antidiscrimination Doctrine, Feminist Theory and Antiracist Politics." *University of Chicago Legal Forum* 1989, no. 1 (1989): 139–167.

———. "Mapping the Margins: Intersectionality, Identity Politics and Violence against Women." Stanford Law Review 433, no. 6 (1991): 1241–1299.

Daniels, Rogers. *Asian America: Chinese and Japanese in the United States since 1850*. Seattle: University of Washington Press, 1988.

Deligman, Scott. *The First Chinese American: The Remarkable life of Wong Chin Foo*. Hong Kong: Hong Kong University Press, 2013.

Deverell, William. "Privileging the Mission over the Mexican: The Rise of Regional Identity in Southern California." In *Many Wests: Place, Culture and Regional Identity*. Edited by David Wrobel and Michael Steiner. Lawrence: University of Kansas Press, 1997.

Diawara, Manthia, ed. *Black American Cinema*. New York: Routledge, 2012.

Dilke, Charles Wentworth. *Greater Britain: A Record of Travel in English-Speaking Countries during 1866–7*. New York: Harper and Brothers, 1869.

Dong, Arthur. Hollywood Chinese: The Chinese in American Feature Film. Los Angeles: Angel City Press, 2019.

Dower, John. *War Without Mercy: Race and Power in the Pacific War*. New York: Norton, 1986.

The Dream City: A Portfolio of Photographic Views of the World Columbian Exposition with an Introduction by Halsey C. Ives. St. Louis: N. D. Thompson Company, 1893–1894.

Dresser, Norine. "Chinatown Militia Units, 1942: Los Angeles and San Francisco." *Gum Saan Journal* 15, no. 2 (1992): 16–25.

Dyer, Richard. *White: Essays on Race and Culture*. New York: Routledge, 1997.

Espana-Maram, Linda. *Creating Masculinity in Los Angeles's Little Manila: Working Class Filipinos and Popular Culture, 1920s–1950s*. New York: Columbia University Press, 2006.

Estrada, William. *The Los Angeles Plaza: Sacred and Contested Space*. Austin: University of Texas Press, 2008.

Fahlstedt, Kim K. *Chinatown Film Culture: The Appearance of Cinema in San Francisco's Chinese Neighborhood*. New Brunswick, NJ: Rutgers University Press, 2020.

Federal Writers Project of the Works Project Administration. *Los Angeles in the 1930s: The WPA Guide to the City of Angeles*. Berkeley: University of California Press, 2011.

Feral, Josie. "Theatricality: The Specificity of Theatrical Language." *SubStance* 31, no. 2/3 (2002): 98/99.

Fine, David. *Imagining Los Angeles: A City in Fiction*. Reno, NV: University of Nevada Press, 2004.

Fogelson, Robert. *Fragmented Metropolis: Los Angeles, 1850–1930*. Berkeley: University of California Press, 1993.

Fong, Tim. *The First Suburban Chinatown: The Remaking of Monterey Park, California*. Philadelphia: Temple University Press, 1994.

Foster, Hal, ed. *Vision and Visuality*. Seattle: Bay Press, 1988.

Fried, Michael. *Absorption and Theatricality, Painting and Beholder in the Age of Diderot*. Chicago: University of Chicago Press, 1980.

Fuller, Karla Rae. *Hollywood Goes Oriental: CaucAsian Performance in American Film*. Detroit, MI: Wayne State University Press, 2010.

Gates, Phillipa. *Criminalization/Assimilation: Chinese/Americans and Chinatowns in Classical Hollywood Film*. New Brunswick, NJ: Rutgers University Press, 2019.

Gevison, Alan. *Within Our Gates: Ethnicity in American Feature Films, 1911–1960.* Berkeley: University of California Press, 1997.

Glenn, Evylyn Nakano. *Unequal Freedom: How Race and Gender Shaped American Citizenship and Labor.* Cambridge, MA: Harvard University Press, 2002.

Gordon, Anna Pegler. "Chinese Exclusion, Photography, and the Development of US Immigration Policy." *American Quarterly* 58, no. 1 (2006): 51–77.

Gow, William. "Building a Chinese Village in Los Angeles: Christine Sterling and the Residents of China City, 1938–1948. *Gum Saan Journal* 32, no. 1 (2010): 39–53.

———. "I Am Chinese: The Politics of Chinese American Lapel Buttons in Los Angeles During World War II." *Western Historical Quarterly* 53, no. 1 (2022): 47–75.

Greenwood, Roberta. Down by the Station: Los Angeles Chinatown, 1880–1933. Institute of Archeology, University of California, Los Angeles, 1996.

Gunning, Tom. "From the Kaleidoscope to the X-Ray: Urban Spectatorship, Poe, Benjamin, and the Traffic in Souls (1913)." *Wide Angle* 19, no.4 (1997): 25–55.

Guerrero, Ed. *Framing Blackness: The African Image on Film.* Philadelphia: Temple University Press, 1993.

Gyroy, Andrew. *Closing the Gate: Race, Politics, and the Chinese Exclusion Act.* Chapel Hill, NC: University of North Carolina Press, 1998.

Hall, Stuart. "Notes on Deconstructing the Popular." In People's History and Socialist Theory. Edited by Raphael Samuel, 227–239. London: Routledge, 1981.

Hartig, Anthea. "Promotion and Popular Culture." In *A Companion to Los Angeles.* Edited by William Deverell et al. Malden, MA: Wiley Blackwell, 2010.

Haenni, Sabine. *The Immigrant Scene: Ethnic Amusements in New York, 1880–1920.* Minneapolis: University of Minnesota Press, 2008.

Hodges, Graham Russell. *Anna May Wong: From Laundryman's Daughter to Hollywood Legend.* Hong Kong: Hong Kong University Press, 2012.

Holmes, Sean. "The Hollywood Star System and the Regulation of Actors' Labor, 1916–1934." *Film History* 12, no. 1 (2000): 97–114.

Hom, Gilbert. "Chinese Angelenos Before World War II." In *Duty and Honor: A Tribute to Chinese American World War II Veterans of Southern California.* Edited by Marjorie Lee, 21–16. Los Angeles: Chinese Historical Society of Southern California, 1998.

hooks, bell. *Black Looks: Race and Representation.* Boston: South End Press, 1992.

Hsu, Madeline. *Dreaming of Gold, Dreaming of Home: Transnationalism and Migration Between United States and South China, 1882–1943.* Stanford, CA: Stanford University Press, 2000.

Isaacs, Harold. *Scratches on Our Minds: American Images of China and India.* New York: John Day and Company, 1958.

Ives, Halsey C. *The Dream City: A Portfolio of Photographic Views of the World's Columbia Exposition*. St. Louis, MO: N. D. Thompson Publishing, 1893–1894.

Jones, Dorothy B. *Portrayals of China and India on Screen, 1896–1955*. Cambridge, MA: MIT Press, 1955.

Keil, Charlie. "Leo Rosencrans, Movie-Struck Boy." *Film History Journal* 26, no. 2 (2014): 30–51.

Kenaga, Heidi. "Making the 'Studio Girl': The Hollywood Studio Club and Industry Regulation of Female Labour." *Film History* 18, no. 2 (2006), 129–139.

Kelley, C. A. *Glimpses of the Far West, 1902*. Americana Collection, University of California Libraries.

Khor, Denise. *Transpacific Convergences: Race Migration, and Japanese American Film Culture Before World War II*. Chapel Hill, NC: University of North Carolina Press, 2022.

Kim, Elaine. *Asian American Literature: An Introduction to the Writings and Their Social Context*. Philadelphia: Temple University Press, 1982.

Kim, Esther Lee. *Made-Up Asian Americans: Yellowface during the Exclusion Era*. Ann Arbor: University of Michigan Press, 2022.

Kim, Ju Yon. *Racial Mundane: Asian American Performance and the Embodied Everyday*. New York: New York University Press, 2015.

King, Barry. "Stardom as an Occupation." In *The Hollywood Film Industry: A Reader*. Edited by Paul Kerr. London: Routledge.

———. "The Star and the Commodity: Notes Towards a Performance Theory of Stardom." *Cultural Studies* 1, no. 2 (1987): 145–161.

Kurashige, Lon. *Japanese American Celebration and Conflict*. Berkeley: University of California Press, 2002.

Kurashige, Scott. *The Shifting Grounds of Race: Black and Japanese Americans in the Making of Multiethnic Los Angeles*. Princeton NJ: Princeton University Press, 2008.

———. "Between White Spot and World City." In *A Companion to Los Angeles*. Edited by William Deverel et al. Malden, MA: Wiley Blackwell, 2010.

Kwong, Peter. *Chinatown, New York: Labor and Politics, 1930–1950*. New York: New Press, 2001.

Kwong, Peter, and Dušanka Miščević. *Chinese America: The Untold Story of America's Oldest New Community*. New York: New Press, 2007.

Lai, Him Mark. "The Historical Development of the Chinese Consolidated Benevolent Association/Higuan System." *Chinese America: History and Perspective* (1987): 13–41.

———. "Roles Played by Chinese in America During China's Resistance to Japanese Aggression and During World War II." *Chinese America: History and Perspective* (1997): 75–128.

Lan, Lawrence. "The Rise and Fall of China City: Race, Space, and Cultural Production in Los Angeles Chinatown, 1938–1948." *Amerasia Journal* 42, no. 2 (2016): 2–21.

Larson, Louise Leung. *Sweet Bamboo: A Memoir of a Chinese American Family* (Berkeley: University of California Press, 1989).

Lee, Anthony. *Picturing Chinatown: Art and Orientalism in San Francisco* (Berkeley: University of California Press, 2001).

Lee, Erika. *At America's Gates: Chinese Immigration During the Exclusion Era*. Chapel Hill, NC: University of North Carolina Press, 2003.

———. *The Making of Asian America: A History.* New York: Simon and Schuster, 2015.

Lee, Heather R. "A Life Cooking for Others: The Work and Migration Experiences of a Chinese Restaurant Worker in New York City, 1920–1946." In *Eating Asian America: A Food Studies Reader*. Edited by Robert Ji-Song Ku. New York: New York University Press, 2013.

Lee, Josephine. *Performing Asian America: Race and Ethnicity on the Contemporary Stage*. Philadelphia: Temple University Press, 1997.

Lee, Cherylene. *Just Like Really: An Uncommon Chinese American Memoir*. San Francsico: Longevity Press, 2015.

Lee, Marjorie. "On the Home Front: Curtis-Wright Technical Institute and an Introduction to the Chinatown Militia Unit." In *Duty and Honor A Tribute to Chinese American World War II Veterans of Southern California*. Edited by Marjorie Lee, 37–38. Los Angeles: Chinese Historical Society of Southern California, 1998.

Lee, Robert. *Orientals: Asian Americans in Popular Culture*. Philadelphia: Temple University Press, 1999.

Lee, Shelley Sang-Hee. *A New History of Asian America*. New York: Routledge, 2014.

Leong, Charles. "Mandarins in Hollywood." In *Moving the Image: Independent Asian Pacific American Media Arts*. Edited by Russell Leong. Los Angeles: Asian American Studies Center and Visual Communications, University of California, Los Angeles, 1991.

Leong, Karen. *The China Mystique: Pearl S. Buck, Anna May Wong, Mayling Soong and the Transformation of American Orientalism*. Berkeley: University of California Press, 2005.

Leong, Karen, and Judy Tzu-Chu Wu. "Filling the Rice Bowls of China: Staging Humanitarian Relief During the Sino-Japanese War." In *Chinese Americans and the Politics of Race and Culture*. Edited by Sucheng Chen and Madeline Hsu. Philadelphia: Temple University Press, 2008.

Lethwaite, Stephanie. "Race, Place and Ethnicity in the Progressive Era." In *A Companion to Los Angeles*. Edited by William Deverel and Greg Hise. Malden, MA: Wiley Blackwell, 2010.

Lew-Williams, Beth. "'Chinamen' and 'Delinquent Girls': Intimacy, Exclusion, and a Search for California's Color Line." *Journal of American History* 104, no. 3 (2017): 632–655.

———. *The Chinese Must Go: Violence, Exclusion, and the Making of the Alien in America*. Cambridge, MA: Harvard University Press, 2018.

Li, Wei. *Ethnoburb: The New Ethnic Community in Urban America*. Honolulu: University of Hawai'i Press, 2009.

Light, Ivan. "From Vice District to Tourist Attraction: The Moral Career of American Chinatowns, 1880–1940." *Pacific Historical Review* 43, no. 3 (1974): 367–394.

Lim, Shirley Jennifer. *Anna May Wong: Performing the Modern*. Philadelphia: Temple University Press, 2019.

———. *Feeling of Belonging: Asian American Women's Popular Culture, 1930s–1960*. New York: New York University Press, 2005.

Lin, Jan. *Reconstructing Chinatown: Ethnic Enclave, Global Change*. Minneapolis: University of Minnesota Press, 1998.

Ling, Susie, ed. *Bridging the Centuries: History of Chinese Americans in Southern California*. Los Angeles: Chinese Historical Society of Southern California, 2001.

Liu, Cynthia. "When Dragon Ladies Die, Do they Come Back as Butterflies? Reimagining Anna May Wong." In *Countervisions: Asian American Film Criticism*. Edited by Darrell Hamamoto and Sandra Liu, 23–39. Philadelphia: Temple University Press, 2000.

Liu, David Palumbo. *Asian/American: Historical Crossing of the Racial Frontier*. Stanford, CA: Stanford University Press, 1999.

Liu, Haiming. *From Canton Restaurant to Panda Express: A History of Chinese Food in the United States*. New Brunswick, NJ: Rutgers University Press, 2015.

Lopez, Caesar. "Lost in Translation." *Southern California Quarterly* 94, no. 1 (2012): 25–90.

Lopez, Ian Haney. *White by Law: The Legal Construction of Race*. New York: New York University Press, 2006.

Lopez, Lori Kido. *Asian American Media: Activism Fighting for Cultural Citizenship*. New York: New York University Press, 2016.

Louie, Ruby Ling. "Reliving China City." In *Bridging the Centuries: History of Chinese Americans in Southern California*. Edited by Susie Ling. Los Angeles: Chinese Historical Society of Southern California, 2001.

Lowe, Lisa. *Immigrant Acts: On Asian American Cultural Politics*. Durham, NC: Duke University Press, 1996.

Lui, Garding. *Inside Los Angeles Chinatown*. Self-published, 1948.

Lui, Mary Ting Yi. *Chinatown Trunk Mystery: Murder, Miscegenation and Other Dangerous Encounters in Turn-of-the-Century New York*. Princeton, NJ: Princeton University Press, 2007.

Lye, Colleen. *America's Asia: Racial Form and American Literature, 1893–1945*. Princeton, NJ: Princeton University Press, 2005.

Mar, Lisa Rose. *Brokering Belonging: Chinese in Canada's Exclusion Era, 1885–1945*. New York: Oxford University Press, 2010.

Marchetti, Gina. *Romance and the Yellow Peril: Race, Sex, and Discursive Strategies in Hollywood Fiction*. Berkeley: University of California Press, 1993.

Markwyn, Abigail. "Economic Partner and Exotic Other: China and Japan at San Francisco's Panama-Pacific International Exposition." *Western Historical Quarterly* 39 (2008): 439–465.

Matsumoto, Valerie. *City Girls: The Nisei Social World in Los Angeles, 1920–1950*. New York: Oxford University Press, 2014.

Mayer, Ruth. *Serial Fu Manchu: The Chinese Super Villain and the Spread of Yellow Peril Ideology*. Philadelphia: Temple University Press, 2014.

Mirzoeff, Nicholas. *The Right to Look: A Counter History of Visuality*. Durham, NC: Duke University Press, 2011.

McClain, Charles. *In Search of Equality, the Chinese Struggle against Discrimination in Nineteenth-Century America*. Berkeley: University of California Press, 1996.

McDougal, Dennis. *Privileged Son: Otis Chandler and the Rise and Fall of the L.A. Times Dynasty*. Cambridge, MA: Perseus Publishing, 2001.

McKenna, Denise. "The Photoplay or the Pickaxe: Extras, Gender, and Labour in Early Hollywood." *Film History* 23. no. 1 (2011): 5–18.

McWilliams, Carey. *Southern California: An Island on the Land*. Salt Lake City: Peregrine Smith, 1946.

Miller, Stuart Creighton. *The Unwelcome Immigrant: The American Image of the Chinese, 1785–1882*. Berkeley: University of California Press, 1969.

Miyao, Daisuke. *Sessue Hayakawa: Silent Cinema and Transnational Stardom*. Durham, NC: Duke University Press, 2007.

Moon, Krysten. *Yellowface: Creating the Chinese in American Popular Music and Performance,1850s–1920s*. New Brunswick, NJ: Rutgers University Press, 2005.

Molina, Natalia. *Fit to Be Citizens? Public Health and Race in Los Angeles, 1879–1939*. Berkeley: University of California Press, 2006.

Hollywood Reporter. *Motion Picture Production Encyclopedia 1950 Edition*. Hollywood: Hollywood Reporter Press, 1950.

Moy, James. *Marginal Sights: Staging the Chinese in America*. Iowa City: University of Iowa Press, 1993).

Musicant, Marlyn. "In Search of a Site for Union Station, 1918–1933." In *Los Angeles Union Station*. Edited by Marlyn Musicant. Los Angeles: Getty Research Institute, 2014.

Nee, Victor, and Brett de Bary Nee. *Longtime Californ': A Documentary Study of An American Chinatown*. Stanford, CA: Stanford University Press, 1986.

Ngai, Mae. *Impossible Subjects: Illegal Aliens and the Making of Modern America*. Princeton NJ: Princeton University Press, 2004.

———. *The Lucky Ones: One Family and the Extraordinary Invention of Chinese America*. Princeton, NJ: Princeton University Press, 2012.

———. "Transnationalism and the Transformation of the 'Other': Response to the Presidential Address." *American Quarterly* 57, no. 1 (2005).

Oh, David C. *Whitewashing and the Movies: Asian Erasure and Subjectivity in U.S. Film Culture*. New Brunswick, NJ: Rutgers University Press, 2022.

Okada, Jun. *Making Asian American Film and Video: Histories, Institutions, Movements*. New Brunswick NJ: Rutgers University Press, 2015.

Okihiro, Gary. *Margins and Mainstream: Asians in American History and Culture*. Seattle: University of Washington Press, 1994.

———. *Common Ground: Remaking American History*. Princeton NJ: Princeton University Press, 2001.

Omi, Michael, and Howard Winant. *Racial Formation in the United States*. London: Routledge, 2014.

Jack Ong. "From Hanford to Hollywood: Remembering Bessie Loo." *Gum Saan Journal* 30, no. 1 (2007).

Ono, Kent, and Vincent Pham. *Asian Americans and the Media*. Malden, MA: Polity Press, 2009.

Outlook Company. *Seen by the Spectator: Being a Selection of Rambling Papers First Printed in the Outlook, under the title the Spectator*. New York: Outlook Company, 1902.

Perry, Louis, and Richard Perry. *A History of the Los Angeles Labor Movement, 1911–1941*. Berkeley: University of California Press, 1963.

Pfaelzer, Jean. *Driven Out: The Forgotten War on Chinese Americans*. New York: Random House, 2007.

Quan, Ella Yee. "Pioneer Families Share Their History." In *Chinatown: The Golden Years*. Los Angeles: Chinese Chamber of Commerce, 1988.

Quintana, Isabella Seong Leong. "Making Do, Making Home: Borders and the Worlds of Chinatown and Sonoratown in Early Twentieth Century Los Angeles." *Journal of Urban History* (2014): 47–74.

Rabinovitz, Lauren. *For the Love of Pleasure: Women, Movies and Culture in Turn of the Century Chicago* 1998.

Raheja, Michelle. *Reservation Reelism: Redfacing, Visual Sovereignty and Representations of Native Americans in Film*. Lincoln, NB: University of Nebraska Press, 2010.

Rast, Raymond. "The Cultural Politics of Tourism in San Francisco's Chinatown, 1882–1917." *Pacific Historical Review* 76, no. 1 (2007): 29–60.

Regester, Charlene. "African American Extras in Hollywood During the 1920s and 1930s." *Film History* 9, no. 1 (1997): 95–115.

Rivera, Takeo. *Model Minority Masochism: Performing the Cultural Politics of Asian American Masculinity*. New York: Oxford University Press, 2022.

Roediger, David R. *Working Toward Whiteness: How America's Immigrants Became White*. New York: Basic Books, 2005.

Roan, Janette. *Envisioning Asia: On Location, Travel and the Cinematic Geography of U.S. Orientalism*. Ann Arbor: University of Michigan Press, 2010.

Robertson, William. *Our American Tour: Being a Run of Ten Thousand Miles from the Atlantic to the Golden Gate, in the Autumn of 1869*. Edinburgh: W. Burness Printer, 1871.

Rony, Fatimah. *The Third Eye: Race, Cinema, and Ethnographic Spectacle*. Durham, NC: Duke University Press, 1996.

Rosaldo, Renato. *Cultural Citizenship in Island Southeast Asia: Nation and Belonging in the Hinterlands*. Berkeley: University of California Press, 2003.

Rosenthal, Nicolas G. *Reimagining Indian Country: Native Migration & Identity in Twentieth Century Los Angeles*. Chapel Hill, NC: University of North Carolina Press, 2012.

Ross, Murray. "Hollywood's Extras." In *The Movie in Our Midst: Documents in the Cultural History of Film in America*. Edited by Gerald Mast. Chicago: University of Chicago Press, 1983.

Rubin, Martin. "Berkeleyesque Traditions." In *Theater and Film: A Comparative Anthology*. Edited by Robert Knopf. New Haven, CT: Yale University Press, 2005.

Rydell, Robert. *All the World's a Fair: Visions of Empire at American International Expositions, 1876–1916*. Chicago: University of Chicago Press, 1987.

Said, Edward. *Orientalism*. New York: Vintage Books, 1979.

Saito, Leland T. *Race and Politics: Asian Americans, Latinos, and Whites in a Los Angeles Suburb*. Champaign: University of Illinois Press, 1998.

Saxton, Alexander. *The Indispensable Enemy: Labor and the Anti-Chinese Movement in California*. Berkeley: University of California Press, 1975.

Starr, Kevin. *Material Dreams: Southern California Through the 1920s*. Oxford, UK: Oxford University Press, 1990.

Schechner, Richard. *Performance Studies: An Introduction*. London: Routledge, 2013.

Schwartz, Vanessa. *Spectacular Realities: Early Mass Culture in Fin-de-Siècle Paris.* Berkeley: University of California Press, 1998.

Schmidt, Bjorn. *Visualizing Orientalness: Chinese Immigration and Race in U.S. Motion Pictures, 1910s–1930s.* Cologne, Germany: Ohlau Verlag, 2017.

Seagrave, Kerry. *Film Actors Organize: Union Formation Efforts in America, 1912–1937.* Jefferson, NC: McFarland & Company, 2009.

See, Lisa. *On Gold Mountain: The One-Hundred-Year Odyssey of My Chinese American Family.* New York: Vintage Books, 1995.

Shah, Nayan. *Contagious Divides: Epidemics and Race in San Francisco Chinatown.* Berkeley: University of California Press, 2001.

Shimakawa, Karen. *National Abjection: The Asian Body on Stage.* Durham, NC: Duke University Press, 2002.

Shoat, Ella, and Robert Stam. *Unthinking Eurocentrism: Multiculturalism and the Media.* New York: Routledge, 1994.

Soule, Frank, John Gihon, and Jim Nisbet. The Annals of San Francisco. New York: D. Appleton and Company, 1855.

Singer, Ben. *Melodrama and Modernity: Early Sensational Cinema and Its Contexts.* New York: Columbia University Press, 2001.

Slide, Anthony. *Hollywood Unknowns: A History of Bit Players and Stand-Ins.* Jackson: University of Mississippi Press, 2012.

Smith, Valerie. *Representing Blackness: Issues in Film and Video.* New Brunswick, NJ: Rutgers University Press, 1997.

Smoodin, Eric. *Regarding Frank Capra: Audience, Celebrity, and American Film Studies, 1930–1960.* Durham, NC: Duke University Press, 2004.

SooHoo, Peter. "Proceedings of the Two Hundred Eighty-First Meeting of the Pacific Railway Club." *Proceedings: The Journal of the Pacific Railway Club* 23, no. 11 (February 1941): 3–6.

Stedman, Raymond William. *The Serials: Suspense and Drama by Installment.* Norman: University of Oklahoma Press, 1971.

Taylor, Diana. *Performance.* Durham, NC: Duke University Press, 2016.

Takaki, Ronald. *Strangers from a Different Shore: A History of Asian Americans.* New York: Penguin Books, 1989.

Tajima, Rene. "Lotus Blossoms Don't Bleed: Images of Asian Women." In *Making Waves: An Anthology of Writings by and about Asian American Women.* Edited by Asian Women United. Boston: Beacon Press, 1989.

Tchen, John Kuo Wei. *New York Before Chinatown: Orientalism and the Shaping of American Culture, 1776–1882.* Baltimore: Johns Hopkins University Press 2001.

Tchen, John Kuo Wei, and Dylan Yeats. *Yellow Peril! An Archive of Anti-Asian Fear.* New York: Verso, 2014.

Teng, Emma. "Artifacts of a Lost City: Arnold Genthe's Photographs of Old Chinatown and Its Intertexts." In *Recollecting Early Asian America: Essays in Cultural History*. Philadelphia: Temple University Press, 2002.

Venman, Barbara. "Dragons, Dummies and Royals: China at American World's Fairs, 1876–1904." *Gateway Heritage: The Magazine of the Missouri Historical Society* 17, no. 2. (Fall 1996)

Wang, Yiman. "The Crisscrossed Stare: Protest and Propaganda in China's Not-So-Silent Era." In *Silent Cinema and the Politics of Space*. Edited by Jennifer M. Bean, Laura Horak, and Anupama Kapse. Bloomington: Indiana University Press, 2014.

Ward, Josi. "Dreams of Oriental Romance." *Buildings & Landscapes* 20, no. 1 (2013): 19–42.

Wild, Mark. *Street Meeting: Multiethnic Neighborhoods in Early Twentieth Century Los Angeles*. Berkeley: University of California Press, 2005.

Wong, K. Scott. *Americans First: Chinese Americans and the Second World War*. Cambridge, MA: Harvard University Press, 2005.

Wong, Eugene. *On Visual Media Racism: Asians in American Motion Pictures*. New York: Verso, 1978.

Wong, Eugene Franklin. "The Early Years: Asians in American Films Prior to World War II." In *Screening Asian Americans*. Edited by Peter X. Feng. New Brunswick, NJ: Rutgers University Press, 2002.

Wu, Ellen. *The Color of Success: Asian Americans and the Origins of the Model Minority*. Princeton, NJ: Princeton University Press, 2015.

Xiao, Zhiwei. "Nationalism, Orientalism, and Unequal Treatise of Ethnography." In *The Chinese in America: A History from Gold Mountain to the New Millennium*. Edited by Susie Lan Cassel. New York: AltaMira: 2002.

Xing, Jun. *Asian America Through the Lens: History, Representation, and Identity*. London: AltaMira, 1998.

Yeh, Chouh-Ling. *Making An American Festival: Chinese New Year in San Francisco's Chinatown*. Berkeley: University of California Press, 2008.

Yep, Kathleen. Outside the Pain: When Basketball Ruled the Chinese Playground. Philadelphia: Temple University Press, 2009.

Yu, Renqui. *To Save China, To Save Ourselves: The Chinese Hand Laundry Alliance in New York*. Philadelphia: Temple University Press, 1992.

Yung, Judy. *Unbound Feet: A Social History of Chinese Women in San Francisco*. Berkeley: University of California Press, 1995.

Zhao, Xiaojian. *Remaking Chinese America: Immigration, Family, and Community, 1940–1965*. New Brunswick: Rutgers University Press, 2002.

Zesch, Scott. *The Chinatown War: Chinese Los Angeles and the Massacre of 1871*. New York: Oxford University Press, 2012.

Zarsadiaz, James. *Resisting Change in Suburbia: Asian Immigrants and Frontier Nostalgia in L.A.* Berkeley: University of California Press, 2022.

Theses and Dissertations

Bingham, Edwin. "The Saga of the Los Angeles Chinese." Master's thesis, Occidental College, 1942.

Chen, Wen Hui. "A Study of Chinese Family Life in Los Angeles as Compared to the Traditional Family Life in China." Master's thesis, University of Southern California, 1940.

————. "Changing Socio-Cultural Patterns of the Chinese Community in Los Angeles," PhD diss., University of Southern California, 1952.

Ferguson, Charles. "Political Problems and Activities of Oriental Residents in Los Angeles and the Vicinity." Master's thesis, University of California, Los Angeles, 1942.

Lee, Mabel Sam. "The Recreational Interests and Participation of a Selected Group of Chinese Boys and Girls in Los Angeles, California." Master's thesis, University of Southern California, 1939.

Louis, Kit King. "A Study of American-Born and American-Reared Chinese in Los Angeles." Master's thesis, University of Southern California, 1931.

McDannold, Tom. "The Development of Los Angeles Chinatown: 1850–1970." Master's thesis: California State University, Northridge, 1973.

Quintana, Isabella Seong-Leong. "National Borders, Neighborhood Boundaries: Gender, Space, and Border Formation in Chinese and Mexican Los Angeles." Ph.D. diss., University of Michigan, 2010.

Tom, Kim Fong. "The Participation of the Chinese in the Community Life of Los Angeles." Master's thesis, University of Southern California, 1944.

Shan, John S. Wu. "Merchandising Chinese Products on the Los Angeles Market." Master's thesis, University of Southern California, 1934.

Yip, Christopher. "San Francisco Chinatown." PhD diss., University of California, Berkeley, 1995.

Newspapers and Magazines

Architect and Engineer
Billboard

California Eagle (Los Angeles)
Chicago Tribune
China Press

Chinese American
Chinese Press
Chinese Digest
The Crisis
Cosmopolitan
Exhibitor's Herald
Film Weekly
Evening Huronite (South Dakota)
Federation News
GQ
Hollywood Reporter
Independent Press-Telegram
Land of Sunshine
Life
Los Angeles Daily News
Los Angeles Examiner
Los Angeles Times
Monthly Labor Review
Motion Picture News
Motography
Moving Picture Weekly
Moving Picture World
New York Times
New York Clipper
North China Herald and Supreme Court & Consular Gazette
Overland Monthly
Omaha Daily Bee
Picture Play
Pittsburgh Courier
Quartz
Reel Life
Rushville Republican (Indiana)
San Francisco Chronicle
Sacramento Union
The Standard, San Francisco, California
Teen Vogue
Variety
Washington Post

Filmography

LISTED CHRONOLOGICALLY

A Trip to the Moon. Dir. Georges Melies, Star Film, 1902

The Adventures of Kathlyn. Dir. Francis Grandon. Selig Polyscope, 1913

The Exploits of Elaine. Dir. Louis Gasnier, George Seitz, and Leopold Wharton. Wharton, 1914

The Hop Smugglers. Dir. Fred E. Kelsey, Reliance Film Company, 1914

Birth of a Nation. Dir. D. W. Griffith, David W. Griffith Corporation, 1915

The Cheat. Dir. Cecil B. DeMille, Jesse L. Lasky Feature Play Company, 1915

The New Exploits of Elaine. Dir. Louis J. Gasnier, Leopold Wharton, and Theodore Wharton, Wharton, 1915

The Chinatown Villains. Dir. John Francis Dillon, Vogue Motion Picture Company, 1916

The Flower of Doom. Dir. Rex Ingram, Universal Film Manufacturing Company, 1916

The Highbinders. Dir. Tod Browning, Majestic Motion Picture Company, 1916

The Yellow Menace. Dir. Aubrey M. Kennedy, Serial Film Company, 1916

Broken Blossoms. Dir. D. W. Griffith, D. W. Griffith Productions, 1919

Mandarin's Gold. Dir. Oscar Apfel, World Film, 1919

The Midnight Patrol. Dir. Irvin Willat, Thomas H. Ince Corporation, 1919

The Red Lantern. Dir. Albert Capellani, Metro Picture Corporation, 1919

Shame. Dir. Emmet J. Flynn, Fox Film Corporation, 1921

Wing Toy. Dir. Howard M. Mitchell, Fox Film Corporation, 1921

East Is West. Dir. Sydney Franklin, Constance Talmadge Film Company, 1922

Toll of the Sea. Dir. Chester M. Franklin, Technicolor, 1922.

Extra Girl. Dir. F. Richard Jones, Mack Sennett Comedies, 1923

The Fighting Adventurer. Dir. Tom Forman, Universal Pictures, 1924

Pied Piper of Malone. Dir. Alfred E. Green, Paramount Pictures, 1924

Thief of Bagdad. Dir. Raul Walsh, United Artists, 1924

The Mystery of Dr. Fu Manchu. Dir. A. E. Coleby, Stoll Picture Productions, 1925

Going Crooked. Dir. George Melford, Fox Film Corporation, 1926

Show People. Dir. King Vidor, Metro-Goldwyn-Mayer, 1928

Welcome Danger. Dir. Clyde Bruckman and Malcolm St. Clair, The Harold Lloyd Company, 1929

Dirigible. Dir. Frank Capra, Columbia Pictures, 1931

Roar of the Dragon. Dir. Wesley Ruggles, RKO Pictures, 1932

Hatchet Man. Dir. William Wellman, First National Pictures, 1932

Shanghai Express. Dir. Josef von Sternberg, Paramount Pictures, 1932

War Correspondent. Dir. Paul Sloane, Columbia Pictures, 1932

The Bitter Tea of General Yen. Dir. Frank Capra, Columbia Pictures, 1933

Eskimo. Dir. W. S. Van Dyke. Metro-Goldwyn-Mayer, 1933

The Cat's Paw. Dir. Sam Taylor and Harold Lloyd, Fox Film Corporation, 1934

The Painted Veil. Dir. Richard Boleslawki, Metro-Goldwyn-Mayer, 1934

Student Tour. Dir. Charles Reisner, 1934

Captured in Chinatown. Dir. Elmer Clifton, Consolidated Pictures Corporation, 1935

The General Dies at Dawn. Dir. Lewis Milestone, Paramount Pictures, 1936

Shadow of Chinatown. Dir. Robert F. Hill, Victory Pictures Corporation, 1936

Outlaws of the Orient. Dir. Ernest B. Schoedsack, Columbia Pictures, 1937

The Good Earth. Dir. Sidney Franklin, Victor Fleming and Gustav Machaty, Metro-Goldwyn-Mayer, 1937

West of Shanghai. Dir. John Farrow, Warner Bros. 1937

Shadows over Shanghai. Dir. Charles Lamont, Franklyn Warner Productions, 1938

Too Hot to Handle. Dir. Jack Conway, MGM, 1938

Torchy Blane in Chinatown. Dir. William Beaudine, Warner Bros., 1939

Daughter of the Tong. Dir. Raymond K. Johnson, Metropolitan Pictures, 1939

Mr. Wong in Chinatown. Dir. William Nigh, Monogram Pictures, 1939

Wake Island. Dir. John Farrow, Paramount Pictures, 1942

Little Tokyo U.S.A. Dir. Otto Brower, Twentieth Century Fox, 1942

Behind the Rising Sun. Dir. Edward Dmytryk, RKO Pictures, 1943

China. Dir. John Farrow, Paramount Pictures, 1943

Destination Tokyo. Dir. Delmer Daves, Warner Bros., 1943

Rookies in Burma. Dir. Leslie Goodwins, RKO Pictures, 1943

Keys of the Kingdom. Dir. John Stahl, Twentieth Century Fox, 1944

The Purple Heart. Dir. Lewis Milestone, Twentieth Century Fox, 1944

Up in Arms. Dir. Elliot Nugent, The Samuel Goldwyn Company, 1944

Blood on the Sun. Dir. Frank Lloyd, William Gabney Productions, 1945

China's Little Devils. Dir. Monta Bell, Monogram Pictures, 1945

First Yank into Tokyo. Dir. Gordon Douglas, RKO Pictures, 1945

Secret Agent X-9. Dir. Lewis D. Collins and Ray Taylor, Universal Pictures, 1945

Soldier of Fortune. Dir. Edward Dmytryk, Twentieth Century Fox, 1955

The King and I. Dir. Walter Lang, Twentieth Century Fox, 1956

The World of Suzie Wong. Dir. Richard Quine, Paramount Pictures, 1960

Flower Drum Song. Dir. Henry Koster, Universal Pictures, 1961

Absent-Minded Professor. Dir. Robert Stevenson, Walt Disney Productions, 1961

101 Dalmatians. Dir. Clyde Geronimi, Hamilton Luske, and Wolfgang Riehterman, Walt Disney Animation Studios, 1961

Chinatown. Dir. Roman Polanski, Paramount Pictures, 1974

Blade Runner. Dir. Ridley Scott, Warner Bros., 1982

Joy Luck Club. Dir. Wayne Wang, Hollywood Pictures, 1993

Crazy Rich Asians. Dir. Jon. M. Chu, Warner Bros., 2018

Better Luck Tomorrow. Dir. Justin Lin, MTV Films, 2002
Everything Everywhere All at Once. Dir. Daniel Kwan and Daniel Scheinert, A24, 2023

Interviews

ASIAN AMERICAN RESOURCE PROJECT, BANCROFT LIBRARY, UNIVERSITY OF CALIFORNIA, BERKELEY AND SANTA BARBARA, SPECIAL COLLECTIONS:

Fong, Benson. Interview by Frank Chin, Nathan Lee, and Jeff Chop, May 9, 1970
Lee, Ching Wah. Interview by Frank Chin and Philip Choy, July 30, 1970
Loo, Bessie. Interview by Frank Chin, May 4, 1970
Yung, Victor Sen. Interview by Frank Chin, April 18, 1971

CHINATOWN REMEMBERED PROJECT, CHINESE HISTORICAL SOCIETY OF SOUTHERN CALIFORNIA:

Chee, Richard. Interview by William Gow, July 7 and October 5, 2008
Fong, Ben. Interview by Annie Luong, May 25, 2008
Hom, Dorothy. Interview by William Gow, September 15, 2007
Johnson, Esther Lee. Interview by William Gow, March 9, 2008
Louie, Ruby Ling. Interview by William Gow, March 28, 2008
Quon, Charlie. Interview by Nancy Thai, April 22 and May 19, 2007
SooHoo, Peter Jr. Interview by William Gow, April 9, 2007
Taylor, Jennie Lee. Interview by William Gow, April 22, 2007, and Scott Chan, May 9, 2007
Wong, Tyrus. Interview by Genie Moon, November 1, 2007

RACIAL MINORITIES SURVEY, FEDERAL WRITERS PROJECT, UCLA LIBRARY SPECIAL COLLECTIONS:

C. H. Yung. "History of C. H. Yung, Pauper." December 2, 1936

SURVEY ON RACE RELATIONS RECORDS, HOOVER INSTITUTION LIBRARY & ARCHIVES:

SooHoo, Peter. "Peter SooHoo Interview by William C. Smith," August 7, 1925

SOUTHERN CALIFORNIA CHINESE AMERICAN ORAL HISTORY PROJECT, UNIVERSITY OF CALIFORNIA, LOS ANGELES, SPECIAL COLLECTIONS & CHINESE HISTORICAL SOCIETY OF SOUTHERN CALIFORNIA:

Chan, Spencer. Interview by Suellen Chan, April 7, 1983
Chung, Walter. Interview by George Yee, January 20, 1980
Hoo, Marshall. Interview by Beverly Chan, May 24, 1980
Hum, Alice. Interview by Beverly Chan, July 28, 1980

Lee, Eddie E. Interview by Jean Wong, January 20, 1979

Lee, Ida. Interview by Beverly Chan, July 29, 1980

Lee, Lilly Mu. Interview by Suellen Cheng, July 24, 1982

Lee, Frank York. Interview by Bernice Sam, July 7, 1980

Lee, Margaret K. Interview by Beverly Chan, April 29, 1980

Leung, Gilbert. Interview by Emma Louie, March 27, 1979

Leong, Herbert. Interview by Jean Wong, December 22, 1980

Loo, Bessie. Interview by Emma Louie, May 6, 1981

Loo, Bessie. Interview by Jean Wong, Beverly Chan, and Emma Louie, February 21, 1979, and January 10, 1980

Loo, Bessie. Interview by Jean Wong, March 21, 1979

Luke, Keye. Interview by Jean Wong, February 23, 1979

Lew, Billy. Interview by Beverly Chan and Suellen Cheng, October 19, 1979

Mock, Allen. Interview by Jean Wong, January 13, 1980

Siu, Dorothy. Interview by Jean Wong, November 21, 1979

Tom, Dick. Interview by Beverly Chan, February 13, 1980

Wong, Maye. Interview by Jean Wong and Emma Louie, May 8, 1979

Yee, Swan. Interview by Suellen Cheng, June 23, 1983

TERMINAL ISLAND LIFE HISTORY PROJECT, JAPANESE AMERICAN NATIONAL MUSEUM:

Miyagishima, Eiichi. Interview, May 1994

PERSONAL INTERVIEW

Chee, Rick. Interview by William Gow, August 12, 2022

Wing, Camille Chan. Interview by William Gow, September 27, 2019

Index

Note: Page numbers in *italics* refer to illustrative matter.

Printed in the USA
CPSIA information can be obtained
at www.ICGtesting.com
JSHW020926130324
59139JS00001B/1